Women who Dare to Believe

mothers, sisters, daughters of God

VOLUME TWO

by Nan Gurley and Bonnie Keen

with grateful hearts this study is dedicated to
our mothers: *Bernie and Gwen*
our sisters: *Alene, Amy, Kay and Margie*
and our daughters: *Courtney, Erin, and Lena*

Published by New Earth Players Press
copyright 2010 - Nan Gurley and Bonnie Keen

No part of this book may be reproduced or transmitted in any form or by any means, electronic or mechanical, including photocopying and recording, or by an information storage or retrieval system, except as may be expressly permitted in writing by the publisher. Requests for permission should be addressed in writing to New Earth Players Press; c/o Nan Gurley; 1105 Brentwood Lane, Brentwood, TN 37027

ISBN 0-9776237-3-4
ISBN 978-0-9776237-3-0

Photography and cover art: Ben Arrowood

Book Design: Ben Arrowood and Casey Fay

Edited by Fiona Soltes

Production manager: Wayne Gurley

To order additional copes of this resource, or information about the accompanying musical of the same name, email at www.womenwhodaretobelieve.com.

Printed in the United States of America

TABLE OF CONTENTS

ENDORSEMENTS .... PAGE 4

WELCOME .... PAGE 6

THANK YOU .... PAGE 7

NAOMI .... PAGE 8

RUTH .... PAGE 24

ANNA .... PAGE 46

ADULTEROUS WOMAN .... PAGE 76

WOMAN WITH THE ISSUE OF BLOOD .... PAGE 102

MARY, MOTHER OF JESUS (PART ONE) .... PAGE 128

MARY, MOTHER OF JESUS (PART TWO) .... PAGE 150

MARY, MOTHER OF JESUS, (PART THREE) .... PAGE 174

EVE (PART ONE) .... PAGE 192

EVE (PART TWO) .... PAGE 218

LEADERS GUIDE AND STUDY QUESTIONS .... PAGE 229

EPILOGUE .... PAGE 242

ENDNOTES .... PAGE 244

"The Women Who Dare To Believe small group study brings the stories of biblical women to life and the application questions powerfully apply to contemporary issues. This study challenges women to take action steps that produce positive change based on the truth of God's Word. It's refreshingly different from other studies--and it will capture the hearts of your group!"

Carol Kent
www.CarolKent.org
www.SpeakUpSpeakerServices.com
wwwSpeakUpforHope.org

"It never occurred to me that these women of Scripture—who I'd passed over with very little thought—had so much to teach me. What an exciting study! These vividly etched characters—these flesh and blood women of God—provide an astounding vision of the Heavenly Father at work then and now, and helped me connect the dots all the way through history from them to me, to better-understand the big picture of redemption."

Sue Buchanan
Author, speaker, cheerleader
www.suebue.com

"If you think Bible studies are dull and laborious, think again. Bonnie Keen and Nan Gurley have developed a women's Bible study that is not only going to teach you about the fascinating lives of the women of the Bible, but it will entertain you in the process. Both women are accomplished actors, gifted communicators, and talented entertainers. Their sense of humor, hopeful hearts, and love of teaching come through every page of this study. This is one women's Bible study your group is going to love!"

Martha Bolton
Emmy-nominated writer and author of
over 50 books of humor, including
"Didn't My Skin Used To Fit?"

"Oh, if you have ever longed to have the Bible come alive for you, you are holding the life-changing key in your very hand. This study of God's Word is like none other on the planet! All the dusty stories of long ago have been dusted off and brought into living color. You will discover answers and applications for living your own life with fresh vibrancy and transformed understanding! Open these pages and begin at once to walk in a new sense of personal joy and direction!"

Glenna Salsbury
Christian Conference Speaker and
Author of Heavenly Treasures
ISpeak4U@aol.com

"This offering is saturated with raw, buoyant, unconditional love. I ache to see the musical! And I'd encourage all to experience this study. It will be marked by a wondrous marriage of excellence and humanity."

Alicia Britt Chole
"painting portraits of truth that refresh the soul"
www.truthportraits.com

"As I previewed Women Who Dare to Believe, I laughed, wept and marveled at the anointing that is all over this brilliant work! I can't wait to see how God will use the stage performance and the Bible Study to rally His Daughters!"

Candace L. Davison
Women's Ministry Coordinator
Sandy Cove Ministries, North East MD

"Women Who Dare To Believe" reminds us that it is God who lifts and sustains us in this world whatever our time in history. It is so much easier for me to believe in his love for me when I experience the answers to my prayers…just like I prayed them. I dare to believe in the Father's love even when his good for me hurts. This study reminds me it is only by his Spirit that this is possible. He continues to work mightily in women to bring about his will and to give glory to the Father who made us for so much more than what we see. Go, girls, but only with him."

Nancy Puryear
Director of Women's Ministry
Christ Community Church, Franklin Tn

"Nan Gurley and Bonnie Keen are the real deal. They're as much "women who dare to believe" as any of those described in their studies. Within these pages, expect wit, humor, authenticity, insight, truth, camaraderie, and a fresh look at inspirational lives."

Fiona Soltes, writer, missionary, friend,
and fellow follower of Jesus

"Bonnie Keen and Nan Gurley have a passion to bring Biblical truth to light. From their wealth of experience and biblical knowledge their latest endeavor "Women Who Dare To Believe" offers a fresh perspective which will encourage and inspire us in our daily walk with the Lord.

Sharleen Dluzak,
Director of Women's Ministry
Church of the Redeemer, Gaithersburg MD

"I have never felt a kindred spirit with women in the Bible till now."

Mary Williams
Great-grandmother and Owner/ President
of Mary Williams Guide Service

"My thanks to the authors for writing this book. I feel like I have had a private, in-depth visit with each woman we studied."

Bernie Arnold
Autor, Mother of 4
Grand Mother of 10

"My wholehearted thanks goes out to Bonnie and Nan for using their God-given gifts to guide mothers, sisters and daughters of our time to know more about His promises. In studying the lives of His chosen women, they dare to create a desire for others to know the depths of God's loving heart."

Gwendolyn Watson

"Our moms wrote this study. It's awesome. Thank goodness it's finished."

Erin and Lena Gurley, Courtney Keen

WELCOME

TO WOMEN WHO DARE TO BELIEVE: MOTHERS, SISTERS, DAUGHTERS OF GOD

Volume Two: A Continued Study for the Girls!

Light a candle beside your favorite comfy place to sit. Set a cup of coffee or favorite tea beside you. Maybe you'd like to stay in your bathrobe a little bit longer, or have music playing in the background. This study is for women, so make it your own special girl experience.

Good for you! We applaud you for taking the time to read. You will be opening two books: the word of God and this study about a few of his beloved women. Ah yes, please read. Reading allows you to imagine the details of their lives, and to walk beside each woman. Hopefully you'll find one or two that will become sisters of your heart.

We live in a culture bombarded with information; reading has met many new rivals. Cable news networks run around the clock with updates of world events. Twitters and tweets now mix with emails and text messaging. We live in a culture obsessed with keeping in touch. There are websites for dating or ones for reconnecting with old friends. Facebook, MySpace, Twitter, and LinkedIn may overwhelm the old-fashioned among us who still prefer emails and cell phones. Before this study goes to print, there will be a flood of new technology on the market, all designed to keep us informed. (The television set of the future will all but wash and dry your clothes, cook dinner, and vacuum your house while doing your taxes.)

Commenting on the influx of relationships fostered on the Internet, Pastor Steve Berger from Grace Chapel in Leipers Fork, Tennessee, noted: "I need to keep my face in the Book to remember the best friend I have."

The women we honor in this study dared to believe God in a time when all they had were the words of prophets and teachers of the Torah. They lived in a culture in which only men could study the word of God. Women were forbidden to touch the holy books. Women were viewed as second-class citizens. Rabbis chose to not look a woman directly in the eye. They were honored for bearing children and keeping the home fires burning, but could be divorced for burning a bagel. A daughter's birth in a Hebrew family brought a smile. A son's birth brought on a party.

Yet throughout history, in harrowing days of moral decay and times of political and social danger, there were women God used in mighty and profound ways. They were simply women who dared to believe. They had fierce faith in the One who promised to keep his word. The line of women who dared to believe God stretches from the beginning chapters of the Old Testament crossing into the final chapters of the New Testament. Each woman we've studied jumps off the pages of Scripture, her choices based on a wild hope in God's covenant.

We're honored that you've chosen to walk beside us in this study. We long to take our place in that crimson line of courageous women who dared to take God at his word, and we want to encourage you to do the same. In the back of the study are leader's guide questions to spark your discussions. Together, we'll walk out our destinies and help each other grow in the grace of our beautiful Jesus.

Let's get started.

In our Jesus, we do wildly and continually hope!
Nan Gurley and Bonnie Keen

A SPECIAL THANK YOU

We are grateful to the following women who agreed to be the first to study *Women Who Dare to Believe: Mothers, Sisters, Daughters of God*. Before the Bible study was in the form that you now have, these women graciously opened their Monday night Bible study to us. For five months, they poured their love and energy into doing each lesson and giving us their feedback. Thank you, dear sisters. Your love and encouragement kept us writing and pressing on, believing that you would be the first of many who would come alongside us and dare to believe.

Pat Ward ~ Diana Reed ~ Bernie Arnold ~ Mary Williams ~ Maxine Bivins
Dele Wilcher ~ Becky Collins ~ Betsy Piper ~ Irene Acuff ~ Debbie Costantine ~ Eva Crothers ~
Jeannie Boshers ~ Glenda Cowart ~ Renee Crawford

WEEK ONE
ANNOUNCEMENTS

BARNS & BORDERS IN BETHLEHEM ANNOUNCES BOOK SIGNING
Best-Selling Author of *Grandmothers Rock with the Ages*

Thursday night from 7-9 p.m., Barns & Borders Bookstore will host Naomi of Bethlehem, first-time author of the best-selling memoir, *Grandmothers Rock With the Ages.* Naomi will be available to sign copies of the runaway hit and also will speak about the events recorded in her riveting book that no one can put down.

"Writing a book was the farthest thing from my mind!" Naomi commented during our interview with her last week. "But when my grandson Obed was born, my friends insisted it was time to go public with our story. It was this same group of grandmothers who gave Obed his name, you know. So I sat down and began and the words came as fast as I could write. I remembered the quote from the book of Job: 'I am full of words and the spirit within me compels me!'" When asked about being a role model for older women, Naomi seemed pleased and answered, "Gray hair is like a crown of honor; it is earned by living a good life!"

Naomi's tale of overcoming clinical depression has attracted a passionate following. Her theme of finding new life in older years has tapped into a fresh new market. Many readers point to Naomi's faith in God and of her journey from despair into hope. They credit her example with renewing a perspective of their own future.

"If a woman like Naomi who lost everything can write a book like this, then it gives all of us the chance to believe our lives aren't over," said a sixty-two-year-old cancer survivor. "Twice I've been told that I wouldn't live past Passover because of cancer." She smiled before concluding, "Of course God is in control. But twice I've beaten the medical prognosis. Say what you want, but I'm with Naomi. It's God who has given me the strength to keep fighting."

Naomi has quite the entourage traveling with her on the press junket. Her daughter-in-law Ruth, son-in-law Boaz, and newborn grandson Obed are scheduled to appear at various book signings and radio and television interviews.

Ruth, a Moab native, describes her mother-in-law's optimism. "She has resiliency in her bones. I think it comes from her heritage. She's a Hebrew woman who has known the faithfulness of God all her life." At this point the lovely, impressive daughter-in-law paused. "Well, there were times when she doubted him. When her husband and sons all died, she wondered if God had forgotten her."

"That was before I stepped in!" exclaimed Boaz, the boisterous, elegant, slightly graying son-in-law as he joined the interview. The love story between Boaz and Ruth has captivated readers across Israel. Naomi weaves her presence carefully through their romance without stealing focus. One cannot read this bestseller without being impressed with the immense adoration Ruth and Naomi have for Boaz. He is obviously God's man for their hour. Over and again he is referred to as the family's kinsman-redeemer.

"Our families were always related," said Boaz as he picked up his young son Obed to quiet his crying. "Only God could have orchestrated the intersection of our lives. To be so blessed to have such a treasure as Ruth for a bride…." Naomi elbowed Boaz gently at this point, "And her lovely mother-in-law Naomi, double the blessing!" Boaz finished as he and Ruth headed away from the interview with Obed happily squirming in their arms.

Obed is indeed a handsome young man even at his tender age. It's not difficult to understand how he inspired a passionate book written by his grateful grandmother. After losing her husband and sons in Moab, she feels fully restored by his birth. And there was no mistaking this young grandson looked as if he knew more than any of us about his coming future.

Please meet this honored family at the signing tonight. Naomi wanted to mention any toys brought will be donated to the Bethlehem Gleaners Guild.

TODAY'S HEROINE:

Naomi

You number and record my wanderings; put my tears into your bottle—are they not in your book? (Ps. 56:8 Amplified Bible)

While Deborah led Israel into battle against Sisera, and Samson rose up to defeat the Philistines; while Gideon put out his fleece and went out to fight the Midianites, two unknown women in Moab were quietly forging a friendship. A mother and daughter-in-law. Theirs is a story that would not likely make front page news. It seems like a mere blip on the timeline of history and would never be known, except for the fact that through their faithfulness they became a part of the crimson line of women in the lineage of the Messiah.

We are about to come out of our collective skins as we study this ever-growing line of women who dared to believe. The connection between our heroines deepens with each passing chapter. Today's lovely grandmother Naomi lived a story that continues to rock with the ages.

Turn to the book of Ruth. As you do, we pray God's Holy Spirit will bring fresh revelations. We've heard this story so many times we may be inclined to think there's nothing new to learn. But God's word is endlessly deep and rich, full and replete with jewels of mystery.

For any of us who have ever wondered if God has forgotten us or turned his back; for those who wrestle with depression, grief or torment from our own choices or those imposed on us by others; for the moments when life drowns out hope, Naomi reminds us that "too late" is not in God's vocabulary. She lived through tremendous loss and, for a time, bought into the lie that she'd moved so far into despair that even God himself could not reach her.

Been there? Done that? Many of us can relate to Naomi's story. In studying her life, once again we are reminded that God is in the business of bringing dead hearts to life.

Naomi's story gives validity to any woman of God who has gone through a deep season of depression. She suffered and she caved in. She knows how we feel when we have experienced the same fear of emotional darkness that even leads us to thoughts of suicide and giving up on life itself.

Most importantly, Naomi represents the people of Israel. Her life points to a God who is ever working to bring them through the valley of the shadow, through the valley of Baca tears, and into his glorious light and hope. Naomi cried a river of tears and found each one had been kept in a bottle, counted like the hairs on her head. Though she wandered through emotional and physical deserts, God delivered her into a season of unexpected joy. Her story was written in God's book in heaven. But she had to hang on through the agony in Chapter One of her life to find God's sweet restoration in Chapter Four.

Like Naomi, in Chapter One of our lives, none of us can see what is coming in Chapter Four! We see through a glass darkly, and sometimes life is so bitter we lose our faith, the gift of seeing what is not seen. When we are in the fog, it's hard to see the hand of God, never sleeping, always moving, always carving out new places of healing for his girls. In our chapter one, he is ever-faithful to work on our behalf. There is another page to turn, another chapter coming. God is working behind the scenes… behind the seen.

So let's look at how Naomi moved from bitter to blessed, from emptiness to fullness.

From Chapter One… to a new chapter in life!

There is so much more to our lives than how things "look." It is only fair to Naomi to take a moment to imagine life in her shoes circa 1380 B.C.

Let's begin with a little background check on Naomi.

NAOMI: CHAPTER ONE

Read Ruth 1:1-3.

Stop.

These first three verses contain a vast amount of information.

All of our lives are impacted by the emotional, physical, and spiritual climate around us. We're going in slow motion here to get as much of a feel for Naomi's early years as possible. The onset of her bout with depression can be traced back to these critical areas in her life. Depression recovery must come on these three levels as well: a healing of the emotional, physical, and spiritual heart.

SPIRITUAL CLIMATE OF NAOMI'S EARLY YEARS

In **verse 1,** how is the spiritual climate of Israel described?

"In the days when the _____ _____"

What would these days have been like? **Turn to Judges 21:25 and put this in your own words.**

_____

_____

Naomi lived in the days when there was "no _____ in Israel."

The story of Naomi and Ruth takes place in the dark times of Israel's history. With no king in Israel, judges ruled the land and it was a free-for-all where everyone did what was right in his own eyes. Idol worship was rampant and the majority of the Hebrew people were morally bankrupt. From our time spent with Judge Deborah in the first volume of *Women Who Dare to Believe,* we have a vivid picture of how this played out.

"There was no king in Israel because in Israel there was no God. The Lord is king…You cannot have a true king if you have not a God. There was no nominal renunciation of God, no public and blatant atheism, no boastful impiety; there was a deadlier heresy—namely keeping God as a sign but paying no tribute to him as a king, worshiping him in outward form but knowing nothing of the subduing and directing power of godliness. That is more to be dreaded than any intellectual difficulty of a technological kind… Dead consciences, prayerless prayers, mechanical formalities—these are the impediments which overturn….This was the case in Israel."[1]

Pause for a moment and let this sink in. Naomi lived in the times when judges came and went through the revolving door of inconsistent faith. There was no demand from Israel to remove God's name from their history books. There wasn't much of any demand for God at all until they were backed against the walls of a self-imposed prison. There was no one like Moses or Joshua to lead them in his ways. She lived in the interlude between Joshua and the coming leadership of the prophet Samuel, and then David.

One of the most sobering verses in the Bible is found in **Judges 2:10.**

What happened after the generation of Joshua died?

_____

_____

We all may have similar questions about this verse. How could they stop telling the stories? How could it be that a generation was born that did not remember the miraculous exodus from Egypt? What happened to encouraging each other by remembering what God had done for Israel? When did the parents stop telling their children? Why?

Read Judges 2:11-13.

Who did the people of Naomi's time serve?

_____

_____

How did the Lord respond?

_____

_____

List the false gods found in **verse 13**:

_____

_____

The Lord had given Israel so many mighty victories over their enemies as he led them to the Promised Land. There was only one major requirement. He asked them to drive out their enemies and utterly destroy the nations they displaced. This sounds somehow un-God-like on the surface. Why wipe out entire nations?

It doesn't take long to see the wisdom in God's plan. He wanted to shield his people from the practice of worshiping false gods. It was a harsh command, but one intended to protect his people from falling into sin.

By the time Joshua had been gathered to his fathers, the people of Israel had disobeyed God's command and inter-married with the Canaanites. Naomi and her family struggled through a time when the people of God were caught up in a secular worldview. Israel had taken fate into their own hands. In what seems an impossible turning of the heart from Yahweh, by the second chapter of Judges they had pledged their allegiance to Baal and Ashtaroth.

The heart of God breaks. Yet the heart of God never leaves his people. Throughout the times that came, during the years when Israel had no king and the judges ruled, God rescued them from their own poor choices over and over again.

EDITORIAL: One commentary notes the following about the last verse of Judges: "It is almost as if the author was weary and refused to dignify the state of affairs with more than, 'Things are bad; they will get better under a king.'" [2]

How many poor choices have we all made, yet God continues, faithful to his nature and word to deliver us from ourselves. So, welcome to our world… and to the world of Naomi, as we revisit the merciful ways of our never-changing God.

CONSIDER: The first three verses of the book of Ruth are replete with information. Naomi's life opens with hopes dashed by death.

Might she have related a bit to this sigh from John Updike in A Month of Sundays? "I have no faith. Or rather, I have faith but it doesn't seem to apply."

PHYSICAL CLIMATE OF NAOMI'S EARLY YEARS

Back to Ruth 1:1-3.

What was Naomi's husband's name?

_____

Name her sons: _____ and _____

What city did they leave and why?

_____

_____

To what city did they move?

_____

Naomi, we want to meet you here. Your husband's name, Elimelech, is translated, "God is King". Let's assume from this that your family was led by a husband who did not forget God was king, even when Israel as a nation had a memory lapse. So, you and Elimelech found yourselves living in Bethlehem during a famine. No food in the grocery stores, no milk in the fridge. In Bethlehem, a city named the "House of Bread," the cupboards were bare. Did the people of Bethlehem wonder why God would allow a famine in their land? It was supposed to flow with milk and honey. Had God withdrawn his promise? Or had the people turned their backs on God? Maybe the store shelves were lined with a few too many statues of powerless gods.

NOTE: Sometimes God allows a "famine" in our lives to get our attention. In his mercy, he takes away our comforts in order to cause us to look up, turn our eyes back to him, and repent. Can you think of a famine in your life that refocused your attention on God?

Naomi, did you and Elimelech and your two sons, Mahlon and Chilion, wonder if you were doing the right thing as you packed your bags? Your boys had been ill since birth. (Their names mean "sickly" and "failing.") This may explain why you left the "House of Bread" in search of a city with a better economy. As parents of fragile sons, you probably left home fearing your sons might not live through a famine.

So off you move to Moab—an interesting choice. Moab is located sixty miles from Bethlehem on the east side of the Dead Sea. It is sixty miles in physical distance from Bethlehem. But you could not have moved farther in spiritual distance from God's people.

MORE ABOUT MOAB

The people of Israel were guilty of the grievous sin of idol worship. God had called his people to separate themselves from the Gentiles around them. Yet the people of Moab were notorious for their worship of Chemosh. Moab's Chamber of Commerce would have had fliers detailing when and where to attend pagan sacrifices. Their ancestors were the descendants of Lot—not from Lot and his wife. Moabites were descended from the children of Lot fathered with his daughters. Of course he was the kind of father who once offered his daughters to be raped by the wild men of Sodom and Gomorrah. After fleeing the city, Lot's daughters got him drunk and each became pregnant. We digress. For more information, see **Genisis 19.** It's a hair-raising, fascinating read.

Naomi, one more important fact for you to consider before staking your tent into Moabite soil. Their Historical Society would want you to know of how they had battled off-and-on with Israel since the first days when Moses led God's nation across the wilderness. The Moabite leader, Barak, once hired an internationally known psychic named Balaam. He was a broker of sorts who was well known for his ability to make a deal between the "gods." He was paid to use his physic powers in an effort to destroy Israel. Of course this plan tanked. Balaam's donkey could tell the rest of that story.

Elimelech, we hope you were aware though there may have been food in Moab, it was also a city that could resort to the practice of human sacrifice, so you'd need to watch your back. Moabite kings Ahab and Mesha were infamous for their barbarism. Ahab went a few rounds with the prophet Elijah in a failed attempt to prove Baal could defeat Yahweh. The Lord had the final word over this day in Moab's history. Yet soon after Ahab's demise, Moab's king Mesha saw defeat again coming their way. So Mesha took his own son who would have succeeded him in office and sacrificed him on the city wall as a burnt offering.[3]

In the larger picture of the book of Ruth, Moab is often likened to the place of human failure. Moab represents the false places we try to find refuge when it seems God has left us. It's the fallen garden, the lies from the enemy, that separated Adam and Eve from God's presence. Moab is counterfeit, empty, and leads to death.

We aren't pointing fingers at the choice of Naomi's family to live in Moab. There are more than enough poor choices made by all of us to go around. It is easy to sit in judgment of them and, from our point of view, criticize them for a lack of faith. But Elimelech and Naomi found themselves in a position that we often find ourselves in as well. They left their heritage at home and went to live among the people of Moab. Scripture does not say that they also worshiped idols. It only tells us they went to Moab in search of food. Was this a lack of faith on their part? If they had stayed in Bethlehem, would God have provided for their needs? Maybe they prayed and asked God to show them what to do. Maybe they felt they didn't get a clear answer.

Maybe they were scared to death.

Can you note a time you ran to "Moab" and away from God?

_____

_____

Let's continue our discovery about the background of Naomi's life, and the culture of her son's lives. In doing so we can sympathize with her situation and realize more fully the astounding deliverance that came from the hand of the Lord. Whatever their reasons, we can be sure the decision to live in Moab wasn't easy for Naomi's family. Thankfully, the book of Ruth is a story of God's choice to redeem their choices and ultimately give them beauty for ashes.

Elimelech and Naomi arrive in Moab and find not only food, but also wives for their sons. God made it very clear to his people that they were not to marry the pagan people around them. He knew their hearts would ultimately be divided and they would end up worshiping the idols of their spouses. Integrated into the foreign culture, Elimelech and Naomi ignored this law and found wives for their sons from the pagan women in Moab. While living in Bethlehem, the people of Israel did not remember the Lord. So let's assume that Elimelech and Naomi had not heard the harrowing story recorded in Numbers 25.

Read Numbers 25:1-2.

These two verses set up one of Israel's greatest defeats.

Israel plays the _____ with the _____ of Moab (Amplified Bible).

What did the Moabite women entice the men of Israel to do?

The Lord was deeply angered by Israel's betrayal. **What the Moabite men could not accomplish, the Moabite women completed.** They brought the Israelites down by the power of sexual seduction. The Moabite women enticed the men to forget the loving protection of Yahweh and convinced them to bow down to foreign gods. Because of their disobedience, 24,000 Israelites died.

This generation was the last to cross the wilderness. They would not enjoy the land of milk and honey. They paid a huge price for marrying the Moabite women and serving their idols. The sandals of this generation would never be used to walk into the Promised Land.

EMOTIONAL CLIMATE IN NAOMI'S EARLY YEARS

In Ruth 1:3, what happened?

_____

_____

In the span of ten years, Elimelech, Mahlon, and Chilion all die, leaving Naomi as a childless widow. We don't know her age, but she's lost her husband and her provider. This is a huge loss for any woman no matter her age, culture, or circumstances. How deeply she may have grieved Elimelech's death seems evident as we learn more about her state of mind. Might Naomi have felt a bit of the following description written by a woman after the death of her husband?

"I didn't faint or lose consciousness. I just felt numb all over. There was a fuzziness, a blurring of all that was going on, like I was walking through a fog. Feelings of helplessness overwhelmed me.... I found it hard to concentrate... confusion ruled my mind."[4]

For Naomi, the confusion mounts.

According to Ruth 1:4, who did her sons marry?

Moabite wives.

How long did they live in Moab?

_____

What happened in **verse 5**?

_____

_____

Verse 5 says "the woman was bereft..." (Amplified Bible). What a perfect word to describe Naomi. Webster defines bereft as in the state of "being deprived or robbed of something." Surely Naomi felt robbed. A decade earlier Naomi had arrived in Moab with her husband, sons, and a heart of hope for a new life. It's safe to say she prayed for sustenance, provision, and dreams for her future. Her life took cruel, unexpected turns. Now she has no husband, no sons, and her life appears to be over.

The words of Job reflect Naomi's grief:

"The thing which I greatly feared is come upon me, and that which I was afraid of is come unto me. I was not in safety, neither had I rest, neither was I quiet, yet trouble came" (Job 3:25-26 KJV).

Her grief not only was the heartache of losing her family, but also included a deep fear for her future. What was it like for a woman back then to have no man in her life? Ancient Middle Eastern culture forced women to be totally dependent on men for their well-being. When a husband died, his property did not automatically go to his wife. It went to the man who owned the family birthright. The wife was left with nothing and therefore was dependent on her sons or a brother-in-law. Naomi is a widow with no one to cover her with protection. She lost both her sons and has no grandchildren in her family; a woman alone facing extreme poverty and starvation.

To make matters even more difficult, Naomi felt responsible for her widowed daughters-in-law. Imagine how fragile and weak her state of mind.

In verses 6-7, what decision does Naomi make?

_____

Go back to your Mom's house and remarry as fast as you can!

It is interesting to note that Naomi believed God would bless her daughters-in-law. She believes God will grant them rest and a new husband.

Have you ever looked at someone else and thought they should receive God's gifts and blessings but you don't deserve them?

Naomi has hope for her daughters-in-law but doesn't believe God has anything good in store for her. She feels outside of his blessing and alienated from his love. It's time to go it alone, without anyone in what's left of the rest of her broken future.

From Bethlehem, the "House of Bread," comes the news that the Lord has "visited his people" to give them food again. Naomi decides it's best to make the sixty-mile trip back to square one... back to where she started a decade before... back to Judah. But did overwhelming sorrow finally catch up with her? As we read the next verses we hear the voice of a woman who loses heart and the will to live.

Describe what Naomi says about herself in verse 13.

_____

_____

SIDEBAR: Since Naomi's life is an open book to many, I (Bonnie) would like to share a little from my own personal journey with clinical depression. I love Naomi from Bethlehem because I believe we have a lot in common. I never have lost a husband from death, but have lived through the death of a marriage. Thank God both of my children are alive and well, but I hit a wall of depression that nearly took me under. Five years after my divorce, my ten-year ministry fell apart in the wake of a national scandal. For years I felt the weight of finances, single parenthood, and the loneliness that comes with uncertainty and lost dreams. Bad choices of my own and of others haunted me during these years, and like Naomi, I found myself wanting to die.

From my book, *A Ladder out of Depression,* I wrote:

"This morning I had thoughts of death again, of how if I didn't have my children, I might just long to be with God. Maybe what I'm saying is that I don't want to face what God is requiring of me here in this world. I just don't want to hurt anymore. His ways are not mine, but his ways seem so hard. When I think of all the men and women in the Bible called to a special walk with God, and what was asked of them, I want to cry out, 'I CANNOT HANDLE THIS! I CANNOT DO THIS! YOU'RE ASKING TOO MUCH!'" [5]

There were moments that only the eyes of my two young children kept me alive. I sincerely believe God used Courtney and Graham to keep me putting one foot in front of the other. Their faces gave me a reason to believe there was a future worth fighting for.

A part of me understands how Naomi felt as she locked arms with Ruth and Orpah and headed toward "help." She was heading home, only sixty miles, but it would have been a hard road to face. And fairly quickly, something snapped in Naomi's spirit. I remember when even walking to the mailbox seemed like climbing Mount Everest. When someone is suffering with depression the smallest effort feels impossible.

"Around 2,400 years ago, the Greek doctor Hippocrates spoke of 'meloncholia,' explaining that a depression was literally caused by 'black, heavy blood passing through the patient's veins.' The Greeks believed depression was caused by too much 'black bile' in the blood. If you have ever experienced this horrible condition, you will be nodding your head right about now as you read these words. There were moments for me when I doubted that my heart would be able to beat through the heavy, black blood… or whether it was worth the effort." [6]

For Naomi, somewhere between her enthusiastic invitation, "Come on girls, let's head for Bethlehem. The Lord (faith-filled covenantal God) has given his people food" and the actuality of making the trip, she lost heart. The black, heavy blood stopped her. The journey seemed too hard, too long, too difficult, too hopeless.

In Ruth 1:8, Naomi hits her wall. What does she say?

_____

_____

Read verses 8-15 and describe the desperate conversation:

_____

_____

When someone is immersed in depression, it makes for some "stinkin' thinkin.'" How did Naomi rationalize sending Orpah and Ruth back to Moab?

Here's our interpretation of Naomi's manic episode:

"Girls, I'm too old and can't get married again, and even if I did marry and have sons, how long would it take for them to grow up and marry you, and how old would you be, and who knows if you would be able to have children, and then they'd have to grow up, and this whole thing makes no sense whatsoever because God has obviously sent me all manner of trouble, so the best thing you can do is leave me and go back to your gods in Moab and your families where you'd have a fighting chance at life again. Save yourselves!"

NOTE TO SELF: How easy is it for us to look at a difficult scenario and say, 'I'm too old… I'm too used up… I'm too unworthy… God has turned away from me… I can't… I can't… I can't….' Have you felt this way? Can you presently relate to Naomi's broken heart? If so, please write a short prayer, even if it's, "Help me, Lord!"

You may find yourself feeling like Naomi. Do you feel empty? Do you wonder at times if the hand of the Lord has gone out against you? Do you feel he has afflicted you? Has he dealt bitterly with you?

The tragedies and heartaches of life can leave us wondering where God is and how he could allow such pain. There are no easy answers, and when others try to comfort us with well-meaning platitudes, it often adds insult to injury.

Psalm 38 is an anguished heart cry from King David. We don't know at what point in his life he wrote this psalm, but we can be sure of how he was feeling when he wrote it. It is twenty-two verses full of pain and grief, and it ends with no answer.

Read Psalm 38 and write out verse 8:

The New American Standard version says, "I am benumbed and badly crushed; I groan because of the agitation of my heart." The Amplified Bible is even more graphic: "I am faint and sorely bruised, [deadly cold and quite worn out]; I groan by reason of the disquiet and moaning of my heart."

In the middle of the outpouring of his soul, David resolves to do one thing. Write what he says in **Psalm 38:15:**

Hoping in God is all any of us can do, especially when answers are not forthcoming. Now turn to **1 Peter 5:9-10** and let these words of truth fall into the broken places of your heart.

What will God do with our suffering?

_____

_____

We must keep our eyes on the unseen, believing he is working even in "Chapter One," in the dry heat, in the losses and pain of a fallen world, specifically to heal our broken places. Suffering is never wasted in God's hands. He holds those tears in a jar, keeps them near your story in his book. All we have to do is keep turning each page, walking into the next chapter.

Now finish reading Ruth 1.

In **verse 14** who went back to Moab?

_____

Orpah returned to Moab. The following observation about Orpah's choice allows us a Selah moment, to pause and calmly think of that.

"How many of us part with Christ at this crossway! Like Orpah they go a furlong or two with Christ, till he goes to take them off from their worldly hopes and bids them prepare for hardship, and then they fairly kiss and leave him."[7]

In contrast, what did Ruth say?

_____

_____

Ruth physically clung to Naomi. She would not take "no" for an answer. In **verses 16-17**, Ruth makes a glorious declaration of her love and loyalty to Naomi right in the middle of Naomi's darkest moment.

Write in your own words what Ruth says to her mother-in-law:

_____

_____

_____

Ruth represents the Gentile nations who would come to know Christ and become his bride. She declared her allegiance to the God of Naomi's people, to Naomi herself, and to live, die, and be buried with the last member of a family she had grown to love in spite of living in Moab, in spite of their desperate times and the unknown future that lay ahead. Basically Ruth said to Naomi, "Stop telling me to go away. I'm not leaving you. Whatever happens, we're in this together. Because of you, I have found God. And only death can keep us apart."

"(Ruth's) assertion that Naomi's God would be her God is especially striking. Ruth's use of the divine name Yahweh translated as "the Lord" in an oath indicates her commitment to the living God. She was choosing to cling not only to Naomi, her land, and her people, but also to her God. In effect, Ruth was forsaking all that she had ever known to follow the one true God." [8]

Her faithfulness shocks and delights us and makes us want to shout, 'Hallelujah!" In this beautiful declaration of love, Ruth is encouraging Naomi to hope again.

What did Ruth see in Naomi that made her choose to stay with this broken woman? What happened in their ten years together that caused Ruth to cling to her? Why did Ruth keep pulling Naomi forward toward hope? Maybe it would help us imagine what Ruth saw in Naomi if we reflect on the women in our lives that have shown us what the love of God is by their actions, their behavior, their conversation, their service, and their faithful friendship.

Please name a friend who has extended grace to you and shown you the love of God. Write what you have learned about God through her love:

_____

_____

_____

Ruth's loyalty is astonishing. It is truly amazing that Ruth chose to stay with Naomi and embrace the Lord. Ruth is exhibiting loyalty not only to Naomi, but also to God. After all, Ruth has seen tragedy strike a family that believed in the lovingkindness of a God named Yahweh. If he was so good, why did he allow all the men in the family to die? Ruth was legally free to start over and make a new life for herself in her own land, but she was willing to give that up and stay with Naomi.

It seems evident that Naomi adored Ruth. She drops the words "in-law" and calls Ruth "daughter." In fact, the word "daughter" is used eleven times in the four chapters of the book of Ruth.

NOTE: To call a woman "daughter" was the highest term of endearment in Jewish culture. Over and again Israel is referred to by God as "Daughter of Zion" and "Daughters of Jerusalem." When Naomi called Ruth "daughter," there was no greater way to express her feelings of love.

After such a passionate plea, how does Naomi respond in **verse 18**?

_____

_____

Hope stifled despair. The glorious insistence of Ruth's love closed the door to Naomi's protests. Naomi couldn't top that speech, not even with another run-on sentence. So the two women make the journey, and enter the city of Bethlehem.

In the larger family photo God is painting, we see the arms of a believing Gentile woman lock with those of a weary Israelite. Together, the two women representing Israel and Gentile nations enter a new beginning by returning to the Lord.

The book of Ruth uses the word "return" twelve times. We all have had journeys where we left places of death (Moab) to return to places of life (Bethlehem, the birthplace of Jesus). We share the sigh of gratitude with Naomi and Ruth as they return to God's loving arms of protection.

What was Naomi thinking as she and Ruth made the journey back to Bethlehem? *My husband and I left home and took our sons to Moab to keep from starving. They all ended up dying anyway. I wish I had died too. When everyone sees me, what will they think? I'm sure they'll wonder what sins I've committed to deserve this kind of punishment from Yahweh.*

As she looked at the young maiden trudging beside her, carrying their meager bundles, what went through Naomi's mind? *What does this headstrong daughter see in me? Why does she cling to me? I'm a dried-up old woman. God is angry with me. Ruth should get away from me before God curses her too.*

Write a brief comment you would have made from Naomi's point of view.

_____

_____

Yet as they come to Bethlehem, what a profound entrance these two women make!

The Word tells us only that the whole city was "stirred" upon their arrival. "What's up with this?" people were saying. "Isn't that Naomi?" Naomi must have weathered her ten years in Moab fairly well, because she was recognized quite easily upon her return.

One has to smile at her description of herself. Naomi is still living in the aftermath of Chapter One, letting that define her present state.

What does she say about her name in **verses 20-21**?

_____

_____

In spite of Ruth's great care of Naomi, their successful entry back into the "House of Bread," she has not fully recovered from her depression. In both verses 20 and 21 she points to heaven and blames God for her pitiful affliction. The events of her life still have convinced her that God is against her. When she reaches her hometown, she greets her old friends and tells them she's changed her name. What she says, in essence, is, "Call me bitter, because God has forgotten me."

Isn't this a typical human response to trials? When things get rough often we default to blaming God. "God could have… should have… would have…." Before we shake a fist in his direction, we might be wise to look first at what we've given God to work with. Naomi might have been wise to think through the choice her family made in leaving Bethlehem and how her family was influenced by moving to a foreign land that worshiped idols. Could she further have noted that, in spite of her loss, God was merciful to give her Ruth? It's doubtful Naomi would have made it back to Bethlehem except for Ruth's loyal love given when Naomi had no will of her own to live.

GIRL ASSIGNMENT: If you have a special "Ruth" in your life, please take time this week to call and thank her for walking you through the places in your life when you wanted to blame God or give up. Or better yet, go to lunch and tell her in person!

CHAPTER ONE ENDS, NEW DREAMS BEGIN

What's happening in Bethlehem in **verse 22**?

_____

_____

It was springtime and the beginning of the barley harvest. Harvest. What perfect God-led timing for Ruth and Naomi to enter Bethlehem during a season ripe with possibilities.

By the end of Ruth 1, God has given Naomi a friend of her right hand. Ruth's beautiful entreaty of love and loyalty comes to Naomi from the lips of a Moabite woman. From the land of Israel's enemy, God allows the hand of Ruth to reach out and give strength and faith to the weak, faint heart of her mother-in-law.

It's not the counsel of a rabbi that entreats Naomi to keep believing. It's not an Israelite sister who declares words of undying love. From the lips of a Moabite daughter-in-law flows the inspiring passage so passionate and powerful it represents the commitment of wedding vows. Ruth saves Naomi's life. A Moabite woman has fallen in love with the God of Elimelech's family.

Ruth is a symbol of the coming church of Jesus. She symbolizes the future Gentile bride of Christ. The church of Jesus Christ will be the one to keep hope alive in Israel, as in the heart of Naomi. It's the voice of Ruth that tells Naomi to keep believing, keep hoping, keep living, to keep dreaming. How unfathomable, merciful, and unpredictable are the ways of God!

TODAY'S DATE: _____

WRITE YOUR OWN HEADLINE: God always is working to lead you through the painful chapters of life. Behind what we see, he is there, working, listening to our prayers, catching our tears that fall, and waiting to rejoice with us when we reach new places of restoration and understanding. Write a headline that describes your personal "Chapter One" deliverance.

_____

_____

> "Behind the seen
> Through the veil
> God reigns on high and all is well
> The angels sing
> Go and tell that all is well
> Behind the seen." [9]

WEEK TWO
You have an **evite**

BABY SHOWER FOR RUTH

Place: Estate of Boaz

Time: All Day Friday

Hosts: Naomi and her YaYa Sisterhood of the Grandmother's Traveling Partners

Colors for Nursery: Tan, Blue, Brown, Rust, Wheat

Please join us as we celebrate the birth of the son born to Boaz and Ruth. He will be called Obed, proudly named by his grandmother's best friends. Jewish mothers are famous for their wisdom on all matters maternal, so come with your best piece of advice. We will assemble a scrapbook of helpful hints our dear Ruth can reference for years to come.

Registered: Babies 'R' Ours, Bethlehem Generational Gems

TODAY'S HEROINE:
Ruth

*My whole being follows hard after you and clings closely to you;
your right hand upholds me (Ps. 63:8, Amplified Bible).*

"Two women looked through bars,

One saw mud, another saw stars." [10]

God bless Naomi. She had plenty of reasons to see a muddy landscape from her prison of loss. But Ruth chose to embrace her loss as a get-out-of-jail-free card. Where Naomi saw a dead end, Ruth began searching the horizon for new life. Grief can make or break us. Losing can only be winning in the arms of God.

If Naomi was a woman who saw the glass half-empty, then Ruth was a perfect best friend to balance out the scales. While the nation of Israel was turning to idols, a Gentile woman in Moab was turning away from idols to serve the living God. As we finish the last three chapters of Ruth, we are given one of the most beautiful pictures of friendship in biblical history.

Ruth was a friend of Naomi's right hand, a friend through life and into death, a friend who symbolizes the everlasting connection of Gentile believers grafted into the lineage of Israel's inheritance.

Who is the friend of your right hand?

Our prayer is that you are doing this study with your closest friend, and even a group of women who are walking with you through life, clinging to Jesus.

We are grateful beyond words to have each other as dearest, best friends in a relationship that spans 30 years. We have seen each other at our best and worst. We have shared countless meals, hours of work, tears, much laughter and our very own book club for two. The funny things our children say make both of us laugh as though they were our own kids. We buy each other lip gloss and scented candles. But there is so much more that knits our hearts together.

Turn to read **Hebrews 10:12** and note who sits at the right hand of God:

_____

Christ is the ultimate best friend any of us will ever know. But God gives us friends here on earth who love us with his love, who share mutual faith in his blood and covering. It's a sweet foretaste of eternal fellowship with Christ to have such a girlfriend this side of paradise.

The cement of our friendship is our love for Jesus. We can tell each other something the Lord has shown us without the fear of being seen as 'weird.' We thrill at his revelations and understand why we cannot wait to talk about them. Together we watch the current headlines and try to analyze the times, talking excitedly about our soon-returning Savior. We anticipate the joys of heaven and know our friendship will continue there. We want God's best for each other. Our friendship is God's gift, and through it we have a glimpse of what Ruth and Naomi must have shared.

Recall from memory what Naomi told Ruth to do while living in Chapter One:

_____

_____

From memory again, how did Ruth respond?

_____

_____

As everyone knows, friendship requires investment. The seeds of a great friendship must be sown in fertile soil, and they take time to be cultivated and nurtured. A committed relationship always costs us something and will often come with struggle and pain.

What was Naomi's state of mind when Ruth made her choice?

_____

_____

What did Ruth's choice require of her?

_____

_____

NOTE: Have you noticed that God gives you strength when your best friend is weak? Have you ever been a "Naomi" who put your "Ruth" through the ringer?

_____

_____

At the end of Chapter One Naomi was not able to contribute anything to their relationship. She was fighting hope and demanding to be left alone. But the friend of her right hand simply refused to walk away.

We don't know what Ruth saw in Naomi that moved her to embrace her depressed mother-in-law with such fierce love. Think about this: Ruth chose Naomi over her own biological mother. Ruth chose to leave her native land of Moab and make a sixty-mile journey to Judah, pulling Naomi along every step of the way if need be. Perhaps she remembered the history of her people, and how Moabite women had been used as pawns to enslave and defeat the Israelite men in times past. No woman of any nationality wants to be sexually manipulated. Did Ruth view marriage to Naomi's son, Mahlon, as a way to move farther from the Moabite culture and closer to the Hebrew God of Jehovah?

How did Ruth learn of Yahweh? Why did she give up the belief system she'd known all her life and put her faith in God? She learned about him in the home of her in-laws. While baking the bread and weaving at the loom, she saw the faith of her mother-in-law and knew she had found something far more satisfying than the worship of Baal. She must have witnessed enough of a difference in Naomi's life and family that convinced her to boldly proclaim allegiance to their Jehovah God, even unto to death.

Can you think of a friend who even in their weakest moment inspired you with their faith?

_____

_____

However this transformation occurred, we know that Ruth made a brave, courageous choice in leaving Moab to go with Naomi to Bethlehem. Frankly, without the faith of her lovely daughter-in-law, it's doubtful that Naomi would have survived the journey. Ruth exhibited a committed love, one that was strong when her best friend was weak. She gave Naomi the pep talk of her life and then walked her despairing mother-in-law out of Moab and into God's land again.

The love Ruth gave to Naomi is translated in Hebrew as "kindly" (Ruth 1:8), representing the covenantal love of God.[11] The book of Ruth is an exclamation point to the overriding theme originated in Genesis 12:1-3. God desires people from all nations, tongues, and tribes of the world be saved. The invitation to his throne room stands open to any who will believe in the work of Jesus and enter there. How we continue to marvel at the lover of our souls. With Ruth, once more God makes clear how he feels about his girls, no matter their background, heritage, or nationality.

Arm-in-arm, Ruth and Naomi have arrived in Bethlehem, looking for their daily bread and a new beginning. They've lost so much, yet Ruth has faith enough for both of them. She trusts that Jehovah God has not forgotten them. When Naomi is down, Ruth picks her up. In showing this steady, gentle loyalty Ruth put herself in a position for favor to fall. And the Lord God is ready to bless her sandals off!

It is springtime, the time of the barley harvest, when they arrive in Bethlehem. These two weary women don't know it, but this spring will be different for them. This spring will bring hope and a new beginning in the "House of Bread."

In the first verse of Ruth 2, hope begins to dawn for Ruth and Naomi. It is found in one word: kinsman.

Delight in reading **Ruth 2**.

Who enters the scene in **verse 1**?

_____

How is he related to Naomi?

_____

What does Ruth volunteer to do in **verse 2**?

_____

In verse one we are introduced to Boaz, a man related to the family of Elimelech. He is wealthy, of noble character and high standing in the community. His name means "swift strength."[12] The author of Ruth places his name at the beginning of this chapter because it is Boaz who will be used by God to orchestrate the fate and future of our two hungry heroines. Not only is he their "kinsman." As the story unfolds, we discover that Boaz is a representative of the Messiah; a kinsman-redeemer.

Ruth asks permission from Naomi to glean in the fields nearby. Gleaning is mentioned thirty-four times in the Old Testament, twelve of these being in the book of Ruth. It was the act of "gathering up" or "picking up."

Turn and **Read Deuteronomy 24:19-22**. What three kinds of people were able to glean from the fields of the Hebrews?

_____

_____

What did God want his people to remember as they were harvesting the fields?

_____

_____

NOTE: By remembering their own poverty and hardship in Egypt, God hoped they would learn compassion for others in difficult circumstances. He hoped they would be generous and with willing hearts would leave the gleanings for the poor.

Throughout his Word, the Lord speaks relentlessly about taking care of the widow, the orphan, and the weak. The picture of leaving some of the harvest behind is a vivid reminder for us today. As we are blessed, we never should clutch the blessing too tightly. We are called to share with those less fortunate. Ruth and Naomi are both widows in need of food.

To her credit, Ruth is not too proud to go out and pick up the leftovers from the reapers in the field. Going out to glean was an act of faith. She knew she was an alien and might not be treated well by the Hebrews. She works hard for the money. And she doesn't go unnoticed.

Describe in your own words what happens in **verses 3-13**:

_____

_____

In **verse 3** the providence of God breaks through. Whose field does Ruth visit?

_____

_____

For skeptics who find it a little too convenient that Ruth stopped to glean on Boaz's property, please note that she did not know who he was. She simply set out to find food for herself and Naomi. Ruth had no idea where she was gleaning because there were no fence rows or mailboxes marking the property lines to reveal the owner of each field. It was dangerous work and she had to be careful. When she happened to come to the field owned by

Boaz, this was unintentional on her part. Yet, with those who follow God, nothing is wasted or coincidental.

Turn to Proverbs 20:24.

Who plans our steps?

_____

_____

God led Ruth to a very special field indeed. Did you know the field of Boaz is the very field that David also walked in while caring for his father Jesse's sheep? It is also the field where the angels appeared to the shepherds when they announced the birth of the Messiah! Oh, glory!

Take a moment and look at the "field" God has led you to inhabit during your life. It's no accident that you are living in exactly the place you live, put together precisely as he made you for your time on the planet earth!

Does this cause anything to rise up in you?

_____

Do you feel faith growing in your heart?

_____

Each simple act of obedience made for the next right choice is honored by God. He has promised to take care of you. He will lead you to his fields of provision where he will generously meet your needs. And he will use you as part of his plan for this world. God always guides the willing child. That's good news, dear daughter.

We are like Ruth, trusting in his covering and purpose for our place in this foreign land. And like Ruth, God has given us far and above more than we can dream, ask, or imagine. He leads us into green pastures prepared for us from the foundations of the world. His only Son, foreshadowed by Boaz, bought us back from the fallen garden to live with him forever.

As we read this beautiful love story, let's walk with Ruth as she meets her kinsman-redeemer and the love of her life!

What do we learn about Boaz's character by how he greeted the employees in his field?

_____

_____

Boaz must have been a terrific boss. When he approached his workers he shouted out, "The Lord be with you!" and was answered with the same greeting. Then his eyes caught sight of a newcomer, following behind the reapers, picking up each kernel of barley. He asked "Who is that girl?" Quickly, he was told that she was a Moabite, living with Naomi. This girl punched in early on the time clock, worked hard without complaining, and only stopped a few times to rest.

In **verses 8-9**, how did Boaz reach out to Ruth?

_____

_____

Boaz immediately gave Ruth his advice about the safest fields to work. He told her to stay close to his female workers. He told the men around her, "Hands off… don't even think about it!" He was more than generous to Ruth by making it safe in his fields while she gleaned. Ruth was a Moabite woman. She could easily have been manhandled or abused. Boaz made sure she was watched and guarded, and he kept a close personal eye on her for protection.

She was undone by this stranger's kindness.

Ruth had a stellar reputation. It was a reputation of loyalty, compassion, strength, and courage. Word traveled fast around the houses of Bethlehem. There was talk about the Moabite woman who left her own people to come and live among the people of Jehovah. Only a short while earlier, Ruth had given Naomi the blessing of perseverance and faith. Now it was Boaz who spoke a blessing over her.

In **verses 11-12**, how does Boaz explain his benevolence?

_____

_____

"A full reward be given you by the Lord, the God of Israel, under whose wings you have come to take refuge" (Amplified Bible).

With his glorious declaration, Boaz is introducing Ruth (the Gentiles) to the workers around him (Israel). We only can imagine how this might have overwhelmed Ruth. The previous verse tells us she is, at the moment, flat on her face on the ground before Boaz, humbling herself because of his kindness toward her. (Sounds like a Gentile heart that is grateful to be included in the inheritance of Israel.)

Verse 11 begins with the phrase, "Boaz answered her…." The literal translation is "Boaz raised his voice." Boaz was speaking at full volume, words loud enough for everyone to hear.

It went something like this: "Look at this woman! And she's not even one of us! All that you have done for your mother-in-law after the death of your husband has been fully reported to me, and how you left your father and mother and the land of your birth, and came to a people that you did not previously know." (Boaz may have replicated Naomi with a few run on sentences).

He shouts to everyone that Ruth has taken refuge under the wings of the God of Israel. He is letting everyone know she has left the idols of Moab and turned to the living God. Boaz then proclaims God will reward her for this choice.

Ruth has taken refuge under the wings of the cherubim that cover the mercy seat on the Ark of the Covenant. She knows she is a foreigner, outside the covenant promises of God. But by faith she has placed her trust in Jehovah and Boaz rejoices in her passion. For a godly man like Boaz, he must have been saddened by the behavior of Israel during this time. When he looked at Ruth, an outsider and the most unlikely candidate for beginning a revival, he must have been thrilled by her faith. In a time when many of God's people were behaving in an ungodly manner, there emerges a Gentile woman from Moab who shows greater loyalty, humility, and strength of character than most Hebrews.

As Christ sees all nations come to him, how do you imagine he feels?

_____

_____

It's interesting to wonder if Boaz knew he was speaking prophetically into both of their futures. In his verbal blessing, Boaz declared that Ruth had coming joys waiting for her. Did he know he would be part of that equation? He must have been impressed with Ruth because she was immediately given a seat at his table during lunch break. After she ate well (and filled a "to go box" for Naomi) she returned to the field to work.

Read Deuteronomy 10:18.

What did Boaz do for Ruth that reflected the character of God?

_____

_____

Boaz ordered his men to leave a little extra barley behind them as they worked so that Ruth would have plenty to take home with her that evening. He did this discreetly and didn't make it obvious. He didn't want to shame her by making her feel like she'd been given a handout. Boaz was generous to Ruth in a way that did not humiliate her. He knew she and Naomi were poor. He let her work but made sure she got all she needed. The Chinese would say Boaz let Ruth "save face."

Imagine Ruth walking behind the men of Israel as they gathered the harvest in the fields. She is ever aware that she comes from Moab, a foreigner and undeserving of the grain she gathers from a God she has chosen to serve. Her childlike willingness to believe in Jehovah over all other gods reminds us of another woman, an outsider to the Jewish heritage. She too believed in Jesus and his power from one almighty source, and was eager to have even the scraps of favor that fell from his table.

Turn for a moment and read Matthew 15:21-28.

Here we find a Greek woman who approaches Jesus, begging him to cure her daughter from demon possession. In one of Christ's more curious responses to a desperate woman, what does he first say to her in **verses 24 and 26**?

_____

_____

In the Greek culture of her day, a pagan would see a "healer" as a magician. "Healing had no necessary connection to holiness. Exorcism in particular was the special province of magicians. In their eyes, supernatural power could only be manipulated by sorcerers adept in occult skills." [13] Perhaps this explains why Jesus did not want her to assume he was just another "wonder-worker" manning a traveling magic show.

How does she let Jesus know that she understands he is God's holy man, and a source of life?

_____

_____

Her acknowledgment of the power of even the crumbs from his table reveals her faith. She knows "that there is indeed an essential difference between the religion of pagans and that of Jews. Magic is not the same as miracle. Connecting wholeness and holiness is crucial. Her reply shows Jesus that she perceives a difference in her own background of occultism and his tradition of righteousness, knowing that her people's gods offer her neither healing nor protection." [14]

In **verse 27** her response is filled with sincere belief. So much so that Jesus replied with passionate approval and grace: "O woman, great is your faith! Be it done for you as you wish. And her daughter was cured from that moment" (Matt. 15:28 Amplified Bible).

Much like Ruth, this woman understood the power of grace that falls on any who come under the covering of God. Exactly like Ruth, she was ready to get down on her knees to receive the leftovers, trusting they would be far better than bowing to any of her culture's false gods.

Read Hebrews 2:14-15.

What did Jesus have to "share in" or "partake of" in order to redeem us?

_____

_____

Read 1 Peter 1:18-19.

What did he redeem us with?

His blood runs in every direction. Different centuries and two women who were outsiders received blessing from God's people. Both women were included in the Jewish heritage of deliverance, sustenance, and loving acceptance at the table of God. Our Ruth, the foreigner to Bethlehem, returns home, not with a few crumbs but a bounteous return.

For a moment, thank God for a time when only he could provide what you needed:

_____

_____

Arriving back in town, Ruth tells her mother-in-law everything! She arrives with what would have been the equivalent of more than half a bushel of barley (enough to feed them for nearly a week). This amount would be what a normal worker would bring home, not someone following behind and picking up the scraps. Naomi was wild with questions and out of her mind with joy at the answers.

Ruth's explanation, paraphrased here, could have inspired another of Naomi's run-on sentences:

"You mean to tell me you have been in the field of Boaz, why that's one of our closest relatives and he has the right to redeem you in marriage my dear, which I'll explain later, but obviously this favor means the Lord has not forgotten us, but most assuredly has placed you in exactly the right place and time, so you do exactly what Boaz tells you and don't let any of the other men near you because he's right, they could get out of line, but my oh my, there might be a levirate marriage right around the corner!"

Well, maybe Naomi wasn't quite so verbose. But her hopes and dreams for the future sprang to life with each passing day.

Read Romans 15:13. Write it in your words on the lines below:

_____

_____

How do we abound in hope? There is no way to measure the power of hope. Hope brings new life to a person who despairs of ever seeing another good day. We move on by the power of the Holy Spirit. We cannot abound in hope by willing ourselves to do it. Only by the filling of the spirit can hope abound in us.

What distracts you from the work of God's spirit?

_____

_____

If we keep our eyes on our circumstances, or on the daily headlines, our hopes will die.

According to **1 Peter 1:3**, to what are we born again?

_____

_____

After something is born, what happens next? Growth! We have a living hope. It is not stagnant. It is meant to increase with every breath we take. We water the living hope within us by reading the word of God.

WATERING WORDS: Look up the verses below and pick one to write on an index card. Carry it in your purse. Read it at stop lights, while waiting in line, during TV commercials, or anytime you need to remind yourself of the hope alive in you!

2 Peter 1:4; 1 Thessalonians 1:3; Colossians 1:27

In the meantime, do as Ruth did. She continued to "glean." The barley harvest was from March to April. The wheat harvest, from June to July. Ruth kept working and Naomi kept planning. Hope to hope, just like us, girlfriend. Hope on in the work of the Holy Spirit. And like the best girl movie we could rent, Ruth lived out a great love story. Naomi played matchmaker to the hilt. She saw great potential in Boaz as a son-in-law, and like every good Jewish mother, she began to plan a marriage.

THREE FUNERALS AND A WEDDING

Now read Ruth 3.

Don't you love this? Naomi was ready to throw in the towel in Ruth 1, and by Ruth 3 she's playing matchmaker with the friend of her right hand. From Chapter One, in which she said, "It's too late, keep away from me, there is nothing I can do for you!" we find Naomi dying her wedding shoes.

In **verse 1**, what does she call Ruth?

"Darling daughter, shall I not now find a home for you that you may prosper?"

Makes one smile! Ruth keeps working and Naomi began planning. She made a plan for a midnight meeting between Boaz and Ruth.

Reading through this chapter, we find a bold and calculated courtship. Naomi's instructions, Ruth's actions, and Boaz's responses are examples of holiness we would do well to heed in our present culture. Naomi sees clearly that Boaz is a potential kinsman-redeemer. She knows the history of levirate marriages in Israel and places Ruth in the position to become a new bride.

LEVIRATE MARRIAGE: This comes from the word "levir," meaning "a husband's brother" as described in **Deuteronomy 25:5-6**. According to this law, if a married man died without having a son to carry on his line, his brother was obligated to bear a son by his widow. The child born to them would thereafter be considered heir to the dead brother's household. This would keep the family tree alive. [15]

A levirate marriage combines the Deuteronomy passages with those in Leviticus. **Read Leviticus 25:25.**

What is now protected in the preservation of a family line?

_____

_____

At first glance this seems like a rather sterile approach to marriage, leaving little room for romance. The closest family member is "obligated" to marry. Yet Naomi wisely observes how God is providing both a kinsman who will redeem Ruth's life, and a man who also brings the added blessing of loving her deeply.

How does this description remind us of our relationship with Jesus?

_____

_____

Christ redeems and restores us to God. But he does so with the greatest heart of love ever known. He poured out his love and heart for us, dying in our place. Nothing is more romantic in the eternal realm than being part of his bride. Who could ever love a woman more deeply or perfectly than Jesus?

As we watch Naomi's plans, it's important to note that she had no position, no money, nothing to work with but faith in God, the Jewish laws, and what she saw happening before her eyes. As a widow in Israel, Naomi owned the field left to her by Elimelech. Yet she could not hire workers for the field and was in no physical state to work the land herself.

But she knew who could change everything.

So Naomi decided to give the Lord a lot to work with! She prepared Ruth for marriage and her field for sale. In doing this, she put everything on the altar and trusted completely in a mighty move of God.

FIELD FOR SALE: SEE FINE PRINT FOR DETAILS

Naomi opened up every possible avenue for God to bless Ruth, Boaz, and herself. Her behavior may make us laugh a bit, but her bold courage in Yahweh paid off.

Do you sometimes wonder how being bold as a woman takes a lot of backbone? Explain:

_____

_____

Several times Naomi referred to Boaz as the "ga'al," the Hebrew reference to a protector or guarantor of the family rights. He could buy back property the family had sold, provide an heir for a deceased brother by marriage to his wife, even buy back a member of the family sold into slavery due to poverty or avenge a relative who had been murdered by killing the murderer.[16]

Read Isaiah 60:16.

Describe "redeemer" as used in this verse.

_____

_____

Now read 1 Peter 1:18-19.

Who is named as redeemer of all believers?

_____

The "ga'al" provided the means by which jeopardized covenant blessings could be regained, redeemed, restored, renewed. Ruth experiences the goodness of such grace in her romance with Boaz.

What does Naomi tell Ruth to do in **Ruth 3:3-4**?

_____

_____

For days Ruth has been out in the fields, sweating in the hot sun, wearing no makeup and having who knows what kind of hair days. She had been seen by Boaz always dressed in her workout clothes. Most of us wouldn't want a potential husband to see us in our sweats until the ring was on our finger or after the bells tolled. Yet Boaz saw into her character. He saw a beautiful, honorable, valuable woman working in his fields. Still, he had yet to see Ruth all decked out and smelling of perfume. Like the sweetest moment between a mother and daughter, Naomi takes great care in preparing Ruth to look her best.

Ruth obeys Naomi's instructions to the letter.

Where did Naomi send Ruth?

___

Ruth was sent to the threshing floor where the animals would trample the husks to separate the grain. This process was called "winnowing" on the threshing floor. The men working for Boaz would be threshing the grain in the evening, from four to five o'clock, when a cool breeze blew in from the Mediterranean Sea. The threshing floor would be located in a public place where the mixture would be tossed in the air so the cool evening breeze would blow away the excess chaff.

Following this work, there would be a celebration, food and wine, and Boaz would sleep the night beside the grain to protect it from thieves. He had no idea who was about to join him on the threshing floor.

By sending Ruth into the night to meet with Boaz, Naomi sent a gentle, clear, and lovely message. Boaz would know that he had the right to redeem the field of Elimelech, to keep the land in their family. And the bonus in all of this would be Ruth, her hand in marriage and redemptive new lives for everyone.

Read verses 7-14.

QUESTION: Do you sometimes feel it takes a clear message from us for men to know how we feel? If so, explain.

___

We'd like to think they can "read our minds" like Superman with Lois Lane. But men are grateful when we are straightforward with them in a respectful way.

What message did Ruth respectfully give Boaz in these verses?

___

Yes, for all practical purposes our sweet Ruth gracefully, quietly proposed! This was a fairly gutsy thing to do. No doubt about it, Ruth had moxie. By going at night, Ruth went in secret so that no one would see her. Some commentaries suggest she did this carefully so as not to embarrass Boaz should he refuse her proposal.

While Boaz slept, what did Ruth do to his feet?

___

Notice she did not lay beside Boaz; she did not uncover anything but his feet. She did not undress, or entice him physically. She showed him with clear choices the intention of her heart. "Touching and holding his feet was an act of submission. This was a daring and dramatic action that would call for a decision on his part to be her protector—and likely, her husband."[17]

What did Ruth ask of him?

_____

_____

In **Ruth 2:12**, Boaz proclaimed in a loud voice that Ruth had taken refuge under the wings of Jehovah. Now, by taking hold of the tip of his garment, Ruth asks Boaz if she can take refuge under his covering.

A more literal translation of what Ruth said would be, "Spread your wing of protection over your maidservant, for you are next of kin."

As far as we know, Boaz had never married. He was much older than Ruth. He probably wasn't accustomed to having a lovely young lady hold his feet around midnight or any other time. He awoke and was startled by her presence. Ruth used his former words in asking him to cover her in marriage.

How would you describe his response?
Overjoyed
Grateful
Overwhelmed
Delighted
Flattered
Determined to do the next right thing to honor her request
ALL of the above and more!

Boaz was well aware that Ruth could have been interested in a younger man, someone more wealthy or perhaps more powerful.

Do you know women who are endlessly attracted to men of power regardless of their character?

_____

_____

Thankfully Ruth wanted a man who would give her true riches: honor, love of God and family, safety, protection, and a heart that would claim her hand in public. In **Ruth 3:11**, he sings her praises: "All my people in the city know that you are a woman of strength (worth, bravery, capability)" (Amplified Bible).

But Boaz goes the extra, extra mile to make Ruth his bride. He doesn't want any single part of the process to be questionable. In doing so, he shows great respect and admiration for Ruth and allows her the precious gift every woman desires: safety and trust with her mate.

What does Boaz say in **verse 12**?

_____

_____

Once again he responds with great generosity. He admits that he is a close relative, but there is someone closer to Ruth than him. This man has the right of first refusal. But if that man cannot redeem her, Boaz promises to do so himself. This all-important matter will be settled by Boaz, first thing in the morning.

In the meanwhile, where does Ruth spend the night?

_____

_____

Ruth lays down at his bidding, on the threshing floor again at his feet. Talk about honoring your lady! Boaz offers her full protection from going out into the night alone. And he never touches her as she lay sleeping at his feet. He is showing himself to be man who will take great care of her on all sides. Early in the morning she wakes to leave so that no one would see her and get the wrong idea. Boaz has also made sure to protect her reputation.

In **verse 15**, what does Boaz give her before she leaves?

_____

_____

He demonstrates his loyal love and kindness to her by another gift of barley grain. This would be the equivalent of an engagement ring. The words "laid it on her" means that most likely he had to help Ruth with how to manage this large amount on her head. This act of kindness seems to be a message to Naomi saying, "I am willing to provide for you in your widowhood not only today, but always."

Speaking of Naomi, can't you just see her looking out the window, watching for any sign of her daughter-in-law? Ruth arrives home just before dawn and tells Naomi everything. What her face must have looked like when she came through the door! She was radiant. Everything was about to change. Once again. let's imagine their conversation.

"Where have you been? It's morning! What happened? Tell me everything!" Naomi must have said as she put away the new gift of grain.

In **verse 17**, please do not miss the beautiful message from Boaz given to the friend of Ruth's right hand.

_____

_____

Wouldn't you have loved to have seen Naomi's face when she heard these words. "Do not go home empty-handed to your mother-in-law!" Naomi might have exclaimed. "Did he truly say this? What a darling man! What a catch, my Ruth! How God has turned my mourning into dancing!"

From emptiness to fullness, from bitterness to joy, Naomi now sees the hand of God move to restore her life. Surely the Lord sees and hears the cries of his people, even two lonely widows making their way back to his covering.

We almost can hear a Jewish mother's excitement in the last verse of Ruth 3. If Boaz was successful in his bid for Ruth's hand, then they would never see another day of hunger and want. It is certain that Naomi looked at Ruth and wondered how God could bless her so richly with such a precious daughter-in-law. Hope is rising and her heart is healing.

"Oh, my! This is wonderful! Simply wonderful! God be praised! You sit down now Ruth, you probably didn't sleep a wink last night with all this excitement. And Boaz, he's the kind of man you can count on. You sit still, dearest. I tell you Boaz will take care of everything this very day, you'll see, or my name isn't Naomi!"

CHAPTER FOUR: MORE AND MORE AND MORE

In Chapter One, Naomi and Ruth never could have imagined the blessings the Lord had waiting for them in Chapter Four. They left Moab arm-in-arm with nothing to hope in but a covenantal God who promised to take care of his people. From Ruth's faith, Naomi drew strength, and with every step in God's direction, they found his faithfulness to be more real than any loss or famine.

Read Ruth 4:1-7.

Boaz the kinsman-redeemer now steps into the role of lawyer, negotiating every detail for the future of Naomi and Ruth.

Where does Boaz conduct the affairs?

_____

_____

Who is the first man to walk by the gate?

_____

_____

Boaz goes to the city gate where business transactions take place. He bids the kinsman pull up a chair and proceeds to invite ten elders of the city to join in as witnesses. He lays out the situation and explains Naomi's desire to sell her land. One of them must either take Ruth's hand or pass on the offer.

Describe the legal proposal before the two men:

_____

_____

Behind Door Number One: Naomi and her land which belong to "our brother" Elimelech.

Not a bad deal.

Behind Door Number Two: Naomi, her land, and Ruth, the Moabitess.

Ruth, from where?

Behind Door Number Three: Naomi, her land, Ruth, and the responsibility of any children you have with Ruth, the Moabitess.

Deal or no deal?

In **verse 6,** how does the primary kinsman respond and why?

_____

_____

His reasons for declining are interesting. He says he doesn't want to marry Ruth, "Lest I jeopardize my own inheritance." What did he mean by this? It could be that he just didn't want the financial responsibility of caring for two more women. He also knew that if he had a son by Ruth, then the field he was redeeming would go to her son and not his. Or maybe he didn't feel comfortable marrying a Moabite woman. Did he fear he would jeopardize his own inheritance by bringing a foreigner into his household?

Moabites were excluded from the family of God. **Read Deuteronomy 23:3-4.**

Who could never enter the assembly of the Lord?

_____

_____

Why not?

_____

_____

Maybe the "nearer relative" had heard gossip about the death of Naomi's husband and sons while in Moab and assumed Ruth might be part of a family "curse."

What's your take on his reasoning?

_____

_____

We don't know his reasons. We only know Boaz must be have been smiling on the inside, if not visibly. Evidently the kinsman first in line for Ruth's hand had no idea he had passed up one of the most amazing women on the planet.

The two men sealed the deal in **verse 7** by exchanging what article of clothing?

Boaz's sandals would have been hard to fill. This ancient custom was a symbolic act and a common practice when property exchanged hands. By giving Boaz his shoe, the man was saying, "I give up my right to walk on the field of Elimelech." Boaz seized this opportunity to make a declaration of his own. Here in the presence of the city elders at the city gate, he made the wedding announcement and declaration of his love for Ruth.

Read verses 8-12.

The people of Bethlehem saw a special spirit in Ruth. They knew she had come to faith in Yahweh and they welcomed her. Boaz redeemed a foreign woman and became a picture of our Savior who redeems people from every tribe, tongue, nation, and people.

What three women we've studied and grown to love were included in the blessing?

_____

_____

Oh, how sweet to hear the names of Rachel and Leah, and the house of Perez, Tamar's son, invoked as a blessing over the marriage and future of Boaz and Ruth. Can you picture them laughing and rejoicing in heaven over this day?

It's easy to understand why they would bring up the homes of Rachel and Leah. These were Hebrew women. But Tamar? We know Boaz was a descendant of Perez, but his mother slept with her father-in-law! Yet think this through.

Like Ruth, Tamar was an outsider, a Canaanite woman and not part of the covenant.

Like Ruth, Boaz' own mother was Rahab, an Amorite (and a former prostitute). God brought these pivotal women to faith. Like Tamar and Rahab before her, Ruth believed in God and was welcomed. She was brought under the protection of Yahweh and woven into the tapestry of his plan. She found shelter under his wings and was given a place at the table in God's "House of Bread."

What happens in **verse 13**?

_____

_____

Wedding bells ring and soon after it's time to decorate the nursery!

Now finish the chapter.

Is this not sheer delight? Can you see the women gathered around Naomi, congratulating her, talking a mile a minute about how the Lord has blessed her life and given her a grandson?

In **verse 15**, what did the neighbor women say Obed would be to Naomi?

_____

_____

For any grandmothers who rock with the ages, what do you feel as you read **verse 15**?

_____

_____

"May he be to you a restorer of life and a nourisher and supporter in your old age" (Amplified Bible). What do we know about Ruth's feelings for Naomi by what is said in this same verse?

_____
_____

"For your daughter-in-law who loves you, who is better to you than seven sons…" (Amplified Bible).

Verses 17-22 bring tears of joy to our eyes. This daughter-in-law was better to Naomi than seven sons! In a culture that craved sons, this was saying a lot! Ruth's faithfulness was used by God to turn Naomi's life around. She had returned to Bethlehem bitter and empty. Now she was full, her cup overflowing with hope and new life.

From the land of Moab, a daughter-in-law became the friend of Naomi's right hand. Ruth clung to Naomi in good times and bad. She never lost faith in the Lord of Naomi's birth. From her loyal lovingkindness, God granted Naomi a grandson, and the grandmothers named him Obed.

Obed's name means, "one who serves."[18]

Naomi's future was bright indeed. What would she say to us as she looked back over the previous ten years? She might say, "Even in your darkest hour, don't doubt God is there and that he can redeem even the worst of circumstances. Don't give up. God is going to write the last chapter of your life. Oh yes, and don't forget the blessings of a loyal friend."

The book of Ruth contains eight blessings. It seems as though God's people took every opportunity to encourage one another and call down the blessings of God in their lives. Let's take a look at each blessing and see what we can glean from them.

Read each one and paraphrase their meaning:

Ruth 1:8-9:

_____
_____

Ruth 1:16-17:

_____
_____

Ruth 2:4, 12, 20:

_____
_____

Ruth 3:10:

_____
_____

Ruth 4:11-12:

_____

_____

Ruth 4:14-15:

_____

_____

In these final verses of this astonishing chapter we are given the full family portrait of how Ruth, a Moabite woman has become a part of the royal line of Jesus. "Her inclusion in the genealogy represents another beautiful illustration of Yahweh's loyal love (hesed) and his commitment to include Gentiles in the covenant community."

Unknowingly, Ruth ends Chapter One with a vow that could have been sung at her own wedding in Chapter Four. Her redemption by Boaz points to the coming full redemption in Jesus for all who will come to him and believe.

Even now, in our days of turbulent headlines and moral decay, there are people of God living out quiet, simple, profound lives of love and loyalty. In spite of the rampant disbelief and apostasy around them, they walk in obedience and do their part, just like Boaz and Naomi and Ruth, in preparing the way for the Messiah.

Behold he stands at the door and knocks, waiting for any willing heart to turn to him. Where we go, he is. Where we travel, live, work, play, suffer and age, he is. Where we are going, he is!

Let's have a little more fun. In your own words, write a blessing to a friend or someone you deeply love. Send it to them in the mail, or better yet, speak it to them in person. Use Scripture to help you write it. Make it personal to fit their circumstances. Commit to pray for them until you see the blessing fulfilled. Our generous father who delights to bless his girls is listening!

BLESSING FOR THE FRIEND OF YOUR RIGHT HAND

_____

_____

_____

_____

Be sure to sign your name! Your father God specializes in making the most of your name.

As we close, have you noticed the evolution of Ruth's name in Scripture? Like you, she humbled herself at the feet of the Lord of the harvest and went from Ruth the Moabitess to Ruth the handmaid of Boaz, to Ruth the great-grandmother of King David, to Ruth the ancestor of Jesus Christ!

Blessings and favor to you sweet one, in the name above all names! Cling to him, wait on him, prepare for him, watch for him!

Precious beloved friends, now fill in your name.

I, _____ from _____,

am becoming _____ the _____,

(a new description)

forever destined to be _____, the bride of Jesus Christ!

TODAY'S DATE: _____

YOUR HEADLINE:
_____
_____

WEEK THREE
BREAKING NEWS

Messiah Watch

Israel 5 B.C.

PROPHETESS IGNORES GOVERNMENT THREAT
Tension in Herod's Court Mounting; Widow in Temple Court Continues Search for Messiah

After eighty years the elderly widow Anna continues to be a one-woman welcome-wagon for visitors in the Women's Court at the Jewish Temple. Anna insists on keeping her vigil to view God's promised baby son in the flesh. Yet King Herod's palace leaked details of a decree that will wipe out every newborn male born in Israel. How will Anna respond to the following news?

"Herod is considering the death of all newborn Jewish males. The Court of Women will be overrun with mourning mothers. There has been no prophecy from God in over 400 years. Will the promised 'Messiah' fade into folklore?"

With little explanation, Anna acts without reason. Is she too old to understand the signs of her times? *Messiah Watch* offers the latest firsthand reports surrounding Israel's oldest female prophetess.

"She continues to greet every new couple that comes to the Women's Court after childbirth," explains an expert on Levitical custom. "After a child is born, a woman is required to submit to an ancient ritual of cleansing at the temple. Some couples continue to have their children circumcised, though the barbaric practice seems highly outdated."

However, a young mother from Nazareth went on record: "Advice from Anna calmed me." Her husband smiled, holding their newborn son as the mother continued. "I came to the temple to have my son dedicated and admit it was a daunting experience to walk into God's house as a new mother."

When asked how Anna responded to the anonymous baby son's circumcision, the father winced a bit. "Any one of God's men would be honored to have his son dedicated to the promise." His wife nudged him with a strange smile. "As for our firstborn son, we are especially grateful for the blessings given him that day! And as for his mother? After watching her give birth, let's just say I have a newfound appreciation for women!"

Messiah Watch requested exclusive time with Anna and the Nazarene parents. Unfortunately, they were whisked away on a rushed vacation to Egypt and unavailable for further comment. Anna, however gave one last statement to the press:

"God's timing is perfect. Don't ask why, just remember the covenant and believe. Open your eyes and behold the coming of the Lord. He is able and he is bringing about all he promised. The Messiah, a baby son, is born in Israel to bring deliverance and bring peace to all men!"

Anna's age will keep her safe from government interrogation. Smiling and calm, she was seen as she has been for decades, sitting in the Women's Court, new mothers gathered around her. Their conversations were off-limits to journalists but the mood was unmistakable. These women were having the time of their lives. They whispered and laughed with sounds of tidings and, dare we say, great joy.

Messiah Watch feels confident that the silence of God has been broken. In spite of Herod's threat on the lives of Rachel's infant sons, someone is coming or has already arrived. The hope of Israel is alive and well. The Promised One may very well be closer than we realize.

OF INCREASING INTEREST: If anyone has news of a new star astrologers have spotted or information pertaining to extraterrestrial activity of a sacred nature, please contact our website.

Time will tell.

Editor's note: The opinions in these articles are those of Israel's prophets and do not necessarily reflect those of the management.

TODAY'S HEROINE:
Anna

Out of my distress I called upon the Lord; the Lord answered me and set me free and in a large place (Ps. 118:5 Amplified Bible).

What is it about a gracious white-haired lady of faith? Why does she have the power to move us? You see her at church, in her home or in the marketplace and she commands respect. Her physical frailty stands in sharp contrast to her dignity and strength of character. She can inspire younger people to keep moving forward in their faith just by her very presence in a room. Her faithfulness speaks for her and causes others to smile and say, "If she can keep going, so can I."

Meet Anna, the prophetess who inspired everyone who met her and even now defines what it means to finish well.

As we begin today's lesson, it's vitally important to set every piece of information about Anna against the backdrop of her spiritual culture. Our understanding of the state of Israel during her life makes even more profound her qualities of courage and perseverance.

Read Amos 2:11-12.

What happened to the prophets in Israel?

_____

_____

Why did God send prophets to the Israelites? He did not want them going to diviners, mediums, enchanters, fortunetellers, and witches. God is the same yesterday, today and forever. His desire is for his children to come directly to the source, to our Creator for instruction and clarity. We aren't to read horoscopes, visit palm readers or call the local psychic hotline. God's word contains harsh warning against such practices. True faith-building wisdom comes from him alone, through his Word and through his prophets.

Read Amos 8:11-12.

What type of famine spread across the nation?

At the close of the Old Testament, there is a 400-year period of silence from God. Israel's refusal to listen to God's prophets and their rebellion against God's guidance resulted in a famine of his word. No canonical records exist between their return from Babylon and the birth of Jesus. From the end of Malachi to the beginning of the gospels of the New Testament, new religious and political parties had risen to prominence. A new world power was in control. As the prophecies of Daniel predicted, Babylon was overtaken by the Persians and the Medes. Rising up after them, Alexander the Great conquered the world with Greek domination. Finally by Anna's day, Rome held a mighty grip of power over every nation, including the Israelites. From one century to the next, the Hebrews found themselves displaced, in captivity, and in a continual battle to retain their nationality.

Yet, after centuries of quiet, we read about our amazing Anna. Her presence in Luke 2 is a shout of undying faith. After centuries of captivity and Diasporas, after years of silence from God, Anna represents the Jews who continued to believe Jehovah was alive and well and on the move. Anna lived in expectation for the God of her fathers to break his silence with a fresh new word, a word made flesh.

Read Luke 2:36-38.

Using our sanctified imaginations and biblical history, let's discover all we can about Anna's inspiring faith.

Luke 2:36-37 gives us the following information:

Her name:

_____

Her tribal identity:

_____

Her father's name:

_____

Her age:

_____

Her marital status:

_____

Her residence:

_____

Her purpose:

_____

Each verse of Scripture is packed with information. At first glance one might read Luke 2:36 and think, "All right, so Anna was an elderly widow from one of the twelve tribes and I can't pronounce her father's name."

Let's dig deeper.

What's in a name? Our names mean everything to God.

Anna's name is an important clue that helps us understand her family's background. We begin by noting that Anna's name can also be written in English as "Hannah." The original biblical Hannah was the mother of the prophet Samuel.

Hannah's name in Hebrew means "grace" or "favor." Anna's name in Latin, "gratia," has the same meaning. Both women were considered to be a prophetess, speaking boldly about the coming king of Israel. Hannah spoke in the Old Testament of what Anna would live to see in the New.

Turn to 1 Samuel 2:10.

Who does Hannah reference in the last words of this verse?

_____

Anna spent her days in the Women's Court of the Temple, peering into every baby blanket, waiting to see the promised anointed king. She was there always, and everyone knew who she was. In Jerusalem she was known as the woman who never left the temple. For over eighty years, from morning until night, she stood as close as a woman could to the Holy of Holies and worshiped with fasting and prayer. Her name represents the grace and steadfast favor of God on man, bringing his son into our world to redeem and save us by his love.

It also is interesting to note the following historical information. Anna was not a common name of her day. As far as we know the name Anna/Hannah was not especially popular in Israel during the late Second Temple Period: "Of the 247 women in Palestine from the period 330 BCE-200 AD, whose names are known, our Anna is the only one who bears this name." [19]

However, among the Jews who remained religious and devoted to God during captivity and as they moved back into the northern regions of Israel, Anna would have been a very honored name. During the Median exile, there are writings from a man named Tobit, a Galilean from the tribe of Naphtali. He often encouraged devout Jews to keep their hope alive in the prophecies God had given them. He continually spoke of the Israelites' return to Jerusalem where all nations would worship the one true God.

Tobit's wife was named Anna. Interesting indeed.

TRIBAL IMPLICATIONS

Turn to Genesis 30:13.

Describe the meaning of this tribe's name:

Anna came from the tribe of _____, which translated into

"_____."

Anna was descended from a legacy of joy. Asher was the sixth son born to Jacob, by Leah's handmaid, Zilpah. When Zilpah gave birth to Asher, Leah had the privilege of naming him. Leah said, "Happy am I! For women will call me happy," and named her son accordingly.

Asher's tribe may have been called happy, yet they experienced years of exile along with the other tribes in Israel's history.

Picture a young Anna, a little girl from the one of the twelve tribes, living in a time when no word of God came from his prophets. For generations, prophecy had been hope and sustenance for Israel's heart. But Anna grew up in a time when no word from God had come for over 400 years; nothing but silence from Yahweh.

Picture how her family would have kept faith alive by telling and retelling stories of God's promises and faithfulness. Perhaps they recalled the Hebrews' deliverance from Egyptian bondage after 400 years. Perhaps they spoke often of the courage of Daniel and Esther, and stories of Deborah's victory in battle. Perhaps she lived on these stories in a time when Heaven was eerily quiet. Perhaps this built Anna's childhood faith and prepared her heart to be used of God to break the silence with revelations of joy!

Now, picture her family living out this faith as part of a group of exiled Jews from the eastern Diaspora of Media. Her people are from the tribe of Asher, taken into captivity by the Assyrians.

Read 2 Kings 15:29.

The tribe of Asher was a northern tribe of Israel and northwestern Galilee was their traditional homeland.

What group is included in the people taken captive to Assyria in 2 Kings?

"Many people from this region were taken captive by the Assyrian King Tiglath-Pilesar about 733 B.C., but others were left behind. When King Hezekiah of Judah ordered a special Passover celebration at Jerusalem about twenty years later, he invited people from the northern tribes."[20]

Read 2 Chronicles 30:6-11.

In **verse 11**, what three tribes are mentioned as returning?

Picture young Anna, whose ancestors were part of the "few" that happily journeyed back to Jerusalem. Most likely her family's tribal identity remained intact in spite of being scattered and taken into captivity. She would have heard stories of how important it was to remember that self-esteem was found solely in Jehovah, no matter your surroundings.

"Awareness of tribal membership may be more likely to have survived in the eastern Diaspora in Galilee. Many exiles in Media, in the midst of an alien culture hundreds of miles from Israel apparently banded together in communities and worked to preserve their Israelite identity. At some point the Median exiles established formal ties with Jerusalem and the Temple."[21]

In this way, Anna was not unlike Tamar or Esther or Naomi. She understood the feeling of being in the minority, surrounded by a godless cultural perspective. Her constancy in pushing into God's promises required trust in his Word even in times of silence and peril.

DADDY'S NAME

What was Anna's father's name?

Turn and read Genesis 32:30.

What happens here, and what is the resulting name?

Peniel or Phanuel means the "face of God." Jacob wrestled all night with the Lord's angel and demanded a blessing. Jacob's name was changed to Israel! And the name of this place bears the story of how God honors true relationship… even if it involves a little pain, questioning, and perseverance.

Did Anna's father teach her patience by his example, bearing down through thick and thin, pushing into the Lord regardless of personal pain? His name would suggest that he was a man of deep faith. He named his baby girl after one of Israel's most beloved women, Hannah. Perhaps he prayed to Yahweh to grant his daughter the favor of blessing her people as well. As a descendant of those exiled by the Medes, he would have been overjoyed when he was able to move back to Jerusalem. This father would have passed along to Anna his love for Jerusalem, the Torah, and the Temple. God's blessing in Numbers 6:24-26 was to shine his face on his people. Surely Anna's father, Phanuel, walked out his hope before her. It's moving to imagine Anna watching her father's face, listening to his conversations with neighbors, looking for any and every sign that God was still alive, active, unchangeable, and working to bring his Promised One to his people.

ANNA'S AGE AND MARITAL STATUS

Anna grew into womanhood with a tremendous sense of faith and identity. From what we learn about her, it's not difficult to imagine that Anna always had been a lady passionate to know all she could about her Lord. Her gifts of prophecy were especially rare in her time, and would only have been placed in a trustworthy heart.

As a young Jewish bride, she would have married according to the customs of her people. As a new wife, Anna would have embraced her role with gratitude and excitement. Yet seven years into her marriage, she finds herself to be a very young widow. Did she recall her father's teachings about God's care for widows when life brought such unexpected tragedy?

Take a moment and gaze at the heart of God toward widows.

Read Exodus 22:21-22.

What three types of people did God warn the Israelites not to oppress?

_____

_____

Now read Deuteronomy 10:17-18.

For whom does God execute his justice?

_____

_____

Lastly, read Deuteronomy 14:29.

What was the purpose of the tithe at the end of every third year?

_____

_____

Twelve widows are mentioned in the Bible. Clearly, God has a big heart for the widow. He warned that he would withhold blessing from people who did not care for widows, orphans, and aliens. The heart that beats in rhythm with God's is the heart that cares for those who are helpless.

TEST QUESTION: (There is no wrong answer.) How would you describe an alien? Think outside the box of a person's nationality.

_____

_____

Let's stop here for a moment and ponder the anonymous years of Anna.

Quite possibly she felt like both a widow and an alien.

She grew up and married at a young age, probably around fifteen or sixteen years. Seven years later she was a widow, probably around twenty-two or twenty-three years old. The next reference to her begins at age eighty-four. A more literal translation of the Greek seems to indicate that the length of her widowhood was eighty-four years. Let's do the math: If she married at sixteen and was widowed seven years later, and lived eighty-four years as a widow, then that would put her age around 107 years.

What happened to Anna between age twenty-three to eighty-four or 107? During those sixty-plus anonymous years, the everyday choices of Anna shaped her into the beautiful, white-haired prophetess whose eyes beheld a forty-day-old Christ child!

How might Anna or any woman respond to being widowed after seven years of marriage? (Circle a few you might have experienced in Anna's situation.)

Bitterness at life's injustice

Anger with God

Depression and shock

Looking for love in other men

Addiction(s) to relieve despair

Turning to God for comfort

Believing life was still worth living

Choosing faith and finding purpose

Combination of the above

At the time we meet Anna she has been a widow for 84 years. There is no mention of her having children or family members still alive. Did she have children and lose them as well? Did this mighty woman of faith bury her mother and father and siblings and outlive them all?

We don't know the details. But it's a worthy exercise to consider Anna's choices given the many years she faced alone.

From personal experience, I (Bonnie) know how strange and horribly alone it feels to be divorced. After my first marriage ended, I was suddenly "uninvited" to couples events, and at church it took years for me to find my place as a single woman. When life throws you into a category you never envisioned, it takes adjustments, grieving, and a period of recovery to start over again. I'm not proud of many of my stops and starts along the way as a divorced, single mom. In thinking about Anna, it's astonishing to imagine the strength of her wise choices. Women who have lost their husbands of any age are hard to face. Women widowed early in their lives are especially heartbreaking. Many times when someone is hurting the first response is to turn away. Any reluctance to reach out to divorcees/aliens and widows in our culture comes from a place of fear. It's frightening to be around people who are suffering openly. Yet when we do as God asks and move toward the hurting, we find ourselves walking on holy ground. Suffering connects us with the passion of Jesus. It's of great eternal worth to get out of our comfort zone and learn to be God's hands and feet to any awkward, lost, lonely soul in need of his love.

As you pray today, ask God to bring to mind anyone who might benefit from a phone call, card, email or message of hope from you _____.

For over eighty years Anna pressed hard into the presence of God for comfort. Eighty-plus years of leaving the past behind her, and reaching out for new joy only God could bring to her future. She seems to have lived a simple lifestyle. It is possible she had a room there on the temple grounds. It could be said she took her role so seriously that she wanted no distractions. After being married seven years and experiencing the death of her husband, she moved into the court of the women and devoted the rest of her life to fasting, prayer, and watching for the Messiah.

Martin Luther gave a sermon on the life of Anna in the year 1522. Three short verses contained in Luke 2 inspired Luther to speak profusely about the implications of Anna's life. The most interesting part of his speech deals with her age and widowhood.

Luther wrote:

"We come now to the more profound and spiritual interpretations. She lived with a husband seven years, and after that was a widow for eighty-four years, without a husband. **Had one sufficient time and skill he might find the whole Bible contained in this number.**" [22]

Hang in there. Luther comments on the heels of this declaration that we "do not need Aristotle of human lore, but have in the Scriptures enough to study for all eternity." He then encourages twenty-first century students of the word, "Let us consider this number in connection with the wonders of Scripture mentioned before." The number seven is commonly used as a reference of completeness, throughout the Bible, and specifically associated with the complete restoration Christ accomplished on the cross. It also is used to signify our temporal life, the life of this body, because all time is measured by the seven days of the week established in Genesis 1.

Seven years as a bride could be viewed in Anna's life as the lives of Israel, children of God, living on earth waiting for the Messiah who would bring the hope of eternity.

Turn to Romans 7:2.

How is a woman bound to marriage?

_____

_____

Paul is using an example here of how a married woman is **bound by law** to her husband as long as he lives.

What happens if he dies?

_____

_____

In this passage Paul uses law and marriage, death and freedom, to reveal what Christ has done to release us from the death of our flesh and unite us to him forever. In the law we are hopeless. Apart from the law, because of his sacrifice, we are now free to live by his grace.

Read Romans 7:4-6.

If Anna's seven years in marriage represented Jewish law, what then would her eighty-four years as a widow allow?

_____

_____

This is not to suggest that widowhood or separation from marriage is to be desired. The point both Paul and Luther are making is to paint a broader picture. Anna's faith represents the complete work of Christ. She was mentioned specifically in Luke 2 not only as an example of a godly woman who rose above the losses of her life, but also as a symbol of what Jesus came to fulfill. When the law brought nothing but death, he died to give us nothing but life. Anna is much more than a precious widow walking the halls of the Women's Court!

Martin Luther was fascinated by the choices Anna made in how she lived as a widow. He notes that she is free to fast, pray, and be near to God's every move solely based on a heart of trusting faith.

"(Luther) points out that besides her life under the law she also walked in the freedom of faith and the spirit, fulfilling the law not only with outward works like a bond-servant but rather in faith. This is signified by the eighty-four years of her widowhood, meaning the spiritual life of faith led by the saints of old. For the widow, the life without a husband, signifies freedom from the law." [23]

Anna is a radical example of spiritual freedom!

Like Deborah and Hannah, describe Anna's spiritual gift:

_____

_____

She was a prophetess. For Hannah, that meant giving her son Samuel back to the priest for dedication and speaking prophetically of the future Messiah. For Deborah, that meant lacing up her combat boots and going into battle. For Anna it meant something entirely different.

What is a prophet's description? What did Anna, this amazing senior citizen of Israel, do every day?

"A prophet is someone who is divinely inspired to communicate God's will to his people, and to disclose the future to them." Different forms of the Hebrew word indicate that a prophet is one who declares or announces, pouring forth the declarations of God. Sometimes prophets were called "watchmen" or "seers." [24]

Isn't God full of surprises? From a generation that had heard nothing from God's prophets for over 400 years, the floodgates suddenly open. And among the chosen few, God uses a widowed, elderly woman to bring glorious news to his people.

Do you wonder if Anna, in her advanced age, ever felt pushed to the side by younger people of her society? Did she ever feel invisible?

Israel had heard nothing from God for centuries, yet here is an old woman who insists on interviewing everyone in her path and talking about the coming Messiah. Did some visitors wonder if Anna was a wee bit senile? After all, the Jews were under the strict, fierce rule of Rome. There had been no word from the Lord longer than anyone could remember. Herod was a madman, and there were rumors that he was on the verge of another murderous rampage.

Did this elderly, vibrant woman simply live in her own little world, out of touch with reality?

Do you ever have "Anna moments" when your faith makes you feel a little bit crazy in our culture?

___

No one likes the feeling of being tolerated. And none of us like the clichés that come with growing older. Yet much humor surrounds the process of growing old and sometimes it helps to laugh a little when faced with the realities of our aging bodies. When a 102-year-old woman was asked about the benefits of living to this advanced age she replied, "No peer pressure."

No kidding! One of the benefits of aging is the ability to say what one feels with childlike freedom. Ironically, the older we become the less we care about what other people might think. People who have lived a lot of life with God have much wisdom to share. Anna surely must have lived out her years shedding layers of inhibition.

She was beyond the problem of peer pressure, but did she feel depressed and unattractive? Was she focused on sagging skin and her wrinkled face? From the description of her actions in **Luke 2:38**, how do you picture her?

___

Contrast Anna's joy and sense of security in God to the issues that are certainly front and center in our culture. Her passion was found in sharing revelations about Jesus. Western culture is consumed with a passionate fear of becoming old. Our society worships youth, perfect skin, and flat abs.

It's fun to imagine what Anna would say about the following *U.S. News and World Report* article that surveyed the baby boomer generations' obsession with the current pursuit of youth.

BABY BOOMERS

> **Bad hair, good wrinkles.** Age is catching up with the baby boomers—the third of the population born between 1946 and 1964—but many aren't ready to admit it. A survey of more than 1,200 thirty- to fifty-year-olds finds that most (seventy-six percent) are convinced that they look younger than their age. Most (seventy-three percent) also believe that people who were fifty a generation ago looked a lot older than do today's fifty-year-olds.

Anna seems to have enjoyed thirty- to fifty-year olds no matter how they looked.

The Louis Harris Poll, financed by OrthoNeutrogena maker of Renova skin cream, also found:

Concerns. As boomers get older, sixty-six percent worry about gaining weight; thirty percent worry about losing hair; twenty-eight percent worry about getting facial wrinkles; and twenty-four percent worry about getting gray hair.

Signs of Age. When judging people's age, most boomers (fifty-eight percent) are influenced by facial wrinkles or brown spots. Lesser numbers are influenced by gray hair (forty-six percent), excess weight (seventy-three percent) and hair loss (thirty-four percent).

Gender. More than a third (thirty-seven percent) of boomers think men age more gracefully than women; twenty-two percent say women age more gracefully. Most (seventy-seven percent) think women worry more than men about an aging facial appearance.

Good wrinkles. Most boomers (fifty-six percent) think facial wrinkles can be assets for a man "because they indicate experience and maturity." But only forty-four percent believe that wrinkles can be assets for a woman.

The typical boomer, the survey finds, thinks middle age begins at forty-one. Older boomers have a much different view of middle age than do younger boomers. "If you could stay one age forever, what age would it be?" the survey asks.

Boomers in their early thirties tend to wish they could have stayed in their twenties. The favorite age cited by boomers from forty-five to fifty is "forty-five or older." [25]

Do we need a hobby in this culture or what? Or worse still, perhaps the fight against aging has become a national hobby.

Can you imagine how Anna would answer the question in this survey?

"Anna, if you could stay one age forever, what age would it be?"

For fun, write her answer:

_____

_____

Among other comments, she might have quoted from the word of God about the beauty of a white-haired woman.

Read Proverbs 16:31, Anna could reply. "Gray hair is a _____ of _____" (NIV). My father knows every one of my gray hairs, and he sees them as a royal adornment on my sweet head. Every age with God is good. I am happy to be whatever age I am!"

Surely Anna would not have missed the opportunity to encourage the interviewer with a little wisdom from the Torah. Picture her taking the arm of the person who asked about her age, sitting them down next to her and smiling with excitement. "Before you go, I want you to hear the words from **Isaiah 46:4. This will help you with your survey.** These verses are the promises of God given to those who love him as they age. You're going to love this!"

Write this verse below:

_____

_____

Imagine the sweet warble of her voice as Anna said, "This beautiful verse is God's promise to see us through all the way from the moment he formed us in our mother's womb to our final breath. The image of him carrying us in his arms, close to his breast, is the ultimate picture of his love. Let the truth of this promise wash over you and fill every place of fear and worry over those wrinkles and age spots and all that talk about graceful aging. Now, let me tell you about the coming Messiah!"

My (Nan's) grandfather lived to be eighty-four. He loved God and he loved to be at church. He served as an elder for more than forty years, and one of his favorite ways to serve was to stand at the door and greet people as they came to worship. Many people have said to me through the years that is was my grandfather's warm handshake and kind words that made them feel welcome when they came to church. My Papaw and Anna have much in common. Surely they already have been introduced to each other in heaven by now, for they are kindred spirits. They shared the platform of welcoming, greeting, excitement, and loving faith to those who gathered to worship the Lord.

Each of us has a platform. It could be in an office, a classroom, a kitchen, or the front door of a church. It is the place God has put us to glorify him and shine as the stars in the universe as we hold out the word of life (Phil. 2:15-16 NIV). Use the space below to describe your platform or place of influence.

_____

_____

_____

Now write a sentence describing how you believe God would have you view the people who come in and out of the place where you serve him.

_____

In the light of eternity, the focus of self-image versus serving God is put into clear perspective. Regardless of age, God uses any willing heart to bring hope to others. One of the purposes of this lesson is to encourage older women in their vital role in the body of Christ and inspire younger women to be like them. In our modern cultural focus on all things "hip," it is often the white haired people among us who go unnoticed. The life of Anna flies in the face of anyone dismissing someone because of their age. Her years of serving God set her apart and made her active involvement at the temple even more spectacular.

Make a list of the women aged sixty and older who have most influenced your life in Christ:

_____

_____

Pick one of these ladies and take a moment to write her a note of encouragement, telling her how much she means to you. Maybe you could name her as a modern-day "Anna" in your life.

My mother (Nan) is a modern day "Anna." At the age of eighty-three, she is now a widow, living alone in the house she's been in for forty-eight years. In 1984, she took her first Precept Upon Precept Bible study written by Kay Arthur. To Mom, it was like finding water in the desert. Her first study was on the book of Judges and ever since then, she has been taking one Bible study course after another, with everything from Kay Arthur to Beth Moore to Bible Study Fellowship and many others too numerous to mention. Mom is a perpetual student of the Word and continually finds joy in the revelation of God through his Word. She inspires me, as Anna must have inspired the younger women in Jerusalem, to never tire of the discipline of sitting quietly before the Lord with the Bible on your lap and listening for his voice with joyful anticipation.

My mother (Bonnie) is a widow, but she has more energy than most people half her age. She is not yet eighty, but Momma thrives on teaching the children's classes at her home church of over fifty years. She delights to tell us about her comments in ladies' Bible class and how salty and fired up she is when they discuss the Word. Yes, Mom likes to throw a wrench into the mix whenever possible just to keep things lively. Momma also cherishes each note of appreciation sent her way. There are notes and gifts all over her house from younger women thanking her for staying the course with God, for being a woman of hospitality and graciousness. And Mom doesn't worry too very much about age. Much like Anna, she's flat-out too busy to bother.

Anna lived a life so full there wasn't time to fret over crow's feet or dry skin. She was on a mission to be stunned, thrilled, and surprised by God's glory. She lived her life in eager anticipation of the first coming of the Messiah. Did she dream about what it would be like to see him? Did she wonder about what she would do in his presence? Meditating on Jesus' return and the anticipation of the joys of life with him in the new earth is the joy of every believer. Anna watched for his first coming. We watch for his second.

ANNA'S PURPOSE AND PASSION

Anna strategically placed herself in a location where she could come in contact with every Jew who came to the outer courts of the temple. It was her platform, her sphere of influence. In this well-trafficked area, she ministered, prophesied, and prayed.

One might say Anna put herself directly in the path of God, hoping, counting on a divine intersection.

Do you ever picture yourself purposefully waiting for a divine collision with the Lord?

_____

_____

In **Luke 2:37**, let's find the weight of each intentional word. In the Amplified Bible translation, this verse reads: "And as a widow even for eighty-four years, she did not go out from the temple enclosure but **was worshiping night and day with fasting and prayer.**"

Eighty-four years she worshiped, fasted, and prayed day and night. Anna was a professional woman of intercessory prayer. She was a professional optimist, a professional lover of her God. There are no accidents with God's timing. It was his perfect will to have both Anna and Simeon, elderly professionals tuned into the Holy Spirit on hand when Mary and Joseph entered the temple with their son.

Before we explore their meeting, let's recall what we know about the role of a prophet in Israel's history. Anna was called a prophetess. What insight does the following information give us about her daily life?

It was the job of the prophet to work hand-in-hand with the priest. The prophets were to admonish and reprove the people of God, and denounce sin and call them to repentance. They also were given God's messages of consolation and comfort. The priests stood ready to administer the daily sacrifices on behalf of the people, and to approach the presence of God on their behalf.

Anna would not have officiated animal sacrifices, but she was as close to the altar as a woman could be. As the people came into the temple to offer sacrifices for their sins, Anna's role would have been to admonish and encourage. She would have been there to greet the women and offer a word of comfort. (Of course she also would have searched every newborn baby's face, hoping—expecting—to see the infant Son of God.) Anna would have been there, day after day, as an ambassador for God, calling the people to turn from their sin, and leading the way in praise and thanksgiving.

We know that what she wanted most in her life was to be near the presence of God. The Holy Spirit was not present in every believer as he is today. His presence was in the Holy of Holies. His Spirit came upon people at certain times, but did not dwell permanently yet in their hearts. By dwelling in the temple night and day, Anna did all she could to be near him.

Anna loved the things of God. As a woman, she could not study the Torah. She longed for a word from God and she lived to see the Living Word. Most likely, she held him in her arms. Like Mary of Bethany, Anna certainly would have sat at the feet of Jesus if she had lived another thirty years or so. Jesus did and said much to elevate the position of women in society. He would have honored Anna as a mighty prayer warrior and would have invited her to sit at his feet as he taught from the Scriptures.

It is interesting to wonder why Anna fasted. What did she pray for beyond her own personal needs? Her list would have included current events and politics, the rule of Caesar Augustus, the way the Jews were being treated, the repentance and redemption of the Jews. Anna was an informed woman. She knew the spiritual tone of her times. She knew how long it had been since anyone had received a word from the Lord.

Let's look more closely at why Anna's choice to praise God was especially brave given the political and spiritual climate of these times.

Read Matthew 2:1-18.

Who was king in Judea?

___

Who visited him?

___

In short order, what did he fear and determine to do?

_____

_____

Herod the Great, as he was called, reigned over Palestine from 37 B.C. until his death in 4 B.C. He was a crafty ruler and lavish builder. Several years ago, I (Bonnie) traveled to Israel to film an overview on the historical background surrounding Jesus' birth. One morning we drove miles away from Jerusalem to one of Herod's palaces. We were stunned by how enormous and elaborate it was. Most telling was the difficult hike uphill to its location and the immense fortification of its walls. Herod used this location as a residence, a palace nearly impossible to invade. He was obsessed with himself and protecting his kingdom of power. It was Herod who planned and carried out the building of the new temple in Jerusalem. He was infamous for being a paranoid, insane leader, bloodthirsty and cruel. Herod feared anyone who disagreed with him politically and killed every descendant of the Hasmoneans (his rivals), including his own wife, Marianne. He also proceeded to murder his own two sons by Marianne. It was this madman who was on the throne when Jesus was born. As signs of Jesus' birth came to him piece by piece, his insecurities mounted resulting in the slaughter of the newborn innocents of Israel.[26]

Historians believe that when Jesus was dedicated at the temple, Herod was still on his fact-finding mission. Yet the Hebrews would have been on high alert with this narcissistic king on the throne in Palestine. And Herod had to answer to the higher Roman rule of Caesar Augustus. The Jews paid a heavy tribute to him in taxes. The Pharisees had taken the law of God and turned them into hundreds of legalistic rules, which they in turn bound on the people. Life for a Jew had become a burdensome ritual of carrying out one set of rules after another while living under Roman rule and authority.

Was Anna discouraged? Did she think her prayers were making a difference? Did she ever wonder if God had forgotten his people? Would anything ever change?

Our understanding of dear Anna was that nothing stood in the way of her joy. Nothing could keep her from being as close as a woman could to the presence of God. Not only was she a widow, not only did she live in times when there had been no word from God, but also she lived as a Jewish elderly woman in the temple built by a madman who had the power to destroy anyone at any time. Still Anna continued to speak openly of her faith in God and to wait for the Messiah.

Hopefully your heart, like ours, is blown away by Anna's sense of optimism and courage. Anna had a heart much like the men of Issachar.

Read 1 Chronicles 12:32.

What did these men understand?

_____

_____

At that time in Israel's history, men from every tribe were defecting from the rule of Saul and coming over to David and forming an army. They knew that God had anointed David to be the new king of Israel. The writer of Chronicles lists the number of men from every tribe who pledged their allegiance to David and makes a point to list the men of Issachar as being men "who understood the times and knew what Israel should do" (NIV).

Men who understood the times and knew what to do! Oh, may that be said of us today! Let us pray to be people who understand the times and know what to do to. Anna did. In the thick middle of personal and political challenges, she devoted her life to prayer and fasting. Following God was not something she took lightly. She gave no casual nod toward the things of Jehovah. He was her life! She was committed, heart, soul, mind, and body to intercession for her people and watching for the Messiah.

Does this backdrop heighten your admiration of Anna's faith? Explain:

_____

_____

Anna understood the times and they weren't pretty. Yet she understood that God was in control of kings and nations. She never let herself look too closely at the world, but kept her eyes on the promises of the Lord. Maybe Anna had been in the temple on the day when Zachariah was burning incense. She could have seen him burst from the Holy Place, speechless after seeing the angel Gabriel. This was not your average day at the temple.

If she stayed there day and night she would have known all about Zachariah. He was from the Levi tribe and part of a select group of men who were allowed into the Holy of Holies once a year. Zachariah had one chance in his lifetime when it was his time to perform the yearly ritual of repentance for the nation of Israel. If the rituals were not carried out perfectly the priest would die. A rope would be tied around his ankle so that he could be pulled from the Holy of Holies if something went awry. Zachariah had an especially unusual encounter with God when he stepped into the Holy Place to offer atonement for God's people. Anna must have learned that after seeing an angel, Zachariah still could not speak, even months after his vision. Then word spread that his elderly wife Elizabeth was pregnant. Anna soon would have heard that Zachariah's tongue was miraculously loosed on the day his son was born. These were not normal events.

To a spiritually sensitive woman, these events would have been very exciting. Did something stir in her spirit, prompting her to pray even harder for the coming Messiah and the redemption of her people? Things were about to get even more exciting. No doubt Anna took a good hard look at baby John when he was brought for dedication at the temple court.

Dr. Luke was the Gentile gospel writer who chose to include Anna's story in his writings. Did you know that Luke has forty-three references to women in his gospel? Three of them are about widows. Luke gives us the wonderful account of Jesus and the widow of Nain (Luke 7:11-15). He also tells of the time a poor widow put two copper coins in the temple treasury (Luke 21:1-4).

Anna was known by the people who came to the temple as "one who sees." What did she see and hear on that blessed day?

_____

_____

Fifteen months after Zachariah was struck dumb, Anna saw baby Jesus brought into the court of the women, just a few feet from where Gabriel stood and announced to Zachariah the birth of his son John, the forerunner of Christ.

Read Luke 2:21-25.

Why were Mary and Joseph coming to the temple?

_____

_____

Jesus' parents were devout Jews who followed the law. They came to the temple forty days after his birth for two reasons. Mary would fulfill the laws of purification and they would present Jesus as "holy to the Lord."

What were the laws of purification? We find them in **Leviticus 12:6-8.**

_____

_____

Once more we are reminded that Jesus was born as a Jewish child to humble Jewish newlyweds. He was brought to the temple by parents who honored God's ways and revered the traditions of their heritage. Jesus was treated just like any other newborn Hebrew child. His mother would need to observe the ritual cleansing and Jesus would be circumcised and dedicated as holy to the Lord.

Who was the first person to meet Joseph and Mary at the temple?

_____

_____

What had been revealed to him by the Holy Spirit?

_____

_____

Simeon took the baby Christ child and held him in his arms. He lifted up the tiny babe and praised God for answering a lifelong prophecy. Prompted by the Holy Spirit, Simeon believed he would not leave the earth before viewing the Messiah.

There was nothing special about Simeon that qualified him to take up the Christ child in his arms and bless him. To our knowledge he was not an ordained religious leader, and he had no credentials or special authority. He was simply a "just and devout" man who had a close walk with the Holy Spirit.

His name means "God hears" and, like Anna, Simeon lived out an example of how God honors those who engage him in prayer and faith.[27] Simeon would likely have had many near misses, chances to have his hope overtaken by doubts. Numerous "would-be" Messiahs sounded false alarms in the land over the years. Yet Simeon had faith enough to watch and wait, and eyes big enough to believe God would bring a Messiah who would do far more than carry a national banner or political agenda. He knew that God's Son would save the human soul and change the world forever.

In Israel, there always has been a group of people looking every day for the Messiah. Anna and Simeon were part of that group. They were in a constant state of alert readiness. Their spiritual ears were open to the voice of the Spirit and they practiced listening to him. Therefore, they recognized his voice, even in a baby's cry!

Read John 10:2-5.

What do the sheep know?

_____

What do the sheep not know?

_____

It is the familiar sound of the voice of the shepherd that guides the sheep. He calls them by name and leads them out. But sheep will literally run from someone with an unfamiliar voice when that person tries to lead the flock. When a stranger comes into the fold, the sheep bolt!

The art of listening to and recognizing the Good Shepherd's voice takes practice. Discernment is required today, just as it was at his first coming. Being immersed in his Word is the work required in order to train our ears to recognize his leading. Going from the milk of the Word to the meat and having our senses trained in righteousness is what prepares us and helps us keep our lamps trimmed and ready as we eagerly watch for his return.

Both Anna and Simeon lived tuned into God's voice. They lived by faith in the unseen, believing God who promised to reveal himself in person. Both of them pushed away doubts and pushed into possibilities. In this passage, Luke makes the point that God used both male and female confirmation to encourage the hearts of Mary and Joseph.

What did Simeon prophesy over Jesus?

_____

_____

Now contrast Anna's actions with those of Simeon in **Luke 2:38.**

_____

_____

Anna's actions are quite different. There is no mention of her taking the baby from Mary's arms into her own. Most women, if given the slightest chance, will reach out to hold a newborn, even for a few moments.

What did Anna do that Simeon did not?

_____

_____

Anna stood near Jesus and then proceeded to tell everyone within earshot about this miraculous child. There is no interchange with Mary and Joseph recorded. (Although it's impossible to imagine Anna would not have had plenty of encouraging advice and well wishes to share.) She was at the temple every day, greeting and watching everyone who came near her. Her spiritual antenna was up and running constantly.

These three little verses of Luke 2 teach us so much about Anna's personality and passion for God's promised one. Anna would surely have stood as close to Mary and Joseph as humanly possible. Surely she would have greeted them and cooed over the newborn baby, giving the child a complete visual check up. Having noted no mention of her own children, she would have been delighted to hold any of the babies and pronounce blessings over them and their parents.

What would it have been like for Mary, this young Jewish woman, to come to the temple? It was a massive, imposing structure and the holiest place of worship in her world. Restricted to the Court of the Women, Mary would have found pleasure in the company of Anna. It is easy to picture the women gathering around Anna, discussing their problems, their dreams, their children. For a woman who had a need or problem, it would have been a great comfort to have an older woman at the temple that was always there to give counsel and comfort. Did Anna comfort and encourage Mary? It's hard to believe otherwise.

How does **Luke 2:38** describe Anna's impression of the baby Jesus?

_____

_____

Anna had no reservations about declaring the redemption of Israel had come!

This precious woman who knew the signs of the times and the voice of her God knew without a doubt she was seeing the Messiah at last. She speaks "of Jesus" immediately by name.

What reference is made to Anna's timing in **verse 38**?

_____

_____

"And she too came up at that same hour, and returned thanks to God and talked of Jesus to all who were looking for the redemption (deliverance) of Jerusalem" (Amplified Bible).

God's timing is spot-on. He knew from before the foundations of the world exactly when Mary would conceive Jesus. He knew when Mary and Joseph would enter the temple and fulfill Simeon's prayer. Our almighty, ever-powerful God also knew exactly when Anna would approach this newborn Messiah and experience the thrill of her life! God's ability to be in the tiniest detail at the same millisecond he is in control of the universe is staggering and comforting.

So one day, into the temple a seemingly simple couple arrives with their new son. Yet nothing could have been more extraordinary on heaven or on earth. Keep your eyes and ears open to the Lord, beloved. Our God is all about thrilling our daily lives and future with unannounced glory.

Joseph and Mary entered the temple for two reasons: purification and dedication. They were following the law that said every firstborn son was to be dedicated to the Lord. Their obedience to God's laws had eternal significance, and fulfilled many prophecies concerning the coming Messiah.

Read Exodus 13:2, 11-16.

Who did the firstborn belong to?

_____

_____

According to **verse 13**, what were they to do to every firstborn male?

_____

_____

What did God want them to remember as they came to redeem their son?

_____

_____

The ceremony in which they redeemed their firstborn sons was to remind the new parents of how God killed every firstborn man and animal in Egypt on the night of the first Passover, and with a powerful hand he delivered Israel from the land of slavery.

In the Promised Land, the firstborn of every animal was to be sacrificed to God, but the firstborn male son was to be redeemed. This was a graphic picture of how God's firstborn only Son would one day redeem us all.

Do you think Joseph and Mary had any real awareness regarding the symbolism of their dedication of Jesus? Why or why not?

_____

_____

In **Luke 2:35,** Simeon spoke a powerful prophetic word directly to Mary. With everything going on around her, do you think she recognized the implications of his prediction?

_____

_____

We know that Mary pondered many things in her heart over the years. Simeon's conversation must have replayed over and again as Jesus grew into manhood. Yet on this day in the temple, a new mother held her firstborn son while Joseph managed to keep two pigeons from flying away. During the ceremony of purification the mother could offer a lamb or two pigeons. The fact that they chose pigeons suggests they were not able to afford to buy a lamb.

To the unobservant, Joseph and Mary would have looked like a small-town couple, a bit out of their league in the big city of Jerusalem at the court of the temple.

Yet when Anna saw them at the doorway of the tent of meeting, she knew exactly why they were there. She had the gift of seeing what others could not see. Anna looked at them and by the revelation of the Holy Spirit, saw the redeemer in Mary's arms. How her faith must have soared in that moment!

For a woman who had devoted her life to God in the very place where animals were sacrificed for sin twenty-four hours a day, nothing could have made her happier than to lay eyes on the One who would be the perfect sacrifice for sin, once and for all! She gave thanks to God as she gazed at the lamb of God who would take away the sins of the world.

Then she continued to speak of him, "to all those who were looking for the redemption of Jerusalem." Do you find it interesting that she spoke to those "who were looking?" Anna sought out those who longed for the Messiah. And she wasn't shy as she joyfully proclaimed that he was here now!

After this most breathtaking day when Anna came up at the very hour when Mary and Joseph were blessed by Simeon and saw the Christ child with her own eyes, do you think she was able to sleep that night? What did Anna pray? Use your sanctified imagination and write a prayer you think Anna may have prayed on the day she saw Jesus.

_____

_____

Anna may have felt the purpose of her life had been fulfilled that day. Surely she was emotionally and physically elated and exhausted. Can you imagine how her heart pounded as she rushed from one face to another to share the news of the baby Jesus? As she lay down to rest that night, when all was quiet and the stars shone above her, did every covenantal promise of God run like beautiful music through her soul? How many years had she been praying for the Messiah to come?

And when the time came, she was there.

We asked author and speaker Barbara Pine to share her insights on dear Anna:

"We're not sure that Simeon would have been there in the temple but that the Holy Spirit prompted him to go. With Anna (I love this hidden 'gem'), 'coming up at that very hour,' we see no need for a spiritual kick in the pants, no command to 'go.' She is where she needs to be because she's where she needs to be! Grocery store aisle, temple… wherever we happen to be, this is where God will surprise us with the opportunity to bless, encourage, testify.

It is not 'consolation' that she awaits; hers is not the need of comfort after some disappointment; her anticipation, her waiting is for the redemption of Israel. She's anticipating the return of something once possessed; waiting for freedom from the debt of sorrow and sin. She knows that release and relief lie in this little guy being jiggled in his mommy's arms. So, leave it to a prophet to anticipate with thanksgiving and praise. She is planning the party."[28]

What redemption are you anticipating from the Lord today?

_____

Allow Anna to encourage you to look eagerly for God to move. As you go through whatever your day holds, keep your spiritual eyes searching each encounter with family or friends, people you work with or sit by at your children's ball games, strangers in the mall or grocery line as an opportunity for God to move. Wait, move, watch, and live in thriving expectation. If nothing else, it will be good for your blood pressure! Luke uses the word "epistasa" with reference to Anna, which means, "she stood over, or beside, or near" that which happened to Christ in the temple. In the Latin text, "superveniens" means she "came near at that time." Quite literally Anna pressed forward with great earnestness to see him.

Living a life of expecting God to be God is hard work. We have head knowledge and we say we believe him. But head faith must be connected to heart faith to have real faith. Anna may or may not have held the baby Jesus physically, but she had made a habit of leaning forward to hear every cry of a child that came into the temple. She lived her life fully prepared to see God's Son in the flesh. She knew it in her eighty-four-plus-year-old bones when she saw the baby Messiah in the arms of Mary and Joseph. With her entire being, Anna embraced Jesus as her Savior the moment she laid her eyes on him.

Can you name a time when you knew without any question God had revealed himself to you?

_____

_____

ANNA'S MESSAGE TO YOU AND ME: "GIRLFRIENDS, FINISH WELL!"

From the beginning of her life to her latter years, Anna lived out her faith and finished well. We don't know how she entered true life in heaven. We do know she gives us a vivid example of how to walk from this world into the next with our boots on, our hope alive, discovering new revelations from God at each turn.

Look at the lovely verses in Psalm 71. It seems the Psalmist could have been looking into the future, and had Anna is mind as he wrote:

> In you, O Lord, I have taken refuge;
>   let me never be put to shame.
> Rescue me and deliver me in your righteousness;
>   turn your ear to me and save me.
> Be my rock of refuge,
>   to which I can always go;
>   give the command to save me,
>   for you are my rock and my fortress.
> Deliver me, O my God, from the hand of the wicked,
>   from the grasp of evil and cruel men.
> For you have been my hope, O sovereign Lord,
>   my confidence since my youth.
> From birth I have relied on you;
>   you brought me forth from my mother's womb.
>   I will ever praise you.
> I have become like a portent to many,
>   but you are my strong refuge.

> My mouth is filled with your praise,
> > declaring your splendor all day long.
> > Do not cast me away when I am old;
> > do not forsake me when my strength is gone.
> > For my enemies speak against me;
> > those who wait to kill me conspire together.
> > They say, "God has forsaken him;
> > pursue him and seize him,
> > for no one will rescue him."
> > Be not far from me, O God;
> > come quickly, O my God, to help me.
> > May my accusers perish in shame;
> > may those who want to harm me
> > be covered with scorn and disgrace.
> > But as for me, I will always have hope;
> > I will praise you more and more.
> > My mouth will tell of your righteousness,
> > of your salvation all day long,
> > though I know not its measure.
> > I will come and proclaim your mighty acts, O Sovereign Lord;
> > I will proclaim your righteousness, yours alone.
> > Since my youth, O God, you have taught me,
> > and to this day I declare your marvelous deeds.
> > Even when I am old and gray,
> > do not forsake me, O God,
> > till I declare your power to the next generation,
> > your might to all who are to come (Ps. 71:1-18 NIV).

Read Luke 2:38 once more. What two things did Anna do when she recognized Jesus as Messiah?

_____

_____

Anna leaves us with a picture of a woman who has spent over eight decades praising God and telling of his mighty works. Dr. Luke tells us that Anna continued to speak of him to all who were looking for the redemption of Jerusalem. Just as the psalmist said, "do not forsake me… till I declare your power to the next generation," Anna was determined, even in her advanced age, to never give up and to finish the work God had given her until he called her home.

Her life wasn't easy. It was riddled with loss, and painting a pristine picture of Anna's faith would be unfair and inaccurate. She had suffered through widowhood and mourning. She suffered the burden of intercession for her people. She longed to see unfulfilled dreams become reality. She had the aches and pains that come with aging. She watched her youthful figure change over the years, and she understood the price a woman pays during menopause.

She lived in a temple where women could only go so far, and then no farther to enter into God's Holy of Holies. She lived in a time when women were considered "lesser" citizens. They were relegated to the outer court of the synagogue and could not sit with the men. Israel suffered a famine of prophecy and the tyranny of Rome. Anna's life was an uphill climb.

Yet through it all, what does Anna do?

_____

_____

Anna praised God and anticipated new beginnings.

Wow! This is so opposite to the prevailing mindset of our time. We think in terms of retirement and taking it easy when we reach a certain age. We are not used to dreaming of reaching new goals, new beginnings, and new adventures with God in our eighties. Especially in America, it is easy to think we deserve to spend our time and money on our pleasures when we reach the golden years.

Can you find a verse in the Bible where we are given instructions for retirement?

_____

_____

(If you do, please let us know!)

One of the strongest women of faith in our generation is an inspiring lady named Kathy Wysong. She spends her time teaching younger women, sending encouraging words from the Lord and continually delights in the mysteries of God. Kathy and her husband serve as chaplains at a local hospital where they meet with strangers who are grieving the loss of family members or friends. Her voice is kind and strong and full of faith in God's love. She has countless "God-stories" from their years spent as hospice prayer warriors. When we asked her to share some of the surprises of God in her life, Kathy sent the following exclamation point.

"Oh for the faith and devotion of Anna!" Kathy began. "Times of surprise in my life of God's love and faithfulness.... He is just so good, even when we least expect it.

On a cold February Sunday morning in 1967, I had a stroke due to birth control pills. My husband rushed me to the hospital where the doctor did a spinal tap. The results came back that my spinal fluid was filled with blood. I was not expected to live and if I did, I wouldn't have a 'viable' life.

Having two young children, the news was devastating. The time came when my husband gathered the children in his arms and told them God may take me to heaven. He relinquished me to the Father, no longer able to hold me from the Father's will. I was going through a struggle to make it each day and especially nights when I prayed to the Father, 'Not my will but thine.'

Three months passed and we went to a healing meeting, invited by a friend. We didn't want to go, but our friend reminded us we had nothing to lose. We sat in the very last row of chairs... (not to get too close)... and our Faith was built as we heard singing that seemed to us to be from the Father, direct words of life for us. In those folding chairs, as far away from the front as we could get, God came in mercy and power and healed my body and weary spirit.

Our spirit was blind to it happening in the now, yet even so he was faithful. He knows our hearts and will be always faithful as we pray, 'Not my will but thine be done.' We have seen him in power… mercy… with healing in his wings… and we were surprised!

What a Savior, to him be all glory!"

Does Kathy's enthusiasm sound like the thanksgiving of Anna?

___

___

Do you have a story of God surprising you with his mercy, power, and healing?

___

___

Kathy is a living, modern-day Anna. She bounds from place to place radiating the glory of God and talking with anyone in her path who is open to hearing stories of his faithfulness and grace. Age doesn't matter to Kathy, any more than it did to Anna. Women like this are such a breath of freedom and fresh release in our culture. In the lives of Anna, Kathy, Barbara Pine, our own mothers and countless other beautiful women who have walked with God for decades, there is a special combination of beauty and boldness. They are unafraid to speak out about his work in their lives. They are fearless in facing the future. They throw down the gauntlet this side of heaven and say, "I believe God no matter my age, my station in life, my bank account, or my culture. I believe him above and beyond this world and will dance into his arms when I leave this world behind."

As Barbara Pine noted, "Well… I do love this…. Anna was worshiping, and she was a prophetess. **Hers** is the voice that according to tradition had better be right! And there, on the campus of the temple (limited for sure, being female) she was neither intimidated by the limitations **or** by the tradition that women had no authority. It seems, doesn't it, that she simply spoke what was clear to her and didn't worry about who heard or didn't. She didn't worry about being female or old. Nice."

Does the study of Anna change the way you see older women of faith?

___

___

Has this made you long for God to bring an Anna into your life?

___

___

Are you an Anna-in-waiting, ready to step out and mentor younger women around you?

___

If you're one of God's "Annas" standing on the sidelines, please jump in and let the rest of us benefit from your years of experiencing God. We need to hear from you. We need emails, phone calls, notes, anything you can share with us that will encourage our hearts as we dare to believe God each day.

Look at Psalm 92:14. What is God's promise to those who are righteous in Christ?

_____

_____

We can be productive at any age. It's part of the mystery of the filling of the Holy Spirit that enables us to still be contributing to the kingdom and glorifying God to our dying breath.

Take a look at some of the stunning contributions made to the world by people who were over the age of sixty-five.

The Earl of Halsburg, for example, was ninety when he began preparing a twenty-volume revision of English law.

Goethe wrote *Faust* at age eighty-two.

Hudson Taylor, at age sixty-nine, was still vigorously working on the mission field, opening up new territories in Indochina.

Caleb took the stronghold over the giants at age eighty-five. (See Joshua 14:10-15.)

"God never intends for us to retire from spiritual activity. The Bible says we can 'still bring forth fruit in old age.' Even as Jesus kept the 'best wine' for the last at the wedding of Cana (John 2:10), so he seeks to gather the most luscious clusters of the fruit of the Spirit from the fully ripened harvest of our lives."

Feeling luscious? Maybe you don't, but that's the way God sees you. You may be past your prime in the eyes of our culture, but to our Father, you are simply moving closer toward the next and most glorious phase of your life with him. You're closer than ever to your glorified body that will never age as you reign with him forever on the new earth.

Anna's message about finishing well applies to any woman, at any stage of life, that is living each day fully and completely to the glory of God. How many of us know young women who walked from this earth into heaven long before we expected their exit? Women who stay the course and believe him at all costs are champions in the eyes of their Father.

In her book, Running the Course: Becoming a Champion in God's Eyes, Kristi Overton Johnson writes of her emotional win as the 1999 World Champion in the waterskiing competition, representing the United States team:

"'It takes a long time to be a champion, baby.'

Those were the words I heard many times when I called my Granddaddy Charlie after competitions. It was his way of encouraging me not to give up on achieving my lifelong goal of becoming world champion. He knew that reaching this standard would take years; it wasn't something that would happen overnight.

As I stood before the best of the best in the world of waterskiing in Milan, Italy, I could hear my Granddaddy Charlie's voice from thousands of miles away whisper, 'You're finally a champion, baby!' Tears of joy ran down my cheeks… it was an unbelievably emotional moment.

Most importantly, I was overcome with a desire and a need to thank God Almighty… it was an opportunity to stop and whisper a prayer of thanksgiving to God.

It was a time to look back on how many ways his fingerprints had been evident in my life, through all the victories, defeats, joys, and pains that had been used by him to bring me to this moment. I clearly saw how God had been working in my life, orchestrating my waterskiing career and all of its experiences to mold me into someone he could use.

It was a moment like few others…when I came face-to-face with God."[29]

Anna was devoted to running her race and finishing the course, even if she had to use a walker to get across the finish line. You may be thinking, I'm too old to be of any good to anyone. God never views anyone as out of commission in his service. He uses everyone yielded to him.

Dream with God and write down something you would like to accomplish before God calls you home:

_____

_____

Write down something you would like to see happen spiritually before you leave this world:

_____

_____

Anna and Kristi, Kathy, Barbara, and godly women of all ages echo the message of the psalmist.

Keep pushing ahead, through the ups and downs, pains and pleasures, joys and sorrows, because in the end finishing well with the Lord is worth more than we can dream or imagine. The champions of faith share one vital practice. They thank God for what has happened in their lives, what is happening and most of all for what will happen in his will and time.

George Burns once said, "Tennis is a game for young people. Until age twenty-five, you can play singles. From there until age thirty-five, you should play doubles. I won't tell you my age, but when I played, there were twenty-eight people on the court—just my side of the net."

There may have been twenty-eight people on the court, but George was still in the game, swinging the racket!

Anna was still in the game too, in the court of the women, proclaiming the goodness of God and the coming of the Messiah. She was a senior citizen who kept her wedding gown on in preparation for the appearance of her bridegroom. Like the parable of the ten virgins, Anna's lamp was trimmed and ready as she watched and listened for his voice. Anna clearly has something powerful to teach us about finishing well. She calls out to generations and reminds us that the woman who waits and watches for her Savior will indeed one day see him face-to-face!

Never stop expecting God to surprise you with new revelations. Surprises in life can be painful. But God overrides pain with unexpected gifts of utter delight!

Today's heroine lived on the edge of her seat, leaning forward, listening, watching, looking for God to come through. We feel her raised eyebrows, her lips curled on the verge of a perpetual smile, a sparkle in her eyes, looking for a miracle at every turn.

Allow Anna to inspire you right here and now in your culture and circumstances today. Hear her voice cheering you on to press in closer, to believe Christ is real and alive and active in your life. Pray an "Anna prayer," however you are led:

_____
_____
_____
_____

Anna chose true life in Christ. She kept her priorities focused on the most important thing of all and this was the secret to her finishing well. Anna had nothing but her faith and an expectation that God wasn't finished. Anna believed God was with her. She lived daily pressing into an unfulfilled promise. She simply and purely took God at his word…even a word given four centuries earlier.

His word was the Word. And Anna lived to see it when his Word became flesh.

TODAY'S DATE: _____

YOUR HEADLINE:
_____
_____

WEEK FOUR

PHARISEE STRAW POLL *FOR WOMEN ONLY*
FRENZIED ACTIVITY CONTINUES DURING FEAST OF TABERNACLES
ADULTERESS SET FREE

The High Council of the Pharisees would appreciate your participation in today's straw poll. This poll is for women only and the results will be available online for public viewing.

Early this morning an anonymous woman was brought before Jesus, charged by the Religious Council with the capital crime of adultery. She was dragged into a huge gathering in the Temple Court to be stoned. However, Jesus deftly turned the situation upside-down. In the end there was no stoning of the guilty party. Once again he broke with Jewish tradition; our teachers never engage in random conversation with a woman. Yet as the crowd dispersed, he was seen speaking quietly with the adulteress. Afterward, she left to return to home, unpunished.

As a woman, how interested are you in what happened to the adulteress?
- ❏ Very
- ❏ Somewhat
- ❏ It's none of my business
- ❏ Depends on how you define "adulteress"

Jesus said, "Let him who is without sin among you be the first to throw a stone at her." Is this an arguable defense?
- ❏ Yes, brilliant
- ❏ No, weak response
- ❏ Depends on how you define "sin"

Regarding the uproar over Jesus, how would do you rate his radical teaching?
- ❏ Extremely powerful
- ❏ Quite interesting
- ❏ Just another zealot
- ❏ Egomaniacal and delusional
- ❏ Life-changing
- ❏ Liberating for women
- ❏ Depends on how you define "radical"

A woman in Samaria spoke with Jesus at length. If he was in your town, would you want to speak with him?
- ❏ Yes, at all costs
- ❏ Never, he's a freak
- ❏ Only with my husband present
- ❏ As a guest speaker for ladies' night out
- ❏ Depends on how you define "speak"

Would you be interested in hearing Jesus debate our top religious leaders about current issues?
- ❏ Yes
- ❏ No
- ❏ Maybe
- ❏ Depends on how you define "current"

How are Jesus' teachings affecting your life?
- ❏ I am beginning to see God's love differently
- ❏ I feel he genuinely cares about women and men alike
- ❏ I never had hope before hearing him
- ❏ He makes sense sometimes and other times loses me
- ❏ I am fine with the laws we have
- ❏ I don't have time for him
- ❏ Depends on how you define "teachings"

Do you think Jesus is running a political campaign?
- ❏ Obviously
- ❏ Possibly
- ❏ Absolutely not
- ❏ Depends on how you define "campaign"

Do you believe he could be Israel's Messiah?
- ❏ With all my heart
- ❏ Open to the idea
- ❏ More and more each day
- ❏ No way
- ❏ Depends on how you define "Messiah"

Are you aware of the threat he poses for our people? Roman authorities are watching for any unrest among us. This week's Feast of the Tabernacles has been a zoo. In light of the adulteress walking free, how do you feel the Sanhedrin should proceed with this Jesus of Nazareth?
- ❏ Treat him respectfully
- ❏ Listen and watch
- ❏ Ask him to tone things down until after Passover
- ❏ Consider the possibility that he is the Messiah
- ❏ Consider trial
- ❏ Arrest and imprisonment
- ❏ Crucifixion
- ❏ Depends on how you define "proceed"

The Pharisee Straw Poll thanks you for your time and participation.
Please feel free to redeem a gift coupon for half-off any Passover sacrifice at our website.

TODAY'S HEROINE:
An Adulteress

"We cannot both judge others and be patient toward them. One cancels out the other."
Beth Moore [30]

John 8 opens like a three-ring circus. It's a human chess game on the steps of the temple and the stakes are high. The players are Jesus, the religious leaders of Israel determined to discredit him, and a "certain woman" found guilty of adultery. Tension mounts with each passing verse. Will Jesus finally be tripped up, trapped by the law, publicly caught in a quandary with no way out? Will the woman be stoned for her sin? Have the scribes and Pharisees finally cornered, tamed, and silenced the teacher from Nazareth? How can an adulteress be called a heroine? Let's dive into this powerful scene and discover what the Holy Spirit will reveal to our hearts.

Turn to 2 Timothy 3:16.

Based on this verse, why do you feel it's important to study this one gospel account of a broken woman's story?

_____

_____

Nothing in the word of God is recorded by accident. Put aside any preconceived ideas about the events recorded in John 8. Clear your spiritual palate. Pretend you've never heard about this woman and her encounter with Jesus. Try not to recall scenes from movies, Easter pageants or flannel-graph figures used in Sunday school classrooms.

With fresh eyes and the ever-present creativity of the Holy Spirit flowing through us, let's study the whole picture. What happened in the days leading up to the moment the adulteress was cast down at the feet of Jesus?

Read John 7:1-10.

What Jewish feast was coming up?

Where was Jesus teaching?

Why did Jesus stay in Galilee?

Who asked him to go to Judea?

What reason in **verse 8** did Jesus give for not going to Judea?

In **verse 10**, note what Jesus did and how.

_____

_____

The Feast of Tabernacles is one of three great Jewish religious holidays; Passover and Pentecost being the other two. It was held in September-October, and was a time each year when the Jews remembered how God delivered them from Egypt. It was a time to recall how their ancestors lived in "tabernacle tents" while making their way through the wilderness to the Promised Land. This feast was a grand week of camping out (minus the RVs). Families would gather by the thousands, staying in makeshift tents in Jerusalem. Imagine the hillsides of Jerusalem covered with people living in shelters made of leaves and branches.

Jesus' brothers taunted him in verses 3-4. In essence, they said:

"Why don't you leave small town Galilee and move on into the limelight! Why perform all your miracles in the middle of nowhere when you could really have a huge impact on the massive crowds in Jerusalem?"

What does **verse 1** tell us about the threat against Jesus waiting in Judea?

_____

_____

The religious Jews in Judea wanted which of the following?

To hear Jesus teach

To ask him more about his connection with God

To arrest him

To kill him

Jesus' life was in danger if he went to Judea. Private opinion of him was turning ugly. The "religious" leaders were questioning his authority and ridiculing him. The chief priests and Pharisees were planning to arrest Jesus. Yet his own brothers sarcastically suggested he go directly into the line of fire.

Verse 5 plainly states the condition of their hearts. For those who have family members who do not yet believe in Christ, he understands your pain. He understands having flesh-and-blood relatives who make fun of your faith. Even God in the flesh was rejected by those closest to him.

SIDEBAR: The good news with God is that no one's story is over until he is finished. James, the brother of Jesus, did not trust him prior to his crucifixion. (This is a different James than the member of his twelve apostles. The apostle James was the brother of John.) However, Christ's brother James later became a leader of the church in Jerusalem. (See Acts 1:14 and 1 Corinthians 15:7.) James wrote a beautiful epistle in the New Testament (James). Jesus' brother Judas authored the book of Jude. [31]

Read Mark 6:1-6.

What happened in Jesus' hometown?

___

Assumptions about Jesus were made in **verse 2**. What conclusion did his neighbors make about him?

___

___

These people saw Jesus grow up as the son of Joseph and Mary. He was a carpenter by trade and may even have practiced this trade to make money during his three-year ministry. Only officials of the temple and religious courts drew salaries. The rest of religious teachers or leaders were either independently wealthy or supported themselves through a trade or profession. Jesus very well might have worked on a few cabinets, tables, and chairs as he made his way through towns performing miracles and teaching those who would receive him. [32]

"Just being a carpenter" labeled and limited Jesus in the minds of those who knew him as their homeboy. How could this small-town man be the Messiah prophesied in the Torah? He wasn't powerful. Messiahs aren't men who work with wood. Messiahs are kings who fight wars and bring down enemies with a sword. Sadly, the very people who taught Jesus as he grew as a child, the ones who came to celebrate his birthdays, passages of manhood in the Jewish faith, the ones who waved a casual "hello" and smiled at his family at the synagogue gatherings, **missed** Him.

It can be hard to allow people we have known the longest to grow and change. They always have lived in a certain part of town and have certain hobbies. They attend the same church and for decades sit in the same seat. They are viewed through a lens of familiarity and assumption, neatly pegged into their own category. If someone breaks the pattern or chooses an unpredictable path, it can be upsetting and uncomfortable.

Do you find it a challenge to keep from judging others by outward appearances and assumptions?

___

___

Welcome to the human race. It's a lifelong battle for all of us. There is a strange sense of comfort in keeping people in their assumed role. It's a false sense of control.

In **Matthew 7:1**, what does Jesus say?

___

___

Christ understood the dangers of finger pointing more than anyone who has ever walked the planet. His entire life was riddled with people who misunderstood, misread, and underestimated his powerful presence on earth.

In **John 6**, Jesus made a shocking statement four times.

What does He say in **John 6:48**?

_____

_____

Jesus was trying to shake up Israel's preconceived ideas of what it meant to be fed from God. God had fed them with manna, protected them even in captivity, and promised to bring them a Messiah. Here he was. Emmanuel. God with them. The true bread of life. But his words upset the status quo. Many of the Jews already had decided what God would do and how God would do it. The radical teachings of Jesus didn't fit the image of God made in their likeness.

What happened in **John 6:60 and verse 66**?

_____

_____

"Many of his disciples drew back (returned to their old associations) and no longer accompanied him" (John 6:66 Amplified Bible).

Do you ever feel like God does not respond to your circumstances like you assumed he would?

_____

_____

Do difficult seasons in life make it seem God is not following his own plans?

_____

_____

Don't be discouraged if you answered, "yes."

The enemy of this world began with one question in the garden and continues to badger mankind with the same old dagger of doubt. (Remember, God is the creator. **Satan cannot create.** He can only repackage the same old lies over and over again. He is the saddest, ultimate wannabe.)

What did Satan ask Eve in the garden? (**See Genesis 3:1.**)

_____

_____

"Did God really say_____?"

When our circumstances look hopeless, the enemy continues to whisper his ancient lie.

"Did God really say_____?"

The word tells us Jesus is the same yesterday, today, and tomorrow.

81

Read Numbers 23:19.

Describe the attributes of God listed there:

_____

_____

The next time you sense the enemy is threatened by your faith, remember that even God's Son was hammered by Satan. After his baptism in the river Jordan, filled with the Holy Spirit, Jesus went into the wilderness. Immediately the enemy began taunting him with questions about God's faithfulness. Talk about nerves of evil steel! Jesus quoted the word back to the Devil and the Enemy decided to wait for a "better time." The word became flesh and used Scripture to shut the Devil down.

Write down a situation in your life in which you feel the Enemy's hammer:

_____

_____

Now say to that situation, "Thus says the Lord: 'All things are possible with God,' according to Mark 9:23. Now get out of my face!"

Satan's pride may have kept him from believing God would do what he promised in his covenant with Israel. Maybe the Enemy saw centuries fly by and began to believe he controlled ultimate power over man. After all, there had been 400 years of silence from God's prophets. Could it be that God would not follow through in bringing the promised Messiah? Not on your life.

God stunned the cosmos with the most outrageous act of love ever conceived. God himself came to man. He came in the form of his only Son. He came as an infant born to a young, unknown, poor Jewish couple in a cave in the middle of the night. He came during the height of Rome's power over Israel. He came as sure as God has been or ever will be, in the glory and humility of a human body.

Satan pulled out the stops to stop God's Son. Still trying to be God, and failing, the war raged on. And Jesus was ready for the fight. Jesus knew the battle would be won on a cross.

By the time we arrive at the temple court where the adulteress is dragged before Jesus, this spiritual battle between Satan and Christ has intensified. Jesus was doing what he purposed to do from before the foundations of the world. He would free men and women from the shackles of sin. He would turn the world upside down and pour out his life to defeat the Enemy.

He had performed many miracles. There had been pivotal encounters between Jesus and women who were touched and healed. He healed them in every way a person can be healed; physically, emotionally, and spiritually. Jesus made a special point to engage in conversation with women who had given up on themselves. Jesus is the knight on the white horse every woman longs for. He is the only one who has the power to fully love, restore, relieve, and revive a woman's heart.

Jesus strides into the crowds gathered at the Festival of the Tabernacles filled with the

Holy Spirit and God's loving heart beating in His breast. He walks into the jaws of danger knowing full well what waits for him there.

Read John 7:11-16.

Who was looking for Jesus?

___

Where were they?

___

How would you describe their conversations about him?

___

When did Jesus begin to teach and where?

___

How did the people react?

___

Who did Jesus credit as the source of his understanding?

___

The climate around Christ was rising to a fevered pitch. It was a time when he was impossible to ignore. Many came to believe he was the Messiah. At the same time, others were convinced that Jesus was a heretic.

With this in mind, read John 7:37-38.

On what day of the Feast does he speak?

How does Jesus speak?

___

What does he say?

___

WE INTERRUPT THIS PROGRAM....

Nelson's New Illustrated Biblical Commentary gives a vivid picture of Jesus' powerful proclamation:

"Jesus' cry was far more dramatic than most modern readers realize. He chose a time when Jerusalem was packed with holiday visitors and a crucial moment in the festivities when he could attract the most attention. It would be as if someone broke into the broadcast of a presidential state-of-the-union address to announce, 'We interrupt this program to bring you a special report.' Jesus chose to keep a low profile but waited for the right moment to declare himself publicly.

On the last day of the festival, the priest took a golden pitcher filled with water from the Pool of Siloam, carried it to the temple, and poured it on the altar as an offering to God. This dramatic ceremony was a memorial of the water that flowed from the rock when the Israelites traveled through the wilderness. On the last day, the people marched seven times around the altar in memory of the seven circuits around the walls of Jericho.

….just after the crowds had not only waved their branches, but as was the custom, literally shook them to pieces in a frenzy of enthusiasm, a voice suddenly cried out; 'If anyone thirsts, let him come to me and drink.' Jesus' timing couldn't have been more perfect or his claim more explicit: He was declaring himself to be none other than the long-awaited Messiah who would pour out the Holy Spirit." [33]

Look up the following Scriptures and see the verses Jesus referenced in his declaration.

Isaiah 44:3: What does the water represent?

_____

_____

Isaiah 55:1: To whom is the water available?

_____

_____

Isaiah 58:11: What does the water produce?

_____

_____

Note the extreme range of reactions to Jesus that day.

John 7:40:

_____

_____

John 7:41:

_____

_____

John 7:42-43:

_____

_____

How did the religious elite respond?

John 7:47-49:

_____

_____

The "little people" were discounted as being unenlightened. The Pharisees accused those who believed in Jesus of being deluded and swept off their feet. The "learned authorities" weren't so gullible. They knew the law. This man Jesus was a definite problem and he wasn't going away. He was gaining control. Many times the Pharisees tried to discredit Jesus as a teacher by using the law as their defense. To their mounting frustration, he had succeeded each time by speaking clear truth. His questions left them feeling foolish.

Part of their frustration with Jesus was the threat he posed to the Jews' stability under Rome's domination. Jesus continually challenged traditional religious law and seemed to have no fear of political chastisement either from his own people or the powers above them. There had been frequent rebellions against the Romans which were often solved by killing Jews and asking questions later.

The scribes and Pharisees had a two-fold problem on their hands. With each passing day, Jesus drew more people to him with his revolutionary talk of a new kingdom based on love, forgiveness, self-sacrifice and mercy. His followers were passionate and his popularity threatened the spiritual power of the Jewish leaders. If talk of new kings and kingdoms turned to rebellion, the wrath of Rome would be unleashed on innocent heads. They had to stop this Nazarene before he upended Jewish theology and brought down Rome's heavy hand on Jewish citizens. [34]

QUESTION: Can you remember a time when church leaders in our culture have been more motivated by fear than faith?

_____

_____

Our focus must be on the kingdom of God, not the kingdoms of the world. Fear will paralyze a heart of faith. Faith frees the heart to live with "ruthless trust," a lovely phrase from author Brennan Manning. We must remember God holds even the most chaotic government in his hands.

The religious leaders around Jesus were more concerned with keeping Rome happy and the status quo in place than in listening to his life-changing words. They simply had to stop him. But how to catch Jesus in a situation in which he would have to retreat?

THE PHARISEES' FOOL-PROOF PLAN

Find someone guilty of breaking the Ten Commandments. Demand Jesus pronounce a sentence according to Mosaic law. Do this in a large gathering and make Jesus out to be a fraud. That ought to clinch the deal. Now, all they needed to do was find the right pawn for the upcoming showdown.

BRING OUT A BIG-TIME SINNER, PREFERABLY A WOMAN

Oh yes, haul out the local adulteress. She can be caught in the very act. What sweet revenge it would be to make this point using a sinful woman, as Jesus had been speaking to all manner of filthy women. An adulteress would serve their purposes perfectly.

Over and again the pious elect missed the message of Christ. He had just publicly offered rivers of living water for those who dared to believe him. The sinful woman they chose to use had a soul parched with thirst. Had the adulteress heard of Jesus? Did she stand at the edge of the crowds earlier in the week and listen when he taught? We don't know. We do know she was in the middle of an affair. She was trapped in a lifestyle of sin. She lived in the dry desert of lies and deceit. By plotting and scheming to have her killed, the very men who felt superior orchestrated her encounter with Jesus. Yet this divine intersection with God's Son would quench her lifelong thirst for all eternity.

Read John 8:1-12.

NOTE: After the uproar Jesus caused the previous day, he did not retreat back to the safety of Galilee's hills. He stayed right in the middle of the hornet's nest and faced danger head-on.

In **John 8:1**, where has Jesus been all night?

___

___

The Son of Man, who had no place to lay his head, stayed the night on the Mount of Olives.

It is the early hours of dawn when Jesus goes to the temple to teach. His presence in the temple is a clear statement that he will not back down from his mission.

Sunlight begins to streak across the walls of the temple. Jesus sits down, as was the custom for respected teachers, and began to speak to the eager faces before him.

Suddenly the morning calm is broken by the cries of a terrified nameless woman, dragged into the center of the court by a group of angry, outraged scribes and Pharisees.

This woman is thrown at his feet. Talk about an awkward moment. The Pharisees have created a dramatic little kangaroo court. Casting themselves in the role of the judge, Jesus must now defend himself and his reputation.

What did they call Jesus in **verse 4**?

_____

_____

Note the contrast between the bullying arrogance of the "religious leaders" and the humility of Jesus. He is sitting with respect to his surroundings and those surrounding him. The men who claimed to honor the law barge in and interrupt Jesus with no regard for respecting either the temple or the people gathered. These religious men were threatened by Jesus and his claim to be God. They were angry that he esteemed the "lesser" people, the ones with no education, no social standing, no credibility in spiritual matters. They were jealous that these people hung on his every word and called him the greatest teacher they had ever heard.

Now imagine the tone of their voices.

What did they say about the woman?

_____

_____

Adultery was a capital crime among the Jewish people. The scribes and Pharisees were rabidly cautious and territorial. They felt responsible for keeping the Jewish people in line, and handed down endless updates on religious laws.

Turn to **Deuteronomy 22:22-24**. What does the Law of Moses actually say about this matter?

_____

_____

No revisions of this crime would be necessary. It was written on tablets of stone by the finger of God and given to Moses and their ancestors. In throwing this woman at his feet, they hoped to offer public proof that Jesus was not divine.

If there had been a commentator in the court of the women that day, he would have been selling tickets to this verbal boxing match. "Step right up, ladies and gentlemen! It's round one of Jesus versus Moses in the Battle of Grace against Law! See the friend of publicans and sinners go head-to-head with the defenders of the Ten Commandments! Watch as the lightweight from Nazareth defends his reputation against the heavyweight champs from the Pharisaical right! Stick around and see who will be left standing!"

"She has been caught in the act—in bed with someone else's husband.... Maybe both of them were married. Whatever the circumstances, it's a clear-cut case of adultery. She is dragged from bed, most likely naked, through the streets and shoved in front of Jesus."[35]

Take a moment to think this through:

We wonder how she was caught. Had this affair being going on for a long time? Was it a regular rendezvous each week? How did the religious men know where to find the woman? Someone had to know because she was caught "in the very act." Did they know about an ongoing affair and decide to step in at this moment to use her for their agenda? Your thoughts:

___

___

If she was dragged nearly naked before Christ, is this not a poignant picture for him? He knows that soon he will hang naked and bloodied on a public cross to pay for all sins. How would this trembling, shamed woman move his heart to rescue and redeem her life?

___

___

The punishment for adultery is found in Leviticus 20:10.

According to the Law, in the case of adultery, who is to be punished?

___

What is the punishment?

___

No method of punishment is given in Leviticus. Death by stoning became the choice used for centuries and still exists in some cultures today. Both the man and woman were to be executed. There has been much speculation about why the man involved is not included in the scene. It takes two to commit adultery, but for some strange and hypocritical reason the Pharisees only brought the woman to Jesus as a visual aid to make their point. Makes a strong case for the "good ol' boys' got-your-back" club.

However, Jesus knows that this is about much more than stoning a guilty woman. The religious leaders could not care less about the fate of this woman, only that she be the catalyst to discredit Jesus. She was being used by self righteous people to trap Jesus into saying something that would incriminate him. When these men looked at her, they were disgusted with who she was and proud of their own reputations. They were religious men who outwardly did all the right things and "fulfilled the law."

Their pride turned to poison.

In **John 8:5**, what gauntlet is thrown down?

___

___

Here the religious men have hit on a problem they themselves have been wrestling with. Rome mandates that a death sentence can only be authorized by a Roman governor. As we see in the case of Jesus' own death sentence, the Jewish authorities had to bend, break, and twist every possible law to land him on a cross.

Read verse 6 carefully.

What end-game result do they seek?

_____

_____

They think Jesus has been backed into a corner. To follow the Law of Moses requires a death sentence. If Jesus agrees, he steps over the line of Roman rule. He dare not bring on the wrath of the Roman authorities. He will then have to let the woman go free. His inability to answer their trick question would incriminate him and prove once and for all that he was not God. If Jesus refused to stone her and was "soft on sin," then they could go home satisfied that once again they had saved the ignorant Jewish masses from following another trouble maker and self appointed Messiah. Either choice leaves Jesus in a no-win situation.

What does Jesus do in response?

_____

_____

His response is amazing. In one of the most startling and tender actions of mercy recorded in Scripture, he stoops down and writes in the dirt with his finger. Jesus restores the dignity of this desperate woman in full view of the "better" men surrounding her. Let them squirm a little. Let them break a sweat. Let them wonder what he will say.

How would his response affect the adulteress?

_____

_____

How would his response engage the crowd?

_____

_____

Jesus took all the attention off of the woman and placed it on himself. He let the moment hang in the air. He let all eyes settle on his fingers, writing, doodling, drawing in the dust of the ground. What did he write? We won't know until heaven, but it's fun to imagine the possibilities. Was it a scripture from the Torah, a simple note to himself, a message to the crowd, a funny picture that kept the focus off the extremely humiliated woman before him? Whatever he wrote, he was clearly making a very dramatic statement by not answering the men who dragged her in. (It's easy to see why crowds loved him. Jesus was unpredictable and so good at putting the pompous in their place!)

The NIV Study Bible has an interesting footnote about **verse 6**. When Jesus wrote on the ground with his finger, "this would seem to recall that the tablets of the law were inscribed in stone by the finger of God." To the very observant on that day, they would have gotten the message loud and clear. Jesus is saying, "Don't quote the law to me. I'm the one who wrote it in the first place!"

Where was Jesus when he drew in the dirt?

_____

_____

When he leaned down, Jesus physically moved to be on the same level as the sinful woman before him. This thrills our very dramatic hearts. If she was on her knees, he was right there with her. If she was standing, he was putting himself in a position even lower than hers. His body language speaks volumes to her. He was saying, "I'm not put off by you. I'm not repulsed by you. You are safe with me."

This is gold. We need to know beyond any doubt that Jesus is eager to welcome us, especially when we are in a mess. He does not stand in judgment but stoops down and looks into our eyes to welcome us into his presence. He knows the messes that riddle our lives. He isn't shocked or disgusted. He isn't angry. He identified with us forever when he chose to leave heaven and wrap his glory in the skin of humanity. He alone uniquely is qualified to pick us up and stand us on our feet again, washed clean. He delights in telling us that he does not condemn. Jesus longs to set us free to live the rest of our lives healed and restored.

God is never afraid to get his hands in the dirt. From the dust of this earth he formed us in his image. Jesus spit in the dirt and made mud balls for the eyes of the blind so they could see. Now with a terrified adulteress before him, and a mob demanding she be punished, he took to playing in the dust of his earth once more.

How would his response affect the accusers?

_____

_____

If a life had not been on the line, this could almost be high comedy. Can you imagine the frustration of the pious men who believed they had Jesus nailed down? He is drawing in the dirt! What is happening? Is he just stalling? Is he confused? This plan had no loopholes! Was Jesus finally at a loss for words?

What a surprise it must have been that Jesus didn't view them as they viewed themselves. Obviously in their minds there was no comparison between men of the law and this sinful woman caught in the very act of sexual infidelity. They were professional men of prayer. They held the most shares of righteous acts in the stock market. The people Jesus was most angry with were the ones who saw themselves as righteous because of their good deeds.

Let's just say this right now: We know Jesus is never put off by our messes. But he is put off by self-righteousness. He never rejects the one who is contrite and lowly of heart, the one who is poor in spirit and in spiritual need. He will, however, rebuke the person who sees herself as spiritually superior to others and lives with a judgmental attitude.

In **verse 7** we find one of the most profound sentences Jesus ever spoke. In verse 8, we read another fantastic move of his hand.

SHAME VERSUS BLAME

The power of shame can be devastating. Are you like the woman caught in sin? Are you caught in a cycle of shame, pointing a hopeless finger at your face in the mirror? The Webster's definition of shame is "a painful emotion caused by consciousness of guilt.... a condition of humiliating disgrace." Shame stifles confession. It stops repentance and healing forgiveness. It paralyzes the emotions and traps the soul in a spiritual deep-freeze. Shame convinces us that God cannot stand the sight of us or the sound our voice. The power of shame will turn us away from God when we are most in need of his intimacy.

Maybe you don't identify with the woman caught in adultery. Maybe you identify more with the Pharisees who brought her to Jesus. We need to ask ourselves if we lean toward the finger pointers, reaching to pick up stones when we see someone in sin. Pointing our fingers at the sins of another takes the focus off our own. The stones we keep ready to throw whenever we feel threatened need to be laid down. It's time. If Jesus doesn't throw them, then neither should we. If we point in any direction it should to the one who took our blame and shame onto himself.

What did the accusers do?

_____

_____

They couldn't leave it alone. They pointed at the woman and demanded a death sentence. They badgered Jesus for an answer as she trembled before the dumbfounded group in the temple court.

Before Jesus spoke what did he do?

_____

_____

Jesus stood up. He faced the "righteous" men and made a brilliant, perfect suggestion. His reply was totally unexpected. Their lives were devoted to being first in line and first in power, position, and authority. Now Jesus gives them another opportunity to grab the blue ribbon for first place.

What gauntlet did he throw down?

_____

_____

"Let him who is without sin among you be the first to throw a stone at her" (John 8:7 Amplified Bible).

Turn to Matthew 5:27-28. According to this definition of adultery, who is guilty?

_____

_____

These famous words from the Sermon on the Mount teach all of us to keep our eyes off the spiritual condition of our neighbor. We would do well to take inventory of the condition of our own hearts.

The self-appointed judges who brought the adulteress to Jesus ended up being the ones found guilty that day.

What did Jesus do in **John 8:8**?

_____

_____

Back down he went to continue writing with his finger in the dirt. Without looking to find out their reactions, continuing to hold the focus of the crowd on him and away from the adulteress, Christ was in complete control.

Read Jeremiah 17:13. Here we find something else written on the ground. Whose names are found in the dust?

_____

Now read Revelation 3:5. Where are our names written?

_____

What a comfort to know our names are written in heaven in the Lamb's Book of Life—in permanent ink! Was Jesus making a point to the Pharisees that day as his fingers wrote in the dirt? Was He giving a subtle warning? Reject me and end up with your name written in the dust. Selah. (Pause and calmly think on this.)

Finish reading verses John 8:9-11.

Who dropped their stones first?

_____

The men are trapped by the very law they had manipulated. Their education and understanding of the law and of their own hearts leaves them unable to hurl a stone at the adulteress. They believe in capital punishment but are unable to carry it out themselves.

It's interesting that none of them continued to argue with Jesus. They could have made a few final protests. "Well, you're right. Technically, we're all sinners, but Moses specifically gave a law about this particular sin. Adultery is a really big one. Don't you think she deserves punishment? Are you soft on sin? What message does this send to our children?" And on and on. They may have been thinking it, but none said a word.

After a few awkward moments, the rocks begin to fall from their hands. The oldest men in the crowd drop their rocks first. They've lived longer than the others. They have had more years of going to bed at night, aware of the dark places in their own hearts. Life teaches us one thing: We need help. We need grace. We need God. The more life that's lived, the more clear the need becomes.

Who was left standing alone before Jesus?

It would have been understandable for her to have exited the scene as quickly as possible. After all, she had been publicly humiliated. Who wants to hang around for more of that? Everyone else left: the Pharisees, the scribes, the crowd that had been listening to Jesus teach.

Some left because they had been humiliated. Some may have left so that this fallen woman could have a moment alone with this man who had kept her from being stoned.

So she stayed. She wanted to be alone with Jesus. This man Jesus was different. Her private encounter with him is heartbreaking in its beauty. What will he say to her? What pain does she bring to the table of this conversation?

What do you think went through this woman's mind as she heard the rocks fall, one by one, and the sound of footsteps leaving?

We don't know why she was having an affair. Most likely it was an ongoing relationship that many others were aware of. No one had done anything about it until this morning.

She could have been reprimanded or counseled to cut off the affair and refused to listen. Psychologists report that the majority of affairs stem from a place of anger. One or both parties feel vindicated to cheat on their spouses because they are angry. The sneaking around, meeting in hidden places becomes exciting and intoxicating. It's a secret passive-aggressive way to get back at one's spouse without them knowing. And it's a lie that hurts everyone involved: the spouses, the ones cheated on and with, any children of either family, and the friends and families of those involved. Most affairs only thrive in the dark. When they are brought into the light, it's not such a thrill. In the light, the pain and heartache come into full view.

REAL GIRL TIME-OUT

Maybe we should stop for a moment and be honest with each other. How do adulterous affairs begin? You don't just wake up one day and find yourself by accident in bed with someone. These things start slowly and the traps our enemy can lay for us happen gradually until a situation one never thought possible has happened.

It often starts like this: A person with an unmet need meets another person with an unmet need and each thinks the other is the answer to everything they've ever wanted. Let's be honest, girls. Temptation is everywhere and we all have unmet needs.

Let's list a few:
The need to be loved
The need to be cherished for who we are
The need to be the apple of someone's eye
The need to be adored by one man
The need to be appreciated
The need to be viewed as desirable
The need to feel safe and protected

What would you add to the list?

The lie of adultery is that unmet needs can be filled by a different set of arms. No one but God will ever "get" you or me. God gets you. He sees you. He knows you. He thinks you rock. You are his dream girl. God is the only one who will ever fully and completely understand us. If we are awake to this reality we can guard our hearts from falling prey to the illusion that someone will be the romantic Tom Cruise character from the movie *Jerry McGuire*. At the end of the film, he stands in a living room full of disgruntled women, stares into the eyes of Renee Zellweger and declares, "You complete me." What a perfectly insane line that hits like an arrow into the heart of every woman. (Thanks a lot, Hollywood.)

How does the enemy use cultural influences to make women believe that a man will fill in the missing gaps in their soul?

___

___

God gives us spouses and relationships of friendship and family, with our children and those we adore. Yet no matter how solid a marriage, how precious a child, how wonderful a group of friends or family, we will at some point fail each other. When we are hurt, or angry with our spouse, it's vitally important to remember we are married to another human being with flaws and insecurities. They will never fully complete us just as we will never fully complete them.

Do you see how unmet needs can build from frustration to anger, then from temptation to a full-blown affair?

___

___

There are situations in which a person suffers with sexual addiction, acting out by having numerous affairs with anonymous partners. Most affairs don't fall into this category. Most affairs start in subtle ways.

FOR INSTANCE:

He's the co-worker or the guy at church who seems to notice and appreciate you, who always laughs at your jokes and tells you how attractive you are. He looks in your eyes when you talk and makes you feel validated, needed, beautiful. It can start with a hug that lasts a little too long. You begin to calculate where he'll be at certain times and make sure you just happen to be there too. Each begins to sense how the other is feeling. Then come conversations about how things are going at home.

MAJOR GIRLFRIEND RULE: If a man starts down the road of asking inappropriate questions about your marriage, put on the brakes and immediately drive in the opposite direction. You can talk to your girlfriends about your man. (Be sure it is kept in confidence and is respectful.) **Never** talk negatively about your man to another man.

As one little inappropriate moment builds on another, the Enemy moves in to whisper, "Everyone deserves to be happy." You go home, where you already feel a bit unappreciated and unattractive. You look at your spouse and begin to feel angry. You think, "Why don't you listen to me like the other man does? You never compliment me. You take me for granted."

These feelings feed off each other like a cancer. It isn't long before you feel you deserve more than you have at home, so why not have it? If your husband really loved you, this wouldn't be happening. It's his fault. It's not wrong for you to have needs. You can only take so much. And so it goes until one finds themselves "caught" in an affair.

The adulteress in John's gospel had been caught up in the lies and darkness of an affair. She was caught in another man's bed, caught by the men of the law.

But now she stood alone before Jesus, caught in the presence of God's Son.

What did Jesus do when everyone left?

_____

_____

He didn't stand up until everyone had left.

Then he stood. She stood. Face to face. Did she dare meet his eyes? Did he cover her torn clothes or nakedness?

This poignant moment is closely reminiscent of God with Eve in the garden. God loves his girls. He wants us to hear him. He wants us to be unashamed and honest before him. He wants to show mercy.

What did Jesus say to her?

_____

_____

Jesus asked her about herself. As with the Samaritan woman, he did not condone or condemn. He wanted to know how she felt, and wanted her to know that he was extremely interested in her heart and life. As women, we deeply desire to be heard. We want to discuss our dreams, our longings and fears. We crave relationship. We were created to nurture and to love. Over and over again it's striking to note that Jesus listened and talked with the women around him.

In this ancient culture, women were treated as second-class citizens. They were not allowed to sit with the men in the synagogue. They weren't allowed to study the Torah. They could be divorced for burning a bagel, while men were allowed tremendous latitude. Yet Jesus made it a point to treat women and men with equal care.

What might Jesus easily have said to her?

_____

_____

He could have said, "I know you've been in an affair with so-and-so's husband and sneaking around to meet him. You know this could mean a death sentence for both of you. What were you thinking?" Yet Christ asked her a question.

"Where are your accusers? Has no man condemned you?"

Jesus asks this as if he's surprised they're alone. These two sentences are packed with concern for her. In essence, Jesus asks her many things.

Where are the ones who want to hurt you?
Where are the ones who know what you've been doing?
Where are the ones who are quick to judge and condemn?
Have you felt under condemnation from men for a long while now?
How do you feel about the fact that they are gone?
Were you shocked to hear the rocks dropping and footsteps leaving?
Are you wondering now what I will do?

What does she say to Jesus?

_____

_____

Three words. Her answer is packed with new hope and faith in him.

"No one, Lord!"

No one has condemned me today.
No one had the courage to say anything after what you said.
None of us have any reason to condemn each other.
You hear me.
You see me.
You are Lord!

What does Jesus say to her as she leaves?

_____

_____

"I do not condemn you either. Go on your way and from now on sin no more" (John 8:11 Amplified Bible).

Jesus is making two points here. He knows that none of the people could condemn her because none of them was sinless. Then he amazes her by saying he doesn't condemn her either. Of all the people present that day, he was the only one who could have condemned her. After all, he is the perfect God/man, the Messiah. He alone is without sin. But he doesn't condemn her, and he doesn't condemn us either.

The words of Jesus apply as directly to you and me as to the adulteress set free that morning on the temple steps. He did not come to the world to condemn, but to save. In just a few days, he would take this woman's brokenness and sin onto his broken body. He would die for her as he died for you and me. Jesus knows where we go, what we do and why. The Father knows all too well that left to ourselves, we would be utterly, hopelessly lost. God knew that the law would only show man his need for grace.

Read Ephesians 2:4-5.

What motivates the Lord?

_____

_____

Who does he love?

___

___

What did he do to satisfy his love?

___

___

What was our condition?

___

___

What did he give?

___

___

What is our condition in Christ?

___

___

He took all our sins to the cross and onto himself. From lying, to dishonoring others, from gossip and slander to murder and adultery, it's a level playing field. None of us has a stone to throw in any direction. We have only knees to bow and grateful hearts to offer to Jesus for his great condescension. As Anne Lamott wrote so beautifully:

"I do not understand the mystery of grace, only that it meets us where we are but never leaves us where it found us." [36]

Jesus lifted the adulterous woman to her feet and sent her on her way forgiven. He told her to choose a different life than the one she'd been living. Was he setting her up for failure? We don't think so. After we encounter the living God, nothing stays the same. If you have looked fully into his face and seen the love he has for you, you are forever changed. When you experience the overflowing cup of grace and feel it pour over you, making all things new, then you are enabled to go and "sin no more."

This does not mean you never sin again. It simply means that you are no longer content or satisfied with a sinful lifestyle that excludes him. You are sorry for your sins and are quicker than ever to repent.

Perfection? Never on this side of heaven. Daily hunger for intimacy with Jesus? Always. That's the difference. And what's so totally amazing is that when our Father looks at us, he sees us as sinless because he never looks at us apart from Christ Jesus!

So where do we go from here? Where do we go to fill the empty places? What does this precious woman have to say to us today? She might start by saying, "Girlfriend, no matter what it takes, get off the merry-go-round of playing with sin. It's not worth it. Stop spinning the sin cycle and begin your life over with the one who changed everything for me! Dare to believe he can do the same for you!"

Have you ever been caught in a cycle of behavior you couldn't stop?

It would be safe to say that for the adulterous woman, being "caught" was the best thing that ever happened to her. It was terribly humiliating at the time, but it ended up bringing her to the feet of Jesus, to forgiveness and a brand new start at life. When her sin was no longer hidden and was brought into the full view of the Good Shepherd, her soul was restored and she was made new.

Staying in full view of our Good Shepherd is the healthiest and safest way to walk with him. When a flock of sheep is close to the shepherd they are safe from predators. It's the sheep who wander off and go it alone that are in danger. Predators hide in the rocks and wait for a lamb to become separated from the shepherd. Without him the lamb is vulnerable and unable to defend itself.

Take a moment and ask the Lord to show you anything in your life he might want you to bring under his loving gaze. He will never shame you. He only wants to heal you. What do you feel you can bring out of the dark and into his light?

By bringing him everything in our lives for his loving gaze and healing touch, our failures, our fears, our hopes and dreams and unmet needs, we are assured of victorious living.

The adulterous woman had all her failures exposed before Jesus. And she walked away healed. She thought only shame awaited her. She must have been so surprised when Jesus turned his loving eyes on her instead of scorn. He gave her hope for her life and healing for her heart.

What do you think her life was like after this dramatic rescue by Jesus?

The adulteress had to return home and make amends. She had to break off the affair, and work to build trust again among friends and family. She had apologies to make to her spouse and any of the offended parties hurt by her actions. She had many daunting challenges to face: how to hold up her head and attend public functions, how to sit with local women in the synagogue and let gossip fly as it might, without offering further defense.

Did she leave Jesus' presence that day thinking she had been given a license to return to her life of adultery? Read Warren Wiersbe's commentary of this New Testament passage.

"We must not misinterpret this event to mean that Jesus was 'easy on sin' or that he contradicted the law. For Jesus to forgive this woman meant that he had to one day die for her sins. Forgiveness is free but it is not cheap. Furthermore, Jesus perfectly fulfilled the law so that no one could justly accuse him of opposing its teachings or weakening its power.

The law was given to reveal sin (Romans 3:20), and we must be condemned by the law before we can be cleansed by God's grace. Law and grace do not compete with each other; they complement each other. Nobody was ever saved by keeping the law, but nobody was ever saved by grace who was not first indicted by the law. There must be conviction before there can be conversion."[37]

As a forgiven woman leaving the temple that day, one has to imagine she walked slowly behind the crowd that began to gather again around Christ. Once again he began speaking. Her life before meeting him had been spent in the pit of lies and sin, low self-worth, and degradation. His words, "Go and sin no more," had fallen deep into the emptiness of her soul. Seeds of grace now had a chance to take root. A short time earlier, traces of dark had framed the day with condemnation and danger. After he bid her entry into a new life, the sun was high in the morning sky. She would hear Christ teaching on into the day, his voice ringing out with promise for all.

"I am the light of the world. He who follows me will not be walking in the dark, but will have the light which is life" (John 8:12 Amplified Bible).

TODAY'S DATE: _____

YOUR HEADLINE:

_____

_____

"At the foot of a soaring mountain
You're still the biggest thing in that picture
Are you really worth counting?
You're still the biggest thing in that picture
Insignificant don't buy it
You're still the biggest thing in that picture
Aim your sling shot at Goliath
You're still the biggest thing in that picture
Don't you feel so small
Don't you feel so small
God doesn't see you that way at all"

Gordon Kennedy and Mark Gersmehl, Ascap

SIDEBAR: Was Jesus A Law-Breaker or Tradition Buster?

"Over the years, the Jewish leaders had amassed thousands of rules and regulations concerning the Sabbath. By Jesus' day, they had thirty-nine different classifications of work. One of these categories of work consisted of carrying a burden, including carrying a needle in one's robe.

They argued over whether a person could wear artificial teeth or a wooden leg. Jesus did not break the law; he violated the traditions of the Pharisees which had grown up around the law." [38]

In one of my travels to Israel (Bonnie) I heard stories from the Jewish people about how present day religious leaders continue to update traditions of the Law. Once a year, new laws are printed in the local newspaper. One of the most recent mandates for the Sabbath was a warning not to pick one's nose. It was determined that a piece of flesh might be accidentally torn in the process.

Obviously this is laughable. Yet it's important to note that for a devout follower of the Law, Jesus came across as snubbing His nose at centuries of tradition. TRADITION is the key word to remember. Jesus violated tradition by fulfilling prophecy. He was the Law, the living Word, walking among His people in the flesh.

Jesus came to prove that Love outweighs Law. He came to fulfil the Law and give freedom to those who choose faith in Him. He came to do far more than keep the Sabbath. He came to redeem the Sabbath and clear the path for all men and women to live freely in His grace.

He grew up as a Law-respecting Jewish man. Jesus knew the Torah and the promises of God. There are so many obvious analogies we can draw from how He put the Law into perspective. Any time we feel that the traditions of our faith are more important than the cross of Jesus and His blood, we get into trouble. As with the leaders of Jesus day, our leaders can take peripheral traditions and make them Law. Jesus abolished the Law because it leads to death. He was a tradition buster and a life giver. Stand guard over this in your own heart. Never let anything rob you of the joy He died to give.

WEEK FIVE
BREAKING NEWS

What's **HOT** & What's **NOT**

MULTITASKING MIRACLE MAN TALK OF THE TOWN
Security Heightened; Record Crowds Expected

Jesus the Galilean is coming our way, bringing with him a firestorm of controversy and growing excitement. You would have to be living under a rock if you haven't heard about Jesus, but then he would be the first to say even the rocks will cry out to tell of his fame and power. Everybody wants face-time with the young, radical teacher. His arrival is expected to draw capacity crowds.

Everywhere he goes, masses of people from all over gather to see and hear what will happen. He's unpredictable and untamed. Jesus comes from Nazareth, a place where nothing noteworthy has ever happened. His family is a lower-middle-class carpenter's clan, somewhat divided about their elder brother's popularity.

He preaches and recruits many to leave everything behind and to follow him. He performs miracles as he travels the countryside. It has been reported that he turned water into wine at a wedding in Cana. He raised a dead man to life in the small town of Nain. Controversy surrounding Jesus has all of Judea talking. Jesus has the Pharisees and scribes wringing their hands and the religious right foaming at the mouth. Lepers have been healed, blind men see, demons cast out, and the hearts of many wonder if he could be the Messiah. This carpenter from Nazareth is quite literally the talk of the town.

Jesus is a man of wildly opposing claims. He calls himself both the Son of Man and the Son of God. He speaks openly about the kingdom of God but lives homeless in the hills. He offers the message of mercy, love, and forgiveness, which makes him a magnet for the needy and poor. At the same time he makes no bones about his disgust for religious leaders who go public with their prayers and records of good deeds.

Already people are lining the streets of our city, prepared to be the first to see Jesus and his followers as they pass through. Please bring extra food with you if you arrive early. Watch to keep your children close by, and beware of scam artists following close on his heels selling their snake oil and miracle drugs.

The ICIDC, Israel's Center for Infectious Disease Control, issued the following notice:

"Due to the claims of miraculous healing, many highly diseased people will descend on the city hoping Jesus will touch them. To the elderly, young children, and anyone with a compromised immune system, we recommend the use of facial masks and that you keep a safe distance from this teacher."

TODAY'S HEROINE:
A woman with the issue of blood

You're blessed when you're at the end of your rope. With less of you there is more of God and his rule (Matt. 5:3 The Message).

"We've all heard the saying that when God closes a door, he opens a window," noted a close friend who lost his wife to heaven after a brave battle against cancer. He paused for a moment before he quietly added, "But it can be hell in the hallway."

The gospel accounts of Matthew, Mark, and Luke contain the story of a woman who lived through twelve years of hell in the hallway. Matthew's account is very limited. Yet both Mark and Luke give us details about this story that we don't want to miss.

We don't know her name. We know she was at the end of herself. We know she lived with great suffering. She was at the end of her rope. Jesus was her last hope. Little did she know there could be no better place.

Before we walk through the hallway with our heroine, let's take a brief refresher course on the culture of Jesus' day. As authors, we have been absolutely thrilled while studying about the women in this collection. We cannot tell you how many times we've screamed with sheer astonishment and delight when our research revealed new insight. God's Word is just rich, rich, rich!

Ready for a little enrichment today, girlfriend?

Turn and read Luke 7:36-50.

Where is Jesus dining?

EDITORIAL: Jesus loved to eat! Everywhere he went he was inviting himself to dinner, or sitting down to dine at the table of anyone willing to break bread. His first miracle was held at a wedding feast. His last meal: the Passover dinner. His first question to the stunned apostles after his resurrection was "What do you have to eat?" Soon after, he was seen cooking up breakfast on the beach. He was passionately human while infinitely divine.

In this Luke passage, Jesus has accepted an invitation to eat with one of the religious leaders named Simon. In the ancient world this would have been arranged so that Jesus sat at the "main table" and the other guests would have been along the outside wall, within earshot of his conversation.

Who came in and what did she do?

_____

_____

Per verse 38, where was she standing?

_____

Per verse 39, how did the host respond?

_____

_____

What does this tell you about how women were viewed in her culture?

_____

_____

Jesus made religious leaders crazy because he continued to speak with women—especially nasty, messed up, loser women. He didn't spend a lot of time with the good little synagogue-attending ladies. (His deep friendship with the family of Lazarus, Martha and Mary, would be one notable exception.) Jesus insisted on interacting with prostitutes and Samaritan women, and now this "sinner" who wept at his feet, spilling perfume and carrying on.

What did Simon conclude about Jesus because he allowed this woman to touch his body? (See verse 39.)

_____

_____

Who overheard Simon's words?

_____

No one. Simon never verbalized his thoughts. Jesus knew exactly what was going through his mind. Simon was quick to dismiss Jesus as being a prophet because he allowed this social out-cast to touch his feet.

Religious leaders were restricted from even speaking to a woman.

"Extensive Jewish religious laws had developed in the first century to ensure moral purity. Many men suspected women of being sexually aggressive and eager to trap unsuspecting men. Teachers of the law in particular—such as Simon and Jesus—were to have as little to do with women as possible." [39]

In **verse 47,** what point does Jesus make?

_____

_____

Those who have nothing to lose have everything to gain. Women would have been especially eager to hear his teaching. For women who had fallen into lifestyles of sin and shame, his words of mercy and forgiveness offered fresh hope. Throughout centuries of Jewish history, women had never experienced such affirmation and attention from their teachers.

"When a daughter was born into a Hebrew family at that time, there was great lamenting. For a daughter would not likely fight for Israel, or win the favor of God. At the synagogue where her family worshiped, the rabbi taught that men were favored by God. Women were prohibited from reading the Torah. If a woman accidentally touched the Torah, it had to be burned because the Torah must be kept pure. The men daily recited the Talmudic prayer which said in part, 'Blessed art thou who did not make me a woman.'" [40]

Yet a "sinful" woman came from behind Jesus to anoint his feet. A woman in this culture would approach a teacher from behind, feeling she was not worthy for a direct encounter. With tears and what was most likely perfume saved for her wedding dowry, she thanked Christ with all she had. She entered the Pharisee home at great peril. We don't know how she managed this. Maybe she simply walked in and fell down behind Jesus. It took great courage for her to risk the scathing glances of Simon's dinner guests.

What does Jesus say to her in **verse 48**?

_____

_____

Here he goes again, forgiving sins! Only God can forgive sin!

To make matters worse, what does he say in **verse 50**?

_____

_____

Simon's mind is swirling. *This woman's faith has saved her? Go in peace? He honored this disgusting, groveling woman who dared touch his feet. What outrageous stunt will Jesus pull next?* Jesus loved all those who heard his voice and had hearts to receive him. The religious leaders were undone by his unconditional love. Jesus broke all manner of traditions. He even dared to heal on the Sabbath. He talked about mourning, meekness, and suffering, calling this a blessed condition. Was he blind to the world around him? Israel suffered her fair share of meekness and mourning under the tyranny of Rome. The firstborn sons of the Hebrew people had been slaughtered thirty years before. Did he have no fear of the clear and present danger around them? Instead of standing with the Pharisees to keep the peace, Jesus lifted up the insignificant people in society, and lashed out at the leaders of the Law. One of the most annoying aspects of Jesus' ministry was his compassionate heart for women.

Let's turn to Mark 5:25-34 and Luke 8:40-56.

It was a glorious time in Jesus' earthly ministry. His popularity was at an all-time high. Everywhere he went, Jesus was the talk of the town. Images of God's Son as a weak, thin, milky-skinned man don't line up with eyewitness descriptions of him in the Word. Mark and Luke describe a strong, passionate, verbal, engaging Savior whose heart was on fire with a mission. Jesus boldly strides through towns and villages, performing miracles and speaking new life to crowds on all sides. His ministry is on the move, full steam ahead and Holy Spirit-led.

Jesus is traveling from one city and village to another with the twelve apostles, teaching them deeper truths about his purposes. He is allowing women into his inner circle: Mary Magdalene, Susanna, Joanna, and others who were financially supporting his needs as he traveled. Crowds gather around him, eager to hear his parables. His apostles have seen him command the Sea of Galilee to "Hush!" during a raging storm. Many have seen him cause a paralytic to stand up and walk. As living water, Jesus pours himself into the people. He redefines who he calls family and travels to a city plagued with demon possession.

What has Jesus been doing before his encounter with our heroine?

He's been busy in Gennesaret, a city on the opposite side of the Sea of Galilee. With great power, Christ cast out a legion of demons from a tormented man. He sent them off a cliff, screaming for mercy.

In **Luke 8:35 and 37**, how do the people of Gennesaret respond to Jesus?

_____

_____

Their reaction to this great act of deliverance leaves us speechless. Go figure. It brings new meaning to his caution about casting pearls before swine. Sometimes, even marvelous miracles cannot move a hard heart.

In **Luke 8:40**, where does Jesus go and how is he received?

_____

_____

As Jesus approaches Galilee this day, he is welcomed with open arms. He is a rock star. The paparazzi are out in full force. People are pressing in on every side to see this amazing teacher. They want a piece of him. They want to see more miracles and healing. He is teaching in parables and revealing the mysteries of the kingdom to those with eyes to see.

We need to have a clear appreciation of what it was like for Jesus as he ministered to those he referred to as "downcast" and "sheep without a shepherd." The Amplified Bible translates **Mark 5:24** this way:

"…and a great crowd kept following him and pressed him from all sides—so as almost to suffocate him."

Mark 3:9-11 describes in vivid detail the way the crowds pressed in on Jesus. It must have been exhausting. Again, let's read the Amplified translation:

"And he told his disciples to have a little boat in constant readiness for him because of the crowd, lest they press hard upon him and crush him; for he had healed so many that all who had distressing bodily diseases kept falling upon him and pressing upon him in order that they might touch him. And the spirits, the unclean ones, as often as they might see him, fell down before him and kept screaming out, 'You are the Son of God!'"

No wonder our Lord had to take time to get away and rest in the lonely places and hills at night. With people falling on him and demons screaming at the top of their lungs, the situation must have been chaotic.

We've all seen celebrities in our culture when they exit a limo to walk the red carpet. A sea of people gathers to touch them or get a photo, shoving microphones in their faces, adoring and shouting. Modern-day celebrities have bodyguards for protection.

On this day, Jesus had no one but his group, a ragtag group of fishermen. Yet in this massive mob of groping people, one woman would not be stopped. No amount of pushing and shoving would keep her from making her way to the feet of Jesus. No one wanted to see him more than one anonymous, brave-hearted woman.

Some things never change: The V.I.P.s are first in line.

Read Mark 5:22-23.

Who gets an audience with Jesus right off the bat?

_____

_____

Why is he special?

_____

_____

What is his posture?

_____

_____

What is his request of Jesus?

_____

_____

Jairus was the main elder of the local synagogue. He would have been the man who conducted the services and kept order. The fact that he was allowed immediate access to Jesus indicates a great respect from those who knew him. Jairus moves first through the crowd to tell the teacher that his daughter is gravely ill. He asks Jesus to come and lay his hand on her and heal her.

HOW LOW CAN YOU GO?

Notice the pattern of people who fell at the feet of Jesus. The woman at Simon's house anointed his feet with gratitude. (The man healed from demon possession in **Luke 8** sits at his feet in his right mind!) Jairus fell at his feet begging for a house call.

Jesus immediately stops teaching, gets up, and begins to follow Jairus home. No sooner had Jairus hit the dirt to plead with Jesus than the people began pressing in and something amazing happens on the way.

Push the hold button on the scene with Jairus. Push hold on the faces in the sea of humanity before him. Zero in on one face. It's the face of an exhausted woman whose faith endured twelve years of hell in the hallway.

END OF HER ROPE MEETS THE END OF HIS ROBE

Read Luke 8:43-48. What was her physical condition?

For twelve years she had suffered from a hemorrhaging flow of blood. We don't know why this woman was bleeding. Maybe she had a miscarriage and never recovered. It could have been a hemorrhage of the womb or bowels. Maybe she had a tumor or cancer. Maybe she had made poor sexual choices earlier in her life that had damaged her uterus. Maybe she went into early menopause and something went terribly wrong. Whatever the cause, she suffered horribly because of her bleeding.

SIDEBAR: As a woman, how do you feel about your monthly cycle?

We would love to hear the various opinions you might have. There are tons of jokes about PMS, but for many women, menstruation can be a dreaded week of pain and inconvenience. The phrase "on the rag" comes to mind, hearkening back to women's lives at the turn of the nineteenth century. All jokes aside, a woman's uncomfortable, bleeding cycle brings with it the ability to bear life. It's a "catch-22." The burden of a monthly cycle allows the opportunity to give birth. But a diseased womb can be debilitating and deadly. We have no way of fully comprehending the agony endured by the Jewish woman we meet in Mark 5 and Luke 8.

Turn to Leviticus 15:19-28 for more information.

At first reading, one might wonder why God would put such harsh restrictions in place for a woman. Is he not the one who created man and woman in his own image? Did he not put a woman together to bleed and bear children? The rules and cleansing rituals seem cruel and shaming. **Nothing could have been further from God's original plan.**

Read Genesis 3:16. What did God say to Eve about childbirth?

God's Plan A provided a perfect bill of health for the human body. We were made to walk in a glorious garden with God, free from any suffering. When both man and woman chose to disobey his commands, they changed the rules. But God's great love provided a way back to him through his Son. Only the perfect blood of Jesus could promise a new garden and redemption from sin.

The Levitical laws were written after the Israelites had been delivered from the pagan surroundings of Egypt. They were preparing to face battle with another pagan culture in Canaan. God's laws for Israel were put in place to set them apart, to protect them and keep them healthy. The temples of the ancient world involved sexual practices and human sacrifice. The laws of Leviticus taught the people of God to keep his temple holy and undefiled. These laws were not intended to shame a woman. They were to give her body strength and protection.

FASCINATING NOTE: Because of their attention to good hygiene, the Jewish nation grew to be extremely resilient and resistant to disease. Even when plagues swept across Europe in the thirteenth and fourteenth centuries, the Jews remained mysteriously healthy!

According to the laws in Leviticus, how long would a woman be secluded after her monthly cycle?

_____

_____

Women in ancient times viewed this seclusion as a chance to rest and be refreshed. They were not required to cook or clean, or tend to daily responsibilities. It was a chance to be still and regain their strength. However, by the time Jesus walked the earth, this Levitical passage had been twisted and turned into something God never intended.

"When a young Hebrew girl began menstruation, it was considered to be the bloody, unclean, sinful curse destined by her foremother Eve. In Hebrew the word 'niddah' was used, which meant height of defilement—a woman's monthly exile from the human race. Therefore, the woman in our text has been niddah, bleeding for twelve years. She was an exile from her family, her society, her religious community." [41]

According to Levitical Law:

What was a woman called when she had a discharge of blood?

_____

What happened to the objects or people she touched?

_____

Leviticus 15:25-28 provides a resume for the woman in **Luke 8**.

What happened to a woman who continued to bleed?

_____

_____

Since her flow never stopped, then she could never go through the steps to purification each month. To be considered unclean meant living a life of isolation from everything and everyone she loved. For twelve lonely years she had lived the life of an outcast.

Let's think this through. Using this backdrop from Hebrew law, imagine what life would have been like for this woman.

If married:

_____

_____

109

If she had children:

_____

_____

Social circles:

_____

_____

Spiritual implications:

_____

_____

If married, her husband would never have been able to share intimacy with her. How long did he stay before that was too difficult? If she had children, she couldn't touch them. She was isolated and unable to participate in a normal family life. She could not mingle with friends and family, for fear of touching someone she loved. She was barred from the temple and was forbidden even to sit on a bench in the synagogue. (No one could even sit on a chair she had been on.) She was like a person with leprosy. She could not touch or be touched.

It would have been particularly interesting to Luke the physician that this woman had gone to every doctor and had tried every cure. In the Talmud, there are at least eleven remedies for chronic bleeding. We can assume she had tried them all. Nothing had worked. She was financially broke from spending her money on "cures." These cures were primitive and superstitious in nature.

"Medicine was not a reliable science in that day. Diseases were not cured by medicines but were exorcised by charms. The physician of Galilee in that age did not differ widely from the medicine man of the North American Indian." [42]

OK. Let's picture this situation accurately. Our heroine is lonely, guilt-ridden, exhausted, and anemic. So she turns to doctors for help. Let's see what the Talmud can tell us about the ancient cures prescribed for an issue of blood.

You aren't going to believe this!

Talmud Cure Number One:
Go to Alexandria, Egypt, and buy gum the weight of a silver coin. Mix it with crocus and alum of the same weight and crush them together. Mix with wine and drink it. If this doesn't work, try...

Cure Number Two:
Boil three pints of Persian onions in wine and drink it while someone behind you says, "Arise from thy flux!" If that doesn't work, try...

Cure Number Three:
Stand in the intersection of two roads with a cup of wine in your hand while somebody sneaks up behind you and scares you and says, "Arise from thy flux!" If that doesn't work, try...

Cure Number Four:
Take a handful if cumin, crocus, and fenugreek and boil them in wine. Drink it while someone says to you, "Arise from thy flux!" If this doesn't work, try...

Cure Number Five:
Take your clothing, tie it to a tree outside your house and when the wind blows, the disease will go into the tree and the health of the tree will leave the tree and go into you. If that doesn't work, try...

Cure Number Six:
Dig seven ditches and burn some cuttings of vines under four years old. Sit over the ditch with a cup of wine. Remove yourself from that ditch and sit over another. As you go from ditch to ditch, have someone say over you, (you guessed it) "Arise from thy flux!" [43]

By this time you should be drunk, penniless, nauseous, feel really stupid, and have said goodbye to your last friend who grew tired of yelling at your "flux." You probably need to attend AA meetings from the consumption of wine. You've shelled out a fortune for travel and spice expenses. "My life is in the ditch," has taken on a whole new meaning. You also might be short on clothes and have become a chronic tree-hugger, especially when the wind kicks up.

Twelve years of this! After trying every possible cure, now our unnamed lady is even more exhausted, financially ruined, and possibly drunk! She tried everything. Then her money ran out.

Let's pause for a moment and think about the empty places we go to find help that end up offering no cure.

What are our diversions?

_____

_____

First try entertainment. If that doesn't work, immerse yourself in work. If that doesn't help, make as much money as possible. If that doesn't provide relief, have an affair or check out some porn sites online. If that doesn't numb the pain, dive into drugs or alcohol, shopping, excessive church activities, gossip. The list of counterfeit cures is endless. These diversions must ultimately drive us to Jesus. He is the only remedy for our brokenness.

Speaking of gossip, let's complete the picture for our precious heroine. To her physical pain, add the scenario of waging tongues. It's important to note how a chronic flow of blood was viewed by the Jewish religious leaders. The Pharisees claimed that any woman who suffered from this malady was being punished by God for immoral sexual behavior. They believed God was angry at her. The literal meaning of the word "plague" is a "scourge or whip in the hand of God to drive you away."

Questions about the woman's "condition" could have turned from sympathetic to downright ugly. Conversation around the well (water cooler) might have sounded like this: "Why is she bleeding? Has she not repented and fasted before God? Has she not seen every medical specialist in Judea? Has she sinned greatly and is being punished by God? Has she had secret affairs? Does she have an STD?"

At the time of this writing, one of our dearest friends in the world is fighting stage four breast cancer for the second time in her young life. For years a prayer posse has lifted her up, fasted for her, and stood by her side. Her husband is a powerful teacher of the Word. They have tried every new form of chemotherapy, radiation, and drug therapy available. They have been in a constant state of believing God for healing. Still her condition deteriorates. At one point, she wept over the phone with words impossible to forget. "I just feel like I'm letting everybody down because the 'wonkies' (cancer) are still here. I'm letting down everyone.... my husband, friends, even God."

Do you know someone with a similar response? Do you have a feeling of hopelessness about any type of ongoing issue in your life? Do you feel you are letting God down because you struggle?

_____

_____

Then the story of this woman is more relevant than you know. He came to give his life to resolve any question about his love for you and for all who call on his name.

At the burial of a thirty-eight-year-old father of three, beloved songwriter and visionary man after God's heart, a pastor spoke quietly into my ear as I wept. "Sometimes life stinks. It just does." He actually used another highly descriptive word, but I think you get the picture. You and I live in a fallen world that many times leaves us overwhelmed by our need for God. There will be unanswered questions about suffering this side of heaven. For now, when God says no, there is only one answer.

Turn for a moment to read 2 Corinthians 1:19-20.

"For the Son of God, Christ Jesus...was not yes and no; but in him it is always the divine yes"(Amplified Bible).

He became sin and disease and humiliation and shame for us. In every situation that presents a "No," Jesus came to be the answer and our "Yes." We cannot understand why some prayers are answered differently than others, but we can stand on the "Yes" of Jesus. He said there would be trouble in this world, but not to fear: He has overcome the world.

For our heroine today, she reached out beyond the opinions of others and the condition of her own body to grasp the "Yes" of Christ Jesus. She was low on money, but full of hope.

Jesus was coming to town.

This broken woman had heard about him. What did she know of him that gave her hope? We wonder who she heard it from. Certainly not the religious leaders. They wouldn't go near her. Who was willing to talk with her? We're guessing it was the other outcasts who told her about Jesus. She learned of him from lepers and harlots and blind beggars and poor people and everyone else on the fringes of society who had been welcomed into his presence and accepted as they were healed and forgiven. In the "Gospel According to Her Day," this woman was as good as dead. Thankfully she reached out to a Savior who was—and is—in the business of bringing dead people back to life.

Maybe this time, she'd find a cure. What she didn't know was that with Jesus she would not only find a cure for her chronic flow of blood, but also the cure for the chronic condition of her sinful nature. She would find salvation for her soul!

Describe her courage in detail after reading **Luke 8:44-47**.

What decision did she make that day?

___

Who else wanted to make the exact same move?

___

What would it take for her to reach Jesus?

___

How did she approach him?

___

What did she touch?

___

What immediately happened?

___

What did Jesus feel leaving his body?

___

How did his apostles explain?

___

How did Jesus explain?

___

She still had faith that God was alive and well and in the business of changing circumstances. Her twelve years of suffering in the hallway were not spent alone. She was still looking for Jehovah to move. After twelve years of no results, she still had hope. Many of us would give up, or become depressed. Depressed people do not easily venture out in public. She was a social outcast. Her body was depleted of iron and hurting. She probably had a smell about her from the constant flow of blood.

What choices did she make that day to brave the crowds and take a bold lunge toward the feet of Jesus? Circle the ones that seem most challenging.

Her decision to leave her house and find Jesus.
Choices of how to disguise herself if possible.
Her decision to face angry people who might recognize her.
Choices about the best approach to Jesus through the crowd.
Hearing screams about her uncleanness.
People pushing her away from Christ.
Mothers shielding their children from her.
Physical exhaustion as she elbowed and pushed inch-by-inch toward Jesus.
Mental taunts of the enemy about how it would make no difference to touch Jesus.
The risk of being trampled and killed in the process.

What are your thoughts about the actions of this courageous woman of faith?

_____

_____

She was barely alive, living on the edge of death. She was desperate for a touch from God.

Have you ever felt this way? Why?

_____

_____

This depleted woman makes a choice. Maybe this is her last chance. If she waits any longer, she might be unable to leave home at all. She had heard Jesus teach, heard about his miracles of healing. If she could only touch even the hem of his robe, she was convinced that would be all she needed. It was worth the risk of the crowd, the price of pushing ahead, the pain of whatever would be required to get to him. She might die in the process, but she would die reaching out for God's man.

Her hands must have been trembling with anticipation and fear as she felt the hem of his robe. Yet at this exact moment, a spiritual earthquake reverberated around her. Power left the body of Christ. Healing flowed into hers. He felt it. She felt it. The demons in the sky fell back and cowered at the victory. Heaven's angels sang with joy. There was something about her touch on the fringe of his garment that was different from all the others pressing in to Jesus that day. We can be certain that there were others touching him at this very moment. What made the brush of this woman's fingers on his prayer shawl cause power to flow from Jesus? When Jesus felt the power flow out of him, he stopped and turned around.

"Who touched me?" Jesus asked.

"Everyone is touching you," replied Peter and the apostles. It is easy to imagine the disciples thinking this was an odd question. "Are you kidding? There are hands and faces grabbing at us from all sides!"

There was so much humanity all around Jesus at the time, a more appropriate question would have been, "Who didn't touch me?"

Picture the people around him stepping back, confused by his question, wondering what he could possibly mean by it. Maybe several people raise their hands. "I touched you!" "I guess I did too, teacher…."

"Maybe it was me?" Jesus kept gazing at the crowd and waiting.

All the while Jairus waits and watches, wondering if Jesus has forgotten about his daughter.

"No, someone with faith touched me. I felt the healing power go forth from me," Jesus insists. He knew the difference between someone just brushing up against him and someone who had touched him in faith. He knew her, and he knew her heart.

Jesus easily could have gone on walking without making a point about the woman who lunged from behind to touch him. He knew exactly what had happened. He knew that she was a social outcast because of her condition. He knew that she had been physically restored but he wanted more for her than physical healing.

Read Luke 8:47 and answer the following questions:

Where was the woman?

_____

_____

What did she notice?

_____

_____

What happened to her body?

_____

_____

How quickly was she healed?

_____

_____

Why was she trembling?

_____

_____

What kind of courage did it take for her to tell the crowd that she had been bleeding for twelve years? The Amplified Bible tells us that she was "alarmed and frightened and trembling."

"In his social contacts, Jesus went out of his way to embrace the unloved and unworthy, the folks who matter little to the rest of society but matter infinitely to God. People with leprosy quarantined outside the city wall, Jesus touched, even as his disciples shrank back in disgust. A half-breed woman who had gone through five husbands already and was no doubt the center of the town's gossip industry, Jesus tapped as his first missionary. Another woman, too full of shame over her embarrassing condition to approach Jesus face to face, grabbed his robe, hoping he would not notice. He did notice. She learned, like so many other 'nobodies,' that you can't easily escape Jesus' gaze. We matter too much." [44]

The tenderness in his eyes must have made the woman feel safe and gave her courage. When no one else admits to touching him and feeling his healing power, she speaks up. Jesus knows what has happened, but he waits for her to declare herself. The unnamed lady knows she is busted and comes forward. For twelve years, people had been disgusted at her touch. Would he be as well?

Mark 5:33 says, "she told him the whole truth." Modern surveys reveal that the Number One fear people have is the fear of speaking in front of large groups of people. We can imagine with what difficulty it all came pouring out of her. Her fear was finally overcome by what he had done for her.

What did she tell Jesus and the people around her?

_____

_____

Here's our version:

"Please forgive me. I have been so sick for twelve years. The bleeding has gone on and on. I have no strength. I have been torn from my family. I've been so alone. My body has grown weaker day by day. I wanted to die. Then I heard about you! You don't turn anyone away. How your power is from God. And now I know it too."

Did she turn and look at the crowd as she spoke of the miracle? "The flow of blood has stopped. I am healed! My strength has returned." Then her eyes back to Jesus. "I'm sorry I touched you. Please don't be angry."

What might the others who came to Jesus for healing have felt upon hearing her confession?

_____

_____

The trembling woman's entire life changed at this very moment. She looked up into the eyes of Jesus and found courage and compassion. Her heart was flooded with hope. She was given a platform at his feet, a voice to tell the ones around her that she was not the same person. She would never be viewed as unclean again. She was a new woman, inside and out, because of the grace and power of Jesus. He allowed her to speak openly about this miracle. Jesus wanted complete healing for her, physically and socially.

Jesus would not let her remain anonymous. He wasn't trying to embarrass her. He wanted her story known and he wanted to acknowledge her great faith. By allowing her to speak openly it's as if he is saying to everyone in the crowd, "Don't think she was healed because my clothes hold magical power. It is my power as God that has healed her. And it is my pleasure to do so."

Every word Jesus spoke was intentional and replete with meaning. In **Mark 5:34**, what does Jesus call her?

"Daughter" was the first tender word out of his mouth. "Daughter, your faith (that is, your trust and confidence in me, springing from faith in God) has restored you to health. Go in peace, and be continually healed and free from your (distressing bodily) disease" (Amplified Bible).

In Israel, no higher word of endearment was used for a woman. The word "daughter" implied admiration, protection, respect, and love. It is the word Jairus had used just moments before about his own little girl. Now Jesus uses it for this woman. How it must have thrilled her. **This is the only time in the entire Bible where Jesus used the word "daughter" for a specific human being.** The unnamed woman is finally named! How long had it been since she had heard anyone call her "daughter?"

She had been known as:
Unclean
Uninvited
Undone
Unable
Unworthy
Untouchable
Unacceptable

Jesus makes it clear: She is now to be addressed as one of God's beloved daughters. No longer will she be merely "a certain woman." Instead of being angry for her "defiling touch," Jesus calls her "daughter" and she is instantly given new credentials. She has been changed from being an outcast on the fringe of society to a cherished daughter of the house of God.

What compliment did Jesus give her?

_____

_____

Her faith in him had healed her. Her confidence and trust in him gave her life. The *NIV Study Bible* tells us that the Greek word for "healed" actually means "saved." She was healed from her disease and told to enter into peace. Jesus took care of all her needs when the power flowed out from him that day. Jesus could have humiliated and accused her of making him ceremonially unclean. Instead, he proclaimed to everyone that she was clean physically and spiritually no longer an outcast. Surprised by mercy, another broken woman in his path stepped from despair into dignity.

Why did Jesus not let her remain anonymous? Warren Wiersbe, in his commentary on the New Testament, writes, "He did it for her sake. He wanted to be to her something more than a healer. He wanted to be her Savior and friend as well. He wanted her to look into his face, feel his tenderness, and hear his loving words of assurance."[45]

People once afraid to touch her now parted like the Red Sea as she stood face-to-face with Jesus. What a beautiful picture to imagine her weeping tears of gratitude and astonishment as she looked into the eyes of God. Standing straight and tall now, she was free to follow after Jesus with the others. She could sit at his feet now and hear his parables without fear of rebuke or shouts of "unclean!" She could watch with expectation about what he might do to heal another.

TWELVE YEARS OF HOLDING ON PLUS A TWELVE-YEAR-OLD TO SAVE

As all this happened in the crowd around Jesus, Jairus waited for an answer for his daughter. Both this young girl and older woman have one thing in common: twelve years. Twelve years of suffering and twelve years of life. Can Jesus handle all of this at the same moment? Can he hear the cries of young and old and everyone in between? He had been on his way to heal the dying daughter of a very important official of the synagogue when he stopped to heal an anonymous, unclean woman. There is no favoritism with our Lord! Everyone is equally important to him. The multitasking Savior we serve is more than capable of hearing your cries and mine. He is never overwhelmed by the needs of his people. And no doubt about it, we are a needy bunch.

What about Jairus? What do you think he was thinking as he watched the miraculous interruption unfold?

_____

_____

When he saw what Jesus did for this woman, was his faith strengthened? Did hope spring up in his heart as he heard the woman's testimony? Did his pulse race with expectation? As Jesus speaks life to the woman before him, a messenger from the synagogue brings news of death. Jairus need not bother Jesus further. His daughter has died.

How do you think Jairus felt about the woman upon hearing the news of his daughter's death?

_____

_____

Did she distract Jesus and steal his miracle? Why did Jesus not take care of his young child instead of listening to this worn-out woman? Or did he believe, even with the news of his daughter's death, that Jesus could bring her back to life?

Jesus knew the emotions running wild in the heart of Jairus.

Luke 8:50 reads as follows:

"Do not be seized with alarm or struck with fear; simply believe (in me as able to do this), and she shall be well" (Amplified Bible).

Believe. Simply believe.

Is this not what healed the woman who fell before him? Was this all that would be required to bring life from death?

Faith.

Let's finish the action-packed chapter of Luke 8. Where do the feet of Jesus travel?

Read Luke 8:51-56.

Who did Jesus allow to enter the house of Jairus?

_____

_____

What was the emotional climate in the house?

_____

_____

What diagnosis did Jesus give for the little girl?

_____

_____

How did the funeral party respond?

_____

_____

Reminds us of the response from Sarah in Genesis 18. God told her she would have a son when she was in her nineties. She laughed at his words. He said them again. She laughed some more. Then he said, "Is anything too hard or too wonderful for the Lord?" (Amplified Bible).

In **Luke 8:54-55**, what does Jesus do?

_____

_____

To prove that she was alive and well, what does Jesus tell the group to give her?

_____

_____

Give her food, let her eat. Normal, healthy young girls are usually hungry. People who are alive and well love food. Just as he would ask, "What do you have to eat?" when he appeared in his resurrected body, Jesus reminds us that feasts await those who live in him.

For those of us who have felt his touch in our lives, we have stories to tell and much to celebrate. The woman healed on this day was encouraged to tell her story in a crowded public arena. Yet the family of Jairus was instructed not to tell anyone of their daughter's healing. Why do think Jesus had such varying instructions about why certain miracles should or should not be shared?

He used the power of miraculous healing to prove that he had powers that could only be given by God. But Jesus was living in a human body. He knew the limitations of our bodies and that even those healed from the dead would eventually face death again. He understood the curse of living life in earth's fallen garden. And he came to overcome more than diseases of the body.

Even more than physical healing, what was Jesus most concerned with?

_____

_____

By the standard of Jewish law, the woman who came to him with the issue of blood was unclean and so are we. She was unfit for the company of others and there was no cure for her flow of blood. Like this woman, we too have the flow of sin in our nature and are unfit for relationship with God. The only cure for our sin is Jesus.

Read Matthew 11:28-30.

What does Jesus call us to do?

_____

_____

We don't have to be "good enough" to come to him. We just need to be desperate. I (Nan) had a friend in college who told me one night that he wanted to be baptized. While he was talking to me about it, I could tell he was hesitant and something was holding him back. I asked him why and he said, "I just don't feel good enough to be baptized." I quickly told him that he'd never be good enough, and that wasn't the point. He couldn't seem to grasp the fact that he could come to Jesus just as he was. He didn't need to get better at anything before seeking a relationship with Jesus. He could come as he was and find love and acceptance and forgiveness.

Do you struggle with the "good-enough" syndrome?

_____

_____

Even a believing Christ-follower can find herself trying to be "good enough" for God's approval. It's comical to think there is a status quo we could meet that would be "enough" to merit God's grace. The mystery of grace is that it is a gift. One cannot earn a gift. All we can do is come like a child and receive what our father has done for us.

Don't wait till you feel "good enough" to approach him. That day will never dawn. You don't have to impress God before you come to him.

What did Jesus give to both the woman and the little girl that day? Think of every possible answer:

_____

_____

Healing. Hope. Intimacy. Life. New names. New future. Dignity.

What condition of the heart did he release for the woman in particular?

"Go in _____."

Peace. How does one find peace in Him? He invites us into a whole new life. Her story encompasses the complete heart of Jesus' mission. Obviously he is concerned with physical healing. She received an immediate miracle of healing. But he didn't want her to sneak away and miss the miracle that would carry her into eternity. Physical healing was wonderful, but what she needed most of all was healing for her soul.

Where do we find the rest that Jesus spoke of in **Matthew 11:28**? Like Ruth, we find it in the house of our Kinsman-Redeemer. **Malachi 4:2** says, "But for you who fear my name, the sun of righteousness will rise with healing in its wings; and you will go forth and skip about like calves in the stall" (NASB). The Hebrew word for wings could also be used to identify the tassels the Jewish men wore on the corners of their robes. There is healing found under the wings of our Savior.

It seems so very sweet that Jesus says we should come to him as little children, with hearts ready to receive. Little children like Jairus's daughter leap, skip, and are quick to dance with their fathers. Both the twelve-year-old woman-child and the woman who had suffered for twelve years were made daughters of God that day. Both received healing under his wings, free from disease, death, and the curse of sin.

"I love those who love me, and those who seek me early and diligently shall find me" (Prov. 8:17 Amplified Bible).

We must mention one other woman healed by the touch of Jesus: Mary of Magdala. Here the woman is named, and her story recorded in all four gospel accounts. Her deliverance was as dramatic as any we can find. Mary was possessed by seven demons. Imagine if you will what Mary's life was like before she met Jesus. Like the woman with the issue of blood, Mary Magdalene was another woman living on the fringes of society. We don't know the manifestations that her demon possession exhibited, but they could have been anything from uncontrollable compulsive behaviors to violent abuse of her body.

"She may well have been a threat to her family. If the Gerasene demoniac's antics are any indication of how people possessed with multiple hostile spirits behave, her family may have had no choice but to bar her from the house.

The Gerasene tore off his clothes, wandered naked among the tombs, and was driven to such violent frenzies that the community had to chain him up. Even that could not always restrain him. He'd been known to break the chains and run howling into the wilderness.

That's the kind of life Mary had before Jesus found her." [46]

If the Gerasene demoniac was a man, think of how the Jews would treat a woman possessed by seven demons? Mary has been characterized as a prostitute in movies and novels. We have no biblical proof this is true. Yet if she was wildly out of control, it's no far stretch to imagine the only way she would have to make any money would be to lift her skirts and allow men access to her body. How else could she have purchased what little food she kept down? What other means did she have for survival?

There is no description of Mary's initial encounter with Jesus. Yet Mary lives out the evidence of this spectacular miracle. Did she writhe and convulse as the demons ran in fear at the sound of Jesus' voice? Were there eyewitnesses? Were his disciples there? Did Jesus instruct them not to write about Mary's miracle? One might speculate that Jesus did not want it recounted in detail to protect Mary from further unnecessary humiliation.

We do know she was obviously a pitiful, miserable woman who found healing, release, peace, dignity, purpose, and salvation when she met Jesus. After meeting him, her life is lived with free and complete absolution. Her passion for following Jesus rivals that of John and Peter. Her heart boldly reached out to him after her deliverance, never to look back. From all the verses we have about her, we know that she never left his side after she was healed. She traveled with him, ministered to him, stood by the cross as he died, and sat by the tomb after he was buried.

John 20:11-18 records the sweetest, most tender interaction between Jesus and Mary Magdalene after he rose from the dead. Turn and read this passage now.

What three ways did the risen Christ speak to His beloved daughter?

_____

_____

In verse 15, what was his first word to her?

"Woman." Jesus' tender attention to Mary of Magdala represents his heart for all women who followed him then and now. He appeared first to a woman and put to rest any question about how much God loves his girls.

In verse 16, what does he say?

"Mary." Jesus spoke her name. He knows his women. He knows you and me. In this breathtaking intimate reconnection, Jesus uses Mary to make the point that he knows us by name. He sits now by the right hand of God and intercedes for us by name. Nothing can ever come between us: no sin, shame, not even death itself.

In verse 17, what does he ask her not to do?

_____

_____

Jesus only would have said this because Mary was physically reaching out to touch him with an outburst of joy. She was not afraid to embrace her Savior. But he had not yet returned to his Father and this time stops her from touching his glorified body.

In verse 17, what precious assignment does Jesus give to this woman named Mary, who loved him with all her heart?

_____

_____

Mary's passion for her Savior was richly rewarded. Jesus didn't choose to hold a press conference first or appear to the most powerful people. Please note the amazing fact that Jesus never appeared in his resurrected body to anyone but those who would believe. He didn't make a trip back to Pilate or Herod, to the Sanhedrin court or those who mocked him. His last words on the cross were a declaration: "It is finished!" Jesus had finished his work. The cross and the empty tomb would be proof enough of God's love and redemption.

Now he chooses a lowly, heartbroken woman to take the news of his resurrection from death to his grieving apostles. A woman's testimony had no legal value in ancient Israel. Jesus chose her anyway! Mary would live the rest of her life with the knowledge that the King of Kings appeared first to her after he conquered death. He called her by name and sent her to spread the good news. Her value in his eyes was something she would never doubt. For a woman who had come so far and lived through such a difficult past, this was the gift of a lifetime.

What does this intentional relationship between Jesus and Mary say to you and me?

_____

_____

We don't need to remain anonymous when it comes to sharing something Jesus has done for us. Let's proclaim his healing power in our lives. Imagine yourself at the feet of Jesus. You have touched the threads of his prayer shawl and have found healing and salvation. Write your own proclamation of joy and thanksgiving for all he has done for you.

_____

_____

In sharing what God has done for us, we help strengthen the faith of others. Look at these victorious words from Psalm 107:2, 20-22. The writer is so full of goodness from the Lord that he couldn't keep quiet even if he tried!

"Let the redeemed of the Lord say so, whom he has redeemed from the hand of the adversary…. He sends forth his word and heals them and rescues them from the pit and destruction. Oh, that men would praise and confess to the Lord for his goodness and lovingkindness and his wonderful works to the children of men! And let them sacrifice the sacrifices of thanksgiving and rehearse his deeds with shouts of joy and singing!" (Amplified Bible).

Turn to read Matthew 14:35-36.

From the information we have in this verse, it seems the woman with the issue of blood continued to share the story of what Jesus had done for her. The news spread rapidly about the power in the fringes of his prayer shawl. As many as touched the edge of his garments were fully healed.

What did all the sick people to do?

_____

_____

"They....begged him to let them merely touch the fringe of his garment; and as many as touched it were perfectly restored" (Amplified Bible).

Jesus didn't advertise the condition of his heart. He lived it. He didn't make grand speeches about all the great things he had done. Many times he told those who received miracles to remain quiet. Jesus walked out his heart of love with sacrificial action.

Now contrast this passage with **Matthew 23:5-7.**

Jesus is speaking to his followers about the scribes and Pharisees. He warns his listeners to avoid the behavior of the religious people who parade their "righteous" deeds for all to see.

What were the Pharisees guilty of when they "made their fringes long?"

_____

_____

WHAT WOULD JESUS WEAR?

Have you ever wondered what kind of clothing Jesus wore? What is an outer garment for a Hebrew man? From *The Victor Journey through the Bible* we learn: "Jesus had to be more careful than his neighbors for he was accepted as a rabbi, and rabbis were expected to dress well, even above their means. A man was expected to cover his head as a sign of respect to those he met. A man also wore an inner garment close to the skin, called a coat or tunic. The outer garment, his cloak, was wrapped at the waist with a wide cloth or leather belt called a girdle. An upper garment, a goltha or tallith was worn with fringes or tassels at each corner. On the feet, he wore sandals. Jesus was probably clothed with the close-fitting undergarments which went down to his feet, as teachers were supposed to do, plus the tallith (prayer shawl) with the four fringes as an upper and outer cloth or covering. A cloth belt secured the clothing at his waist. His head was covered with the outer cloak, brought up over his head or by a separate cloth wound around his head." [47]

In Ancient Israel, tassels were tied to the four corners of the outer tunic. This outer garment eventually evolved into a formal prayer shawl.

Let's turn to the Old Testament to discover the spiritual meaning behind this fashion statement.

Read Numbers 15:37-41.

What was the purpose of the tassel and the cord of blue on the outer garment?

_____

_____

Now read Deuteronomy 6:4-9.

What primary command would the tassels have reminded them to obey?

_____

_____

The tassels were there to remind a Jewish man of his responsibility to fulfill God's commandments. They were tied together in 613 knots representing the 613 laws of Moses. The tassels hung openly on the outer garment and were originally used to remind the wearer to walk in the ways of God's laws. These tassels were made of blue cord; thus the term "royal blue."

Blue dye was extremely expensive. It only could be found in the shell of a Murex snail. It took 12,000 snails to fill a thimble full of blue dye and a pound of this dye would cost about $36,000! The blue tassels represented the divine royalty of being God's people.

It's humorous to think of Jesus wearing tassels to remind himself of the commands that he Himself wrote! God had commanded Moses to write into law a way of dressing that would help the Hebrews to remember the holiness of their God and his desire for them to keep his commandments. Jesus, being a proper Jew, was wearing the clothing of a rabbi. His outer garment had fringe and tassels at the four corners. But he needed no reminder that he was the very fulfillment of God's promises. His prayer shawl was worn in obedience and submission. It covered the body of God's Son. His robes would soon be torn and bloodied as he went to the cross. Jesus would become the new law of liberty.

Yet by his day, the spiritual hierarchy viewed their tassels as an outward show of superiority. Add to this 400 years of silence from God, and the prayer shawls were no longer honored as a garment invoking humility.

"By the end of the Second Temple period, tassels had become a symbol of social status. The wealthier you were, the more grand your tassels might appear...."[48]

The longer the shawl, the closer to God.

The woman with the issue of blood was not trying to touch the hem of the garment of a Pharisee. They offered her only a life of guilt and loneliness. She longed to touch the garment of the One she'd heard of who welcomed the outcasts of society. When we are self-righteous, we make it impossible for those outside of Christ to see Jesus in our lives. They see only an outward show of good deeds instead of a genuine trust in God who welcomes the poor in spirit.

We can be guilty of dragging the streets with a prayer shawl that could use a shorter hem.

How about an exercise in humility? Write down a specific example of healing that Jesus has done in your life. It can be physical, emotional or spiritual. Give him the glory and share this with a friend.

Is there any "hemorrhaging" situation in your life? Are you desperate for him? What do you have to push through to get to him?

In the South where we come from, there is a phrase we use when we want someone to get a really firm grip on something. We say, "Just grab a-holt of it!"

Just like the woman with the issue of blood who grabbed the hem of Jesus' garment, we hope you will "grab-a-holt" of everything he stands willing to give you. Write a prayer to Christ and ask him for the help and healing you need:

_____

_____

_____

_____

Throughout the gospels we read about women Jesus touched and healed. Many of them followed after him to support his ministry. Could it be that this woman, in the company of other mothers, sisters, and daughters of God followed Jesus even to the cross? Could it be that she saw him shed his blood to heal the world? Her bleeding had been a curse. His blood would heal every wound and restore mankind to the heart of God.

Imagine for a moment what life choices this woman made after her miraculous healing:

_____

_____

_____

_____

Early church tradition says that the woman with the issue of blood was named Veronica. It is also written in early church history that she had a bronze sculpture made and placed in the front of her house. It was a statue of a woman kneeling at the feet of Jesus.

We can't be certain if this is true. One day we'll know every detail of her story. One thing is certain: Keep your eyes on the feet of Jesus. Wherever he walks, he brings new life. Even nailed to a cross, his feet could not be stopped.

Falling at the feet of Jesus always brings results. Whatever motivates a bending of the knee, be it worship or prayer, pleading or quiet adoration, there is no greater place of power than being submissive and grateful before him. At the feet of Jesus we find endless acts of mercy and healing for our souls.

As we live between the now and the not yet, we can be certain that this anonymous woman in the Bible was never anonymous to God.

And neither are we.

We need you, Lord. We press in to touch you, Lord. We need to hear you call us "daughter."

TODAY'S DATE: _____

YOUR HEADLINE:
_____

_____

WEEK SIX
BREAKING NEWS

Messiah Watch

VIRGIN TEEN GIVES BIRTH TO ALIEN

Herod's Armies Search Judea; Local Shepherds Report UFO

Unconfirmed accounts of an alien child born to an anonymous teen in the hillsides of Bethlehem pour in. Rumors run rampant. Details about the bizarre birth are sketchy.

Shepherds from a nearby field insist they witnessed a visitation of unidentified representatives from an unknown universe.

"We were counting sheep and it was late when these... uh... these... I'm sorry but all I can say is that we saw angels appear!" one shepherd blurted out. "By God, the sky lit up and they were singing!"

Another shepherd commented, "I know we sound like we've lost our minds but nothing has ever been so sure and clear as what happened in Bethlehem last night." The humble laymen attempted to describe a choir of heavenly beings.

"Our God has been silent for 400 years," said a young shepherd named Jeremy. "Last night the skies broke apart to announce the birth of our Messiah. He is here at last!" After a moment of silence, Jeremy finished, "Shepherds are always the last to hear about anything. To think that God would give us this news first leaves us nearly speechless!"

The appearance of a strange star has kept Messiah-watchers on high alert for months. These new reports from the Shepherd's Guild only serve to heighten expectations of a Messianic birth in Judea.

Conversely, mothers in Bethlehem have refused comfort since the recent loss of their newborn sons. All males under the age of two have been eliminated per mandate of the Palestine governor, King Herod.

Herod's office issued the following explanation:

"Herod's administration felt it necessary to eliminate the existence of any Hebrew male born in the last two years. Our objective is to keep order in the provinces and to maintain a status quo for the growing demographic of our population. Measures were imposed to protect the citizens of Judea from fraudulent imposters."

News of a rival child-king's birth will indeed upset Herod's apple cart here in Judea.

Messiah Watch reporters will keep their ears to the ground and eyes to the sky. Our staff is dedicated to bring you the whole truth and nothing but the truth, so help us God!

TODAY'S HEROINE:
Mary, the mother of Jesus

For with God nothing is ever impossible and no word from God shall be without power or impossible of fulfillment (Luke 1:37 Amplified Bible).

"Time. A footspan on eternity's trail. Time did not exist until he wrote it. He, himself is timeless, but his story will be encased in time. The greatest mind in the universe imagined time… it was love that gave Emmanuel, God with us. The author would enter his own story. The word became flesh. He, too, would be born. He, too, would be human. He, too, would have feet and hands. He, too, will have tears and trials."[49]

Every woman who dared to believe in the promises of Jehovah trusted that at the exact time in history, Messiah would be born. God's Son would be given to the world through the body of a woman. Heaven's clock would strike "Now!" when at last the time came. On eternity's trail enters a young maiden from Nazareth. Her feet intersect with the "now-time" of God's plan. She will give birth to his heart, his Son. We invite you to take a most spectacular journey with us into the world of Mary, the mother of Jesus.

She has been immortalized in stained glass, exquisitely sculpted in marble and painted by the finest artists throughout the centuries. The eyes of all women who dare to believe gaze with us as we study the woman God chose to be the mother of his only Son. Let's zoom in for a close inspection. Maybe we can get a realistic picture and even find some common ground with her.

NO GIRL IS ORDINARY

Who was this flesh-and-blood woman? Did she live a saintly and exalted life, living on a higher plane than most of us? Was she flawless as a person and unequaled as a mother? The Scripture gives us several moments in Mary's life to meditate on. These glimpses reveal a woman more like you and me than we imagine. Let's dig in, and treasure each glimpse of her as Mary learned to treasure the wonderful and awful moments in her life.

The next time you are tempted to think of how little you matter in the scheme of "big things," close your eyes and remember Mary. The first time we see her in Scripture, she is an ordinary teen-age girl living at home with her parents. She is engaged to a carpenter. She lived in Nazareth.

"Can anything good come out of Nazareth?"

Nathanael asked this question in John 1:46 when Philip told him he had found the Messiah who came from Nazareth. Why would Nathanael, a guileless man, say something so negative about this town?

Nazareth is situated on the southern mountain ranges of Lower Galilee. Picture the wrong side of the tracks. The southside of Chicago. The badlands of Harlem. Trouble. Mary's hometown was a common village which housed a garrison of armed forces. Roman troops were literally in their back yard. "Jewish hatred of the Romans was so extreme that most Jews avoided any association with Nazareth."[50]

Yet from the hilltops surrounding the basin of Nazareth, there was a spectacular view thirty miles in every direction. From atop these hills was the view of historical battlefields. In one direction lie the fields where Barak and Gideon led the Israelites into battle. One could see the fields of Saul's and Josiah's defeats. One can see Naboth's vineyard and where Jehu got his revenge upon Jezebel. You can see Shunem and the house of Elisha, Mount Carmel in the distance and the place of Elijah's sacrifice. The history of the Israelites was played out in the territory surrounding Nazareth. [51]

Though surrounded by places of historical notoriety, Nazareth itself was small and insignificant. It was a small stop on a caravan route from the seacoast to Damascus. These Galileans were famous for what they lacked: culture and sophistication. Their dialect was coarse. They had a way of talking that would have been called "hick" in our time. Our culture would have referred to Nazareth as a "hole in the wall," a wide spot in the road, a truck stop where you gas up en route to some place better.

Think of a place in your own town where real estate is cheap because most people would never want to live there. A place where the adults never got much education, maybe not even a high school diploma. A place where the people use bad grammar, never see a dentist, and wouldn't know a symphony from a crude rap song. Now imagine the mother of Jesus came from such a place.

Mary grew up among people with a reputation for being irreligious, rebellious against authority, and having loose morals. To service Rome's security forces, brothels were common in Nazareth. The town was full of flop houses. The red light district of Nazareth enjoyed a steady stream of Roman soldiers who stopped in to get drunk and see a hooker. The town and people who lived there were looked down on by everyone.

Native Nazarenes were red-neck, backwoods, low-life homeboys from Galilee. If you called someone a Nazarene, you were basically calling them a "despised one." Does this phrase have a familiar ring to it?

Turn to **Isaiah 53:3**. Who is described in this verse and how?

_____

_____

Isn't God's word amazing?

Isn't the love of God astonishing?

Nathanael's question about anything good coming from Nazareth was understandable. Put together the whole picture of what we know about Mary's hometown and the question could have been more to the point: "Can there even be any virgins in Nazareth?"

God chose a virgin, teen-age girl from a hick nowhere place in a town despised and disgraced to carry the fetus of his Son. No one saw this coming.

The world is quick to give importance to the wealthy, the rich and famous, highly-educated and culturally sophisticated "beautiful people." Just as quickly, this worldview is equally ready to put down or dismiss anyone or anything that doesn't measure up to an inflated idea of worth. Does anything of significance come from insignificant or notorious places?

Can you note someone you admire who came out of a most unlikely background or circumstance?

_____

_____

The great artist, Thomas Kinkade is one such example. His paintings are loved because they radiate hope and light. Years ago I (Bonnie) sang at an event where Mr. Kinkade spoke. Presumptuously I expected to hear a boring, one-dimensional keynote address. I was humbled and stunned as Kinkade opened up about his past. He grew up in a "broken home," rejected by his father. As a young boy he was impressed with the suffering of his single mother and the fallout his siblings shared because of their dad's absence. This painful place of lack gave Thomas his artistic focus. From the smallest to the largest commission, he would infuse light into every painting.

Into dark circumstances, God delights to invade our preconceived notions and surprise us. He chose an unknown girl in a town famous for nothing but immorality to be the mother of the Savior of the world.

ONE VERY ROMANTIC DAY

When we first encounter Mary, the unsavory reputation of her hometown would have been the last thing on her mind. Ah, the glorious ability of a teen-ager to live in the moment.

What do we know of Mary's character and personality? What did Mary's parents make sure she knew before she became engaged to Joseph? We meet her on the day of their betrothal ceremony.

Mary would have been a teen-ager, between the ages of fourteen and seventeen. When a Hebrew girl began to have her monthly cycle, the next thing on the agenda would be marriage. Young Mary is now a woman. She has arrived at the exciting culmination of her girlhood dreams. She is betrothed to Joseph, a carpenter from Bethlehem. According to the Law of Moses the marriage contract had been negotiated by both families and the dowry settled.

Knowing what we do about Nazareth, how do you think Mary's family responded to her betrothal to a man from Bethlehem?

_____

_____

In Jewish culture, the betrothal of a couple was binding and very much like a modern wedding day in our culture. There was feasting and celebration. The bride-to-be met her fiancé under a canopy where oaths of commitment were pledged. It was during the betrothal service that a ring would be placed on her finger. Mary was legally promised to Joseph before a crowd of family and friends. She had been claimed by a man of honor and respect. She was awash with excitement about the coming months. Now Joseph would prepare a home for them, and when all was ready, he would make the covenant complete. Until then, there would be preparations for becoming a bride and special gowns to be sewn for her wedding night.

ONE EXTRAORDINARY MESSENGER

If you're married, think back to a favorite memory from your wedding engagement. After you came home from a party or shower, or special dinner with your fiancé, how did you feel as you prepared to sleep that night?

___

___

Mary had just been the center of everyone's congratulations. She had looked into the eyes of Joseph and wondered if he felt the same joy that filled her heart with anticipation. They would spend their lives together! When Joseph took her hands into his, she noticed they were rough and strong. Her promised husband was an accomplished carpenter. Secretly she longed to be held in his arms, to fall asleep in the embrace of a godly man. She wondered how his powerful arms would one day hold their firstborn child. What a lucky girl! She was soon to be married to a man from the line of David!

Could she possibly fall asleep after such an exciting day?

Luke 1 answers this question. We have Dr. Luke to thank for his particular attention to details. It's nice to have a doctor's diagnosis, especially because women enjoy having as much information as possible. Matthew's account of Mary's betrothal centers more on the groom's perspective. Dr. Luke takes us into the heart of young Mary.

The words Mary speaks to the angel Gabriel tell us volumes about her character. It's fun to picture Dr. Luke interviewing Mary later in her life to ask about the details of the day Gabriel appeared to her.

The good doctor wrote his gospel account with one purpose. Like any respectable physician, he wanted to deliver a complete, solid report. In **Luke 1:4**, he writes, "(My purpose is that) you may know the full truth and understand with certainty and security against error the accounts (histories) and doctrines of the faith of which you have been informed and in which you have been orally instructed" (Amplified Bible).

In other words, what you may have "heard" is one thing. Rumors about the birth and life of Christ will run wild. What you are about to read is God-breathed truth.

Let's go to the word and see what we can find out about this teen-age bride-to-be from Nazareth.

Read Luke 1:26-31.

Who visits Mary?

___

Who sent him?

___

Gabriel, the angel who has appeared throughout history, is given the most treasured assignment of all time. Imagine Gabriel in heaven, waiting, inquiring before the throne of God, "Is it time yet? Is she ready? Can I take the news now?" At last the time came and God released Gabriel to slip through the veil of unseen dimensions and into the small room of a teen-age girl. Gabriel did not appear to a wealthy girl of privilege, but to teen-age maiden in a nowhere village on the fringes of Galilee.

What medical point does Dr. Luke make extremely clear about Mary in **verse 27**?

_____

Three times we are told in one verse that Mary is a virgin.

She was a virgin, a virgin who had never been married. A virgin who was to be married to Joseph, a descendant of the house of David. The doctor makes it impossible to miss the fact that God's miracle is about to take place in the body of a pure maiden.

What are the first words Gabriel speaks to Mary in **verse 28**?

_____

_____

Excitement bursts forth from Gabriel in his salutation to the startled maiden. It's as if even the angels could not contain the joy. From before the foundations of the world, Jesus had waited to make his entrance on earth. At last the time had come! The young girl was before him and Gabriel showers her with praise.

Turn to **verse 45** for just a moment. Why does Elizabeth say Mary is blessed?

_____

_____

This could be the very reason she was chosen by God to bear the Messiah. She simply believed. Mary wasn't chosen because she was rich or famous or beautiful or educated, talented, or even a good person.

She simply believed and loved God. This must have been a refreshing assignment for Gabriel.

How does **Luke 1:29** describe Mary's initial response?

_____

_____

Please keep in mind that Mary was fully human. She was a young teen-ager excited about her upcoming wedding. Her room was in a small home located in a nasty village with a crummy reputation. Her heart was pure but unprepared for an angelic visitation. The Amplified Bible tells us that her thoughts were reeling…."revolving in her mind what such a greeting might mean."

What do angels always say when they appear on earth? (See verse 30.)

_____

_____

"Do not be afraid." *Mary, don't pass out on me, just keep breathing. This is all very strange but you will survive.* Gabriel looks into the astonished eyes of the young maiden and explains the glorious assignment God has given her. Surely he was pleased with this young girl's faith as he told her what would soon take place.

Read Luke 1:31-37.

What has Mary found in God's eyes?

_____

_____

Grace! Free, spontaneous, absolute favor, and lovingkindness with God! Gabriel's enthusiasm spills out again.

"And listen!" (Could Mary have suddenly pulled the covers over her head and ducked under for a moment?)

What is about to happen to her body?

_____

_____

With whose child?

_____

Who will the child become?

_____

Where will he reign?

_____

What would be his name?

_____

Gabriel has given Mary more information than she can possibly take in. The Son of God would be born to her and she would call him "Jesus." Jesus was a common enough name in her day. It was the Greek form of the Hebrew name Joshua which meant "Yahweh saves." Yet this common name would belong to a most uncommon child who would grow up to be the king of Israel? Mary's young mind hit overload.

Wait... wait... wait a minute. Whose child? What are you saying? A pregnancy? Give birth to a king who will do what? Adrenaline pounded through her veins but finally she caught her breath. Mary speaks to her angelic visitor for the first time. She interrupts Gabriel with a profound question.

What does she ask in **verse 34**?

_____

At this point Mary does not seem troubled by the presence of an angel in her room, but was troubled by his words. Mary's question to Gabriel, "How shall this be since I am a virgin?" tells us **she believes** what he is telling her. She just **doesn't understand** how it can be possible. She wants to know how this can biologically take place in a body that has never had intimate relations with a man. Gabriel is happy to answer her question and does not condemn her to nine months of silence as he did Zacharias (Luke 1:20).

"Oh yes, of course," he might have said. "Obvious question, my dear. Sweet Mary, your virginity poses no problem for God. He specializes in doing the impossible, especially with a woman's reproductive cycle. The womb of a woman is where he does some of his best work, knitting together each life with intimate care."

How does Gabriel explain how Mary will conceive? (See verse 35.)

_____

_____

When Mary was overshadowed by the Holy Spirit, the "thing" that was conceived was the very seed of God himself.

"The Holy Spirit will come upon you, and the power of the Most High will overshadow you as a shining cloud; and so the holy, pure, sinless thing (offspring) which shall be born of you will be called the Son of God" (Amplified Bible).

Who had ever heard of such a thing? Maybe Mary had. Maybe her Mom and Dad made a point of teaching her the prophesies about the coming Messiah.

Turn to Isaiah 7:14. What did Isaiah say the sign of the Messiah would be?

Turn to Exodus 40:34. What covered the tent of meeting?

_____

_____

The Shekinah Glory, God's visible presence in the form of a cloud, covered the Tent of Meeting and the glory of the Lord filled the tabernacle! In the same way, this is the very One who overshadowed Mary, a young girl who believed God was able. A young lady who was willing to be his handmaid.

The Holy Spirit will hover over her to bring the baby into her womb. The third part of the Trinity has hovered to birth miracles since the beginning of time. It was the Holy Spirit that hovered over the earth in Genesis to birth order from chaos. The Holy Spirit births truth in the innermost places of the heart. This is extremely tender and intimate. God himself will fill Mary's womb. The time has come for the shining glory of God to hover and birth his pure and sinless Son in the body a virgin.

Why was it important that the mother of the Messiah be a virgin?

Our dear friend and theologian Glenna Salsbury teaches on this subject. In her CD SOMETHING TO THINK ABOUT/Fascinating Facts To Build Your Faith, she makes it very clear why the birth of our Savior had to be from the womb of a virgin.

"A strange phenomenon occurs in the development of the blood. Blood appears within a fetus only after the sperm enters the ovum. In the womb, no blood passes from the mother to the child. The Bible says that God made all men of one blood and that blood is in our flesh. It became diseased when Adam sinned, thus all humans die. For a human to be born sinless, it would have to be conceived without the introduction of the male sperm. The Bible says Jesus Christ was born of a virgin without the introduction of a human sperm."

Does this make you roll your eyes with a bit of skepticism? Don't just take Glenna's word for it. "Google it," dear one! Find out. Do your own research. Do some "blood work." Science confirms the Word of God.

Conception is the start of a new and separate life, totally independent from the mother. At the beginning of a human life, one sperm from the father enters the ovum (egg) from the mother.

Debate continues about the virgin birth of Jesus. In the end it's a personal choice to take God at his word. Mary was a pure, precious-hearted young lady. But she was born with a sin-nature just like you and me. **Jesus was born without a sin-nature because he did not have an earthly father. Not even Mary's blood was running through his veins.** The blood flowing through his body was the blood of God (Acts 20:28). He was fully human in flesh, but his blood was sinless. If Jesus had not been born of a virgin, then his death on the cross would be meaningless. He would simply be a martyr, not a Savior capable of forgiving sin. Only God's perfect blood could be shed when Jesus gave his life as God's perfect lamb.

"The work of God in Mary introduces something unknown before or after: the birth into the human race of one who is both God and man." [52]

Think it through, girlfriend. The deeper our understanding, the more powerful will be our witness!

Stop here to catch your breath. If this blood data is new to you, please write about how this moves your heart:

_____

_____

Back to Mary and Gabriel. What's not to love about the angel Gabriel? How Father God must have smiled during this conversation.

"And listen!" Gabriel says again. (*What choice do I have?* Mary might have thought.)

In **Luke 1:36,** Gabriel tells Mary of another miraculous birth. What other miraculous pregnancy is in motion?

_____

_____

At last Mary takes it all in. Her heart willingly accepts the will of God, no matter how inadequate she may feel. Her words are ones we would do well to say over and again as he works in our lives.

What simple statement of faith does Mary speak in **verse 38**?

_____

_____

Be it done unto me as the Lord wills.
Be it done unto me as the Lord sees what is best.
Be it done and may I view myself as a handmaiden after his heart.
Be it done, Lord, no matter the cost.
Be it done, Lord.

Matthew's gospel account describes the child young Mary will soon feel growing in her body: "….for he will save his people from their sins (that is prevent them from failing and missing the true end and scope of life which is God)" (Matt 1:21 Amplified Bible).

At Mary's prayer of acceptance, Gabriel exited earth.

Mission accomplished.

ONLY COUSIN ELIZABETH WILL TRULY UNDERSTAND

Read Luke 1:39-56.

God intentionally chose the young woman who would birth and mother his beloved Son. We can assume that Mary's parents taught her the ways of the Lord and discussed verses of prophecy and promises around the dinner table. Four hundred years of silence from God did not dampen the faith of her family. Mary must have had an especially sweet relationship with her mother.

Yet, in **Luke 1:39** where does Mary go and with what urgency?

_____

_____

Mothers like to feel our daughters can come to us under any circumstance. We can handle anything. How often do we tell our girls to believe God for the impossible? Moms are the unshakeable cheerleaders in their daughters' lives. We want them to dream big dreams because their God is huge. Mary's mother would certainly have had many conversations with her about the promises of God and how he would move mountains in her future.

So let's cut Mary's family some slack. Imagine being at the breakfast table the day after they have just thrown a celebration to honor the betrothal of their daughter to Joseph. Think for a moment about the stress/joy combination that packs a punch for the parents of the bride. Mary's mom has gone to bed the night before with a sigh of gratitude. The betrothal was lovely. Now she can relax a bit as they wait for Joseph to finish building a new home.

The next morning she wakes to find her daughter breathless and excited. Mary insists that an angel of the Lord came in the night to tell her that she is pregnant with the promised Messiah child from God. Talk about bringing a room down.

Mary pregnant? An angel appeared? How will Joseph and his family respond? Lord help us, what will Mary's father say when he hears about this? What will the neighbors say? How will we keep this a secret? Do we tear up the marriage paperwork here and now? Our rabbi is going to have a coronary!

How do you think Mary's mother processed this information?

_____

_____

FOOD FOR THOUGHT: When God actually does the impossible thing he has promised, how do we respond? Mary's mother knew Jehovah's Messiah would be born of a virgin. Her daughter was as good a candidate as any to receive this great destiny. Did Mary's mother believe her? Are we prepared to embrace the possibility that God will do what he says?

_____

_____

Was Mary able to accurately describe her angelic conversation with Gabriel and the visitation of God's Holy Spirit hovering overhead? Did she convince Joseph when she told him she was pregnant? Could she explain to her parents that Isaiah's prophecy had come to rest on their daughter? Or was the glory of it too precious and breathtaking to ever be fully disclosed?

"Stepping from the throne, God removed his robe of light and wrapped himself in skin; pigmented, human skin. The light of the universe entered a dark, wet womb. He whom angels worship nestled himself into the placenta of a peasant...."[53]

Mary was engaged to Joseph at the time the angel Gabriel appeared to her. The period of engagement in Israel was one year. The punishment for being unfaithful during the espousal period was death by stoning. The people of the town would stone the unfaithful woman, then cover her with dung and plant a tree in that place to remind everyone of the cost of adultery.

When Mary said, "Behold the handmaid of the Lord," she accepted a great risk. In being willing to bear the Messiah, she basically said, "I am willing to let Christ be born in me." She knew she would be scorned and accused of having an illegitimate child, but she was willing to pay the price.

Matthew's gospel tells us that when Mary told Joseph, he wanted to break off the engagement quietly. He was a good guy. He didn't want Mary to be publicly shamed or stoned. He sought to protect her. Joseph knew Mary's character. She was a pure, honorable girl. The news of her pregnancy shook him to the core. Mercifully, God dispatched another angel to calm Joseph's heart. This angel appeared to Joseph in a dream to reassure him that Mary was telling the truth. Indeed, her womb had become the Holy of Holies.

Thankfully in the end, Mary's family and especially her fiancé believed that she was part of God's plan to birth the Messiah. But Mary doesn't stay home. With great haste she goes straight to the house of her cousin Elizabeth.

Why do you think Mary felt drawn to stay with Elizabeth?

_____

_____

Probably to escape gossip, questions impossible to answer, and for moral support, Mary wastes no time in traveling to see her cousin Elizabeth.

Elizabeth has received a miracle. Surely Elizabeth will believe Mary.

Why was it so important to see Elizabeth? Why did her family let her go? Gabriel told Mary that Elizabeth ("well-stricken in years") was pregnant. Mary wanted to share her news with another woman who certainly believed in miracles. She wanted to be in the company of a woman who would share her joy without judgment.

With the haste of a teen-ager on a mission trip, Mary left Nazareth and traveled to a town on the western edge of Jerusalem now known as Ein Karem. Was this trip a nice stroll down a country lane? Hardly. This road was dangerous and definitely unfit for a pregnant woman. Mary traveled about 100 miles. It was a road used by people living outside the law. Mary grew up in the roughshod streets of Nazareth. Perhaps this now served her well. She would need to navigate the hill country terrain full of deserts, canyons, and cliffs. The road was rocky, full of hills and valleys. Did she walk? Ride a donkey? Was she alone? We don't know. But she could only have traveled at the most ten miles a day, which made it a ten-day journey to see Elizabeth.

We have a perfect chance right here and now to see what this young girl was made of. Forget the dainty, fair-skinned, frail-looking images of Mary. What does this one journey tell us about her character, inside and out?

_____

_____

Read Luke 1:39-46.

At last, Mary enters the home of Zacharais. What is the first thing Elizabeth hears?

_____

_____

What happens to Elizabeth at the sound of Mary's greeting?

_____

_____

When Mary walks in the door unannounced, Elizabeth begins to prophesy and the baby John leaps inside Elizabeth's womb. It's fun to think about tiny John doing a flip in his mother's womb when Mary walked in. A fetus can hear by the time it is sixteen weeks old. John heard Mary's "hello" and immediately knew who she was. The Holy Spirit was already filling John, and at sixteen weeks he recognized the voice of the mother of Jesus.

Does this boggle your mind? How does this make you feel about the unborn babies around us and what they hear? (No stock, law-ridden answers, please. Think about the wonderful implications here.)

___

How is Mary greeted by her cousin Elizabeth?

___

What does Elizabeth say in a loud voice?

___

If there had been hushed whispers in Nazareth, Mary finds none of that in the home of Elizabeth. With a loud voice Elizabeth shouts confirmation to Mary's wondering heart. All it took was the sound of Mary's voice to cause the baby in Elizabeth's womb to leap for joy. "Blessed, favored of God, above all other women is Mary!" Elizabeth's declaration would be words that would comfort Mary throughout her entire life. "Blessed is she who has believed that what the Lord has said to her will be accomplished!" (Luke 1:45 NIV).

Young Mary's heart now leapt with ecstatic joy. She dared to believe the angel Gabriel brought the word of God. She desperately needed another woman who would understand this miraculous visitation. How encouraged Mary would be by the proclamation of Elizabeth. The revelation to Elizabeth by the Holy Spirit meant that Mary didn't have to worry about whether or not Elizabeth and Zacharias would believe her story.

What does Elizabeth call Mary in **verse 43**?

___

This was the first time Mary heard herself called, "the mother of my Lord." Elizabeth praises God for this privilege. One day her son John would publicly announce Jesus to be the Son of God. Elizabeth now mirrors the same humility telling all around her that her young cousin carries the Messiah. Mary may not enjoy this salutation again until many years later after the resurrection of Jesus.

She lived her whole life bearing the reproach of being an unwed mother. It was a reproach that followed Jesus throughout his life.

Read John 8:41.

Here we find the Pharisees seeking to discredit Jesus because of his family background.

Who do they say is his father?

___

How do they accuse him of being born?

As an adult, Jesus hears the echoes of gossip that surrounded his mother's pregnancy. Thirty years later, religious leaders attempt to destroy him with rumors about his birth.

"The mother of my Lord" is a title Mary never dreamed she'd have. It was a role she may have felt unfit to fill. It carried with it a weight she may not have chosen to bear, had she known the price. How in the world did this poor young teen-ager think she would be able to live up to the challenge? We get a true picture of how Mary felt about being the handmaid of God and the mother of Jesus when she responds with abandoned praise.

Mary is now fully free to celebrate the glorious impossibility of the child conceived within her. With childlike faith, Mary embraced the calling God lavished upon her.

This lovely passage is called the Magnificat. Mary begins by saying, "My soul magnifies the Lord." Magnify is translated "magnificat' in Latin and this is why these verses have been called the Magnificat for generations.

As you read Mary's song of faith, picture her dancing and weeping with joy. Picture Elizabeth clapping and praising God at the sound of Mary's spontaneous singing. Picture the angels joining with her, rejoicing in heaven. Picture the mothers, sisters, and daughters of God who believed this moment would come. Picture the laughter of God ringing through the halls of eternity as a pure-hearted maiden from nowhere Nazareth delighted to receive his miraculous Son. Mary quoted prophecy and scripture as she danced and sang before God.

Let's feast upon her words in Luke 1:46-55.

> "My soul magnifies the Lord
> And my spirit has rejoiced in God my Savior.
> For he has had regard for the humble state of his bond slave.
> For behold, from this time on generations will count me blessed.
> For the Mighty One has done great things for me
> And holy is his name.
> And his mercy is upon generation after generation
> Toward those who fear him.
> He has done mighty deeds with his arm;
> He has scattered those who were proud in the thoughts of their heart.
> He has brought down rulers from their thrones,
> And has exalted those who were humble.
> He has filled the hungry with good things;
> And sent away the rich empty-handed.
> He has given help to Israel his servant,
> And in remembrance of his mercy,
> As he spoke to our fathers,
> To Abraham and his offspring forever" (NASB).

What does Mary's song tell us about her?

_____

_____

Mary knew the Torah! She must have been taught by her father.

Why would she have been taught by her father and not her mother?

_____

_____

Girls were not allowed to study the Scriptures on their own. Her Son would one day change all that. But as Esther learned from Mordecai, so Mary learned from her father. From what Mary proclaims in these verses, what does she know about the character of God?

List as many adjectives as you can find that Mary uses to describe God:

_____

_____

Being asked to mother the Messiah could safely be called a challenge. It is the truth you know about the character of God that will sustain you through the challenges of life. Mary seems to have been anchored in the sovereignty and power of God enough to be willing to walk down a road what would be anything but easy.

Look at the verses of praise again. As you read them, remember what a small town Mary came from and how despised were the people of Nazareth.

Let's take a sweet, forward glance into how Mary's humility influenced the heart of Jesus.

According to the Magnificat:

What does Mary say God does on behalf of the humble and oppressed?

_____

_____

Read Matthew 5:3,5.

What does Jesus call those who are humble?

_____

_____

Magnificat:

What does Mary say God does for the oppressed?

_____

_____

Magnificat:

What does Mary say God will do for those who hunger?

_____

_____

Matthew 5:6:

What does Jesus call those who hunger and thirst after righteousness?

_____

_____

Magnificat:

What does Mary say all generations will call her?

_____

_____

Matthew 5:10-11:

What does Jesus call those who suffer for the sake of righteousness?

_____

_____

"Blessed!" Please read all the definitions included in this one word. According to the Amplified Bible: Happy, enviable fortunate, and spiritually prosperous—possessing the happiness produced by the experience of God's favor and especially conditioned by the revelation of his grace, regardless of their outward conditions.

Gabriel called her "blessed." Elizabeth called her "blessed." Mary called herself by the same endearment. One day, Christ would call blessed all who would be like his mother: humble, meek, merciful, gracious, long-suffering, and willing to believe.

Did Mary sing parts of the Magnificat over her infant firstborn son at two a.m. feedings? Did she tell him that God blessed the misunderstood and those looked down on? Did she sing of God's endless mercy and favor to those who lived in the light of his grace? Was he not the source of her heart's happiness?

Do you remember a special song you sang over your children? Or a song sung over you by your mom or someone who loved you? What were your favorite words?

_____

_____

Mary only had to look into the face of her baby son to gaze upon God's love and unconditional revelation. Her Son was the God she believed. Jesus was the living proof of his mother's faith!

Read the last verse, Luke 1:55, one more time.

Mary ended her song with on a spiritual high C! She is rejoicing in the fulfillment of God's promise to Abraham.

Read Genesis 17:19 and Galatians 3:16.

What is Jesus called in Galatians?

___

Three thousand years before she was born, God promised Abraham a **seed**. She knew this seed was the Messiah and that she had been chosen to be his earthly mother. It's interesting to note that Abraham was living in the same hill country as Elizabeth when God spoke this promise to him. When Mary steps through Elizabeth's front door and praises Jehovah she proclaims that God has fulfilled his promise.

"Mary breaks forth in song, stitching scraps of psalms together with words remembered from the Old Testament thanksgiving of Hannah.... She is, in fact, echoing Gabriel's message that her Son will be the king who restores Israel, affirming publicly what she has been told privately." [54]

What a wonderful girl-visit Mary must have shared with Elizabeth. Both of them were free to sing and rejoice and share pregnancy stories. Do you have a friend who allows you the freedom to be a little Jesus-crazy?

___

Honestly, if not, we hope you find one soon. One of God's greatest gifts to us is a girlfriend who gives us room to sing and dance before him. We run to those women when we have a breakthrough with God, or want to brag on how he loves us! Beside every great girl is a girl-friend who loves God.

FABULOUS SIDEBAR: There is a church in Ein Karem called The Church of the Visitation, commemorating the meeting of Mary and Elizabeth. Set into the stone are fifty-seven ceramic tiles, each with Luke 1:46-55 written on it in a different language. People who make the pilgrimage can read Mary's beautiful proclamation of faith in everything from Swahili to Portuguese to Vietnamese.

Could you use a "Mary-Elizabeth" visitation right about now? If so, call your "M" or "E" and set up a time for some good girl-talk about your faithful God.

On rare occasions, it's not our momma's turn. Hard as it is to write this, we know it's true. At certain junctures in our lives, we might turn to another female confidant. Often we pray for the woman God will make available if one of our daughters needs to talk to someone other than us. We pray for God to bring a wise, alert, real lady of his heart into their path. Other times we pray to be that person for someone else's child.

Do you have a momma figure that you confide in? Are you this woman in a younger girl's life?

___

Elizabeth was this safe place for Mary.

The authors of this study continue to be a safe place for each other. I (Bonnie) recall specific times in my life when being with Nan was the safest place for me to come apart at the seams with joy.

JOURNALS OF A MOTHER

When we began to study Mary's life, I pulled out a journal I kept during my first pregnancy. With teary eyes I opened the dusty little blue book in which I wrote about the miracle of becoming a mother. A human life was being formed in me! What could be more miraculous?

Mary may have lived over 2,000 years ago, but she would have felt the same ageless emotions any pregnant woman feels. Here are some excerpts from my pregnancy journal. Every entry is addressed to my baby.

TO MY UNBORN CHILD

"Today I found out that you are going to be a Christmas present for me and your father. I'm absolutely shocked, numb, happy, and terrified all at the same time! What an incredible day!"

"There are so many things I cannot wait to share with you.... I hope you'll love the Lord like I've grown to. I'm sure you will teach me so much about his incredible power and wisdom."

(While reading, I came across the next entry.)

"I was afraid I wouldn't be able to find Nan and I wanted her to be the first person to know about you. The good Lord worked it out wonderfully. I went to Nan's house on the way to lunch. (I can't wait for you to meet my precious friends.) She was so excited too! She laughed and cried and we hugged and jumped up and down."

Nan's memory is much more detailed. While studying about Mary's surprise visit to Elizabeth she wrote:

"This reminds me of a time when someone came to my door unannounced. It was twenty-seven years ago and I was in my tiny kitchen at home. Our kitchen had a window over the sink and a door that went out into our driveway. The door had a window on it too, making my little kitchen a sunny, warm place.

I was at the sink and didn't hear a car come in the driveway. Suddenly I heard a tiny tap at the door and I looked over to see Bonnie leaning over and looking in the window to see if I was home. I saw her before she saw me. She was wearing a yellow sweater and she had a funny look on her face. Knowing her as well as I do, I knew that something was up. It wasn't like her to just pop over unannounced.

I quickly opened the door and the first words out of her mouth were, 'Nan, I wanted to come and tell you. I just found out I'm pregnant!'

This was quite a visitation for me! I was thrilled and excited and full of joy for Bonn. If I'd been physically able to do a back handspring I would have."

Neither of us can do a handspring, but for the past thirty years Nan and I continue to laugh and cry at God's surprises. I'm grateful to say we excel in spontaneous singing, lots of jumping around and for many reasons keep a stash of Motrin nearby.

While staying in the joyous home of Elizabeth, Mary would have experienced her first signs of pregnancy. Did Mary have the usual symptoms? Elizabeth would have known exactly how to talk her through the stages of exhaustion and nausea.

From my journals, I wrote the following:

"I'm exhausted to the bone; you really need a lot from my body….That scares me. I want to be so healthy and careful…. I feel so strange….The Lord is going to prepare me for your life. It's an awesome thought."

"We had a very long day, and you must have gotten really tired. You wanted me to sit down and gave me a terrific headache. I felt like I was getting the flu. I'm trying to slow down and rest more for you, little one. I pray you are growing strong and healthy…."

"You can't believe all the things we've been doing. I'm rehearsing for a new show and you've been such a good little tadpole during these rehearsals. I think the choreography I'm doing will be good for you. Maybe you'll come out step-kicking and singing, 'Brand New Day!' I do so want you to love music!"

OK. We have to do this. Take a minute and pull out a baby book, grand-baby book, a journal or two of your own. What were some of your first thoughts about being a mother/grandmother/aunt/godmother?

_____

_____

You and Mary have a lot in common. Surely she felt the same wonder and prayers all women feel as they ponder the child they carry, with one **huge** exception. Mary knew she carried the holy Son of God.

Was it a combination of a pure heart and tender age that caused Mary's open embrace to motherhood? Mary seems to be very excited about being God's handmaid. This is a term we don't often use. It would be extremely politically incorrect in our culture. It would be a term too derogatory to say in public.

In Mary's generation, a handmaid or maidservant was someone humble and ready to give obedient service. A handmaid was considered to be the lowest kind of female slave. A handmaid had no rights and was the property of her master. A slave and a master. This terminology was used deliberately by Mary to bind herself to God and his call on her life.

The apostle Paul used the masculine form of this word to describe himself in the opening words of Romans: "Paul, a bond-servant of Christ Jesus, called to be an apostle and set apart for the gospel of God…" (NIV).

Mary was set apart. She was humble. She was willing to set aside her own agenda for her life and go down a different road. She knew that an unexplained pregnancy would jeopardize her reputation and her relationship with Joseph. She was willing to risk it.

She would have to face decades of unanswered questions about the birth of her Son. She would marry Joseph, but it would not be the wedding night she imagined. Most likely it was a quiet affair, without the usual dancing and celebration. She would never be able to explain why she left town so soon after her betrothal party. Whatever happened next would be a lifetime of faith, trusting in God's faithful character. Baby showers? Maybe not. Remembering the merciful right hand of God? All the time.

Mary's magnificent song had to carry her through years of the unknown. She held onto what she knew to be true.

She had grown up all her life knowing that the Hebrew people were set apart, a nation belonging to Yahweh. She grew up surrounded by Roman armies but her eyes saw beyond them and believed in the power of the one Ruler of all. She knew it would be through Israel that God would bless the world. She knew the Lord Almighty had conquered more than Rome dared to dream. Jehovah had subdued nations and exalted the humble.

She could trace the lines back as far as the mind could go. The mighty deeds of God always included the least likely bond-servants to do his will. Was David not a young shepherd boy chosen to be king by Samuel? Was Esther not an orphan living in an exiled country when she saved her people? Was Hannah not barren? Was Sarah not old?

Mary knew what God promised he would do. She may not have felt up to the task in her own strength, but she trusted the one who had the power to bring it all to fulfillment in spite of her frail humanity.

LUKE'S INTERVIEW WITH MARY: DAY ONE

To write an accurate account of the life of Jesus, Dr. Luke would have interviewed Mary late in her life after Jesus' death and ascension to heaven. We wonder what questions might Dr. Luke have asked.

Luke: Mary, did you feel worthy to birth the Son of God?

Mary: Worthy?

Luke: When Gabriel appeared with the news, did you wonder if you were just dreaming? Why would God choose you?

Mary: Oh… well… I thought, Why not me?

Luke: That might sound a bit arrogant to some.

Mary: Arrogant? I don't understand. It was an honor. I knew Israel's history. I was his handmaid, a slave to God's will. His will was to use my life. All I had to do was accept his will.

Luke: Weren't you afraid?

Mary: Afraid of…?

Luke: Afraid of everything. Bearing the shame of a strange pregnancy, bearing the child, raising him, motherhood?

Mary: God did all the work. He gave the strength. He provided the daily manna of grace. It was I who received the blessing!

Has God asked you to do something that is beyond your strength and ability?

_____

_____

Most likely he has. He seems to delight in using us in ways we never dreamed possible. If he has put you in a situation that challenges you beyond your ability to cope or endure or succeed, then take heart.

Remember Mary. He has put you there to help you learn to lean on him.

Bind your heart to his. Become a bond-servant.

He wants to accomplish his purposes through you. He desires to mold you more and more into the image of his Son. As you yield to him and co-labor with him, the impossible will be made possible. The result will be your faith increasing and his glory proclaimed.

What did the angel say to Mary in Luke **1:37**?

_____

_____

Take a moment to describe a situation in your life that feels impossible:

_____

_____

Write a prayer of crazy faith to God! He wants you to trust him to help you in this exact place in your life:

_____

_____

Mary doesn't ask the angel Gabriel for details about the life of the child she will bear. **Read Luke 1:31-32** and list the details Gabriel reveals about Jesus' destiny:

_____

_____

The cost for God was the heartbeat of his Son.

The cost for you and me is a heart saying, 'Be it done unto me as you will.'

Death for life.

Life forever.

Life from a tiny baby born to a simple girl who believed.

"Mary didn't know whether to give him milk or give him praise, but she gave him both since he, as near as she could figure, was both hungry and holy. Joseph didn't know whether to call him Junior or Father. But in the end, he called him Jesus, since that's what the angel had said and since he didn't' have the faintest idea what to name a God he could cradle in his arms…

Don't you think… their heads tilted and their minds wondered, 'What in the world are you doing, God?' Or better yet, 'God, what are you doing in the world?'

Rest well, tiny hands. For though you belong to a king, you will touch no satin, own no gold. You will grasp no pen, guide no brush. No, your tiny hands are reserved for works more precious:

> to touch a leper's open wound,
> to wipe a widow's weary tear,
> to claw the ground of Gethsemane." [55]

TODAY'S DATE: _____

YOUR HEADLINE:
_____

_____

> "From God's heart to our side
> Came the promised child
> Flesh and bone
> Lamb of life
> Simple, holy Christ
> Born a sacrifice."

Bonnie Keen, Lowell Alexander, Ascap [56]

Week Seven
BREAKING NEWS

Hebrew Gazette

Nazareth Weekly Calendar

The monthly meeting of Hebrew Mothers of Pre-Schoolers (H-MOPS) will host a special guest at their upcoming meeting in the home of Golda Avram, the wife of our beloved Rabbi.

The guest speaker is Mary of Nazareth, wife of Joseph and mother Jesus.

"The seminar is titled "Treasures of the Heart," said Golda. "We invited Mary to share some of her secrets of scrapbooking."

The Gazette was able to catch Mary between feedings and laundry to find out what she plans to teach the H-MOPS.

"Motherhood is a wild ride and I feel like I'm holding on for dear life," Mary said while changing her son's diaper. "Things happen fast. I want to remember the cute things my son says and document his milestones. Scrapbooking is the perfect way to preserve the treasures of childhood."

When asked why she created the art of scrapbooking, Mary replied, "My heart has always been a scrapbook. I've always been the type to ponder things that happen to me, and I've always journaled. Life is full of sweet and difficult moments. Each is a gift in its own way. Looking back in the pages of a diary, I can better see the hand of God in my life. Scrapbooking was the next logical step when I became a mom."

Mary says those attending the seminar should bring photos, your kids' artwork, drawings or scribbles, scraps of outgrown clothing, report cards, old Mother's day cards, growth charts, anything with sentiment or special meaning. She promises attendees will leave that day with something they will treasure the rest of their lives.

The seminar is free but a love offering will be taken to benefit needy moms of Nazareth.

TODAY'S HEROINE:
Mary, part two

"Mary treasured up all these things and pondered them in her heart."
Luke 2:19 (NIV)

"Through chattering teeth, arctic scientists inform us that only one-eighth to one-tenth of an iceberg is visible. As much as ninety percent is submerged in the unseen. Because of their enormous mass, and with that proportion, icebergs are virtually indestructible.

Ten percent seen plus ninety percent unseen equals an indestructible life.

The most influential life in all of history reflected the iceberg equation. Ninety percent of his life on earth was spent in obscurity. Ten percent of his earthly life was spent in the public eye.

And all of his life was, and still is, absolutely indestructible." [57]

The anonymous years of Jesus' life remain a mystery. In Scripture, we are allowed to see only the tip of the iceberg. John's gospel concludes by saying the largest library on the face of the earth would be insufficient to contain all the details of his earthly life.

What was he like as a child? What do we know about his family? Did he have a favorite fruit to eat or game to play with his friends? How did Mary feel as she watched her holy toddler grow from adolescence into manhood? What were her memories of the night he was born?

Virginia Stem Owens writes:

"The Christmas cards always clean the scene up, concealing any signs of her struggle, the bloody rags, and discarded placenta. Instead of picturing her with swollen lips and sweat-matted hair, they show Mary serene and sanitary. Yet the cave floor would have been littered with manure and urine-soaked straw, and the feed-trough where she laid her baby filled with moldy hay." [58]

Jesus was fully God and fully human.

Jesus cried.

Jesus may have had diaper rash.

Jesus had to learn to crawl and then sit up and finally take his first steps.

Jesus cut teeth and occasionally scraped his knees.

Jesus laughed and giggled, cooed, and got grumpy when it was nap time, just like every other toddler.

Jesus had hormones when he grew into manhood.

Jesus came as a human being, the greatest condescension in history, to prove God's great love.

And when the time came, he bled real blood, shed real tears, and died a fully human death on a hideous cross on a craggy hill to redeem the sins of man.

To sanitize his life is to discredit his sacrifice.

Mary was fully human and not God. To make her more or less is a discredit to her very real experience of motherhood.

What would you like to know about the unrecorded years of his life?

_____

_____

Mary's heart held the memories of these anonymous years. Her life as his mother was fueled by faith. She trusted God one day at a time. We have the advantage of reading the word and seeing an enlarged photo of the earthly life of Jesus. We know that he will reign forever in the new earth as King and Lord of all. Yet like Mary, we don't' know every detail about what will happen between then and now.

Take a moment to think about what Gabriel didn't tell Mary.

He focused on the details of the ultimate victory of Jesus and his reign on the throne of David for all eternity. Gabriel did not say anything about his ministry, the three hardest years of Jesus' life. He omitted any mention of how the Pharisees would harass him or how the Sanhedrin would call for his crucifixion. He didn't reveal the coming heartbreak she would bear. There would be no preparation for the day she watched her firstborn son scourged, mutilated, and hung naked on a cross like a common criminal.

Thank goodness Gabriel was told only to reveal the bigger picture and the ultimate victory of the child Mary would bear. Speaking further would have been too much for her. Sometimes seeing the big picture is more merciful than seeing snapshots along the way.

Think of an event in your past when you look back with hindsight, you are grateful that you didn't know what was coming.

_____

_____

We share Mary's leap of faith. It's a daily walk we have in common with every dear saint that has gone before us and everyone that will come after. We all know what **will** happen; we just don't know **how** it will happen.

What does this day-to-day faith walk cause us to do?

_____

_____

Faith gives us freedom to live without fear.

Faith allows the heart to embrace questions without having to understand the answers.

"Intellect, when not informed by the heart, is evil." [59]

Spiritual disconnection between the head and heart leads to a life of frustration. Head knowledge without heart acceptance is the breeding ground for legalistic death. At some point we must believe God's word and let go of what we don't understand.

What experience have you had that could have used more of a head-heart integration?

_____

_____

Mary doesn't ask Gabriel for more details. She doesn't press him for "the rest of the story." She sets aside her rights to know the future and says yes to God. But this young lady is a thinker. She ponders life and the ways of God. Her mind is at peace with the unknown. Mary stores up these treasures of faith in her heart.

She stayed with Elizabeth until baby John was born. Then she traveled back home. By this time, Mary was three months pregnant, most likely lonely, and beginning to show physical proof of God's growing Son. Surely she clung to the truth of Scripture and to the message of Gabriel.

Six Months of Expectation

What is it like when a woman is "expecting?" Mary lives the next six months with an extreme case of expectation. Pregnancy is a wild experience, filled with wonder and awe. It's a puzzling and perfect time watching the fascinating changes in your body.

If you're a mom, what was the funniest moment you experienced during pregnancy?

_____

_____

I (Nan) have never been pregnant. Both of our children are adopted. But I can speak to what it means to live in expectation of the arrival of a long-awaited child.

Wayne and I adopted Erin and Lena from China. From the moment we decided to do this, I was "pregnant" with joy! Every moment of every day in the whole process of endless paperwork, my thoughts were filled with anticipation of what my daughters would be like. I couldn't wait to put my arms around them. (Some mothers get stretch marks. I got paperwork.)

We adopted the girls four years apart. At this point, adoptions from China took eighteen months. Most moms have a pregnancy of nine months. Mine was more like the gestation period of an elephant!

The adoption process can best be described as an exercise in the loss of control. It seems that everyone but you has power in the situation. Each day as I waited to receive the picture of our baby and permission to leave the country to bring her home, I tried to do something to prepare for her arrival.

NESTING

I was in major nesting mode. I prepared their bedrooms, choosing wall color, fabric for curtains, painting bookshelves and filling them with children's classics. I dreamed of reading them books and rocking them to sleep. I started their baby books before I even met them and filled the pages with notes from friends who anticipated their arrival almost as much as I did.

I began to pray for my child, telling God that he simply **had** to protect them until I got to China! I could not wait for the "joy that was set before me" to be in my arms at last. It was a blessed time of waiting that God used to birth something new in me before I became a mother.

Describe your nesting process:

_____

_____

PONDER THE "TIP OF THE ICEBERG:" MARY'S BIRTH STORY

Moms like to compare notes with our birth stories. None of us has one that holds a candle to Mary's.

What were the first signs of your baby's arrival?

_____

_____

The next time we read about Mary, she's in those ready-to-drop days of her third trimester. No Bethlehem General Hospital with nurses stood by. Epidurals wouldn't come along until centuries later. There would be no luxury hotel, mid-wife or soft bed waiting for her tired body. Our nine-month-pregnant heroine is traveling on a donkey en route to Bethlehem. She and Joseph must register for the census in his ancestral hometown. Caesar Augustus has mandated this registry for the entire civilized world.

Did Mary and Joseph know they would fulfill a major prophecy as they arrived in Bethlehem?

Read Micah 5:2-3.

> "'But as for you, Bethlehem Ephrathah,
> Too little to be among the clans of Judah,
> From you One will go forth for me to be ruler in Israel.
> His goings forth are from long ago,
> From the days of eternity.'"
> Therefore he will give them up until the time
> When she who is in labor has borne a child.
> Then the remainder of his brethren
> Will return to the sons of Israel" (NASB).

O Little Town indeed!

Western culture often presents the birth of Jesus like a "once-upon-a-time" scene from a fairy tale. How dismissive this is of the human experience involved in his birth. It's maddening to see pageants at Christmas and Easter where Mary looks like she stepped out of beauty salon, perfectly put together, calm and serene as she holds her newborn babe. On stage, the set involves a cute little stable. Joseph smiles and shepherds and wise men bow and gesture like they were overacting in a Disney drama.

Nothing could be further from biblical truth.

Mary was nine months pregnant when Rome required that she and Joseph travel seven to ten days to Bethlehem. Caesar Augustus mandated this census be taken for the entire civilized world. The census would facilitate the payment of taxes.

How would you respond to a government demand for a census and taxes and an ungodly long trip when you needed to be home and close to your mother?

_____

_____

Most of us would have risked facing a little jail time. What courage it took for these two newlyweds to make this journey. We can have a little fun, imagining how Joseph attempted to put a positive spin on things. *Come on honey. I know this trip is coming at a bad time, but keep a positive attitude. (Mary might have wanted to knock his attitude into next week.) Let's get packing and get this over with. We'll get you back to Nazareth before... before... well, who knows, maybe we have a major prophecy to fulfill!*

How did Mary pack for this trip? Did she tuck baby clothes into her bag? Did she feel the onset of early symptoms?

Maybe you've pictured Mary as some kind of super-spiritual wonder woman with a close walk with God. She was a remarkable teen-ager. But Mary was just like you and me. She had to trust God to be in every detail of her life and help her walk it out. Mary would most likely be the first to tell us she didn't do it perfectly. She would encourage us to keep on keeping on even when we're not sure how things will unfold.

Read Luke 2:6-7.

No doctor would be attending, ready for any emergency. And no Apgar test would measure the baby's aptitude and potential! (Thank goodness! Can you imagine trying to "measure" God's potential?) When Mary dilated to ten centimeters she was laying on the dirty floor of a cave.

"Along caravan routes there were some public buildings in New Testament times, where travelers could stop for the night with their animals and find safety with others. In some cases, these inns had a lower courtyard for the animals, with upper space for the travelers to sleep, certainly not with a private room, bath and restaurant! In some places, inns were little more than guest rooms adjoining a private home. Such may have been the inn of Bethlehem."[60]

And more:

"Jesus was probably born in a stable or in a cave that served as one. The inn was most likely a reception room in a private home or a space at a public shelter, not a large building with several individual rooms. The manger was probably a feeding through for animals." [61]

Thousands were in Bethlehem, the little city bursting at the seams with people who claimed it as their ancestral home. It is likely Joseph inquired at the door of whatever type of "inn" he found, desperate to find a private place for Mary. Every spare bed was taken and the upper floors were full of people. The only option was to stay on the first floor with the animals or in one of the stable/caves located in the field outside the city.

I (Bonnie) have been in this field, the one place between Jerusalem and Bethlehem where these caves are located. After walking in this field, I found spindly needles from the undergrowth stuck to my skin and clothes. Rocks and steep inclines made it difficult to find a clear path. I cannot fathom being in labor and navigating this terrain. Remove from your mind any image of Mary and Joseph finding a low rate room from a B.C. version of Motel 6. Mary climbed into a dark cave and gave birth to Jesus in a space used to house animals.

Did Mary think, "*This is not what I had in mind*" Or was she grateful at last to have a place to lie down, even if it meant sharing the space with some four-footed friends?

How would Mary respond to the second verse of "Away in A Manger?"

"The cattle are lowing, the poor baby wakes,
But little Lord Jesus no crying he makes...."

Ladies, what is the first thing we long to hear when a child is born?

_____

_____

Crying. Crying is a sign that the child's lungs are healthy and working fine. Crying is a baby's way to communicate:" I'm hungry, I'm sleepy, I'm wet, I want to be held." Jesus was born in a cave to a teen-age momma. We assume Joseph did the best he could to help Mary as she birthed her firstborn son and laid him in a manger used to hold cattle feed. Jesus was fully human and fully God. We can safely assume that Jesus was not silent on that night, lying in his makeshift crib by the cattle.

Let's make some personal application from Mary's birth story. She is a shining example of submission to the will of God. It meant some inconvenience to her, but she wanted to be the "handmaid" of the Lord.

What does the word "submission" mean to you?

_____

_____

Submission is an unpopular word and an even more unpopular lifestyle. Simply put, it is placing God's agenda ahead of our own.

Does it ever frustrate you that God does not ask your opinion on how to accomplish his purposes? We may say we're willing to be used by him. Are you willing for him to do things his way? How challenging is it to say, "Be it done unto me according to your will?"

_____

_____

We have it in our heads that submission to God will end up condemning us to a drab and colorless life full of hardship and rejection. With fearful hearts we whisper, "Not my will but thine be done" and wonder if we have signed up to live in a third-world country for the rest of our days. If we give over our Plan A, surely God will make sure we're on a foreign mission field, deprived of hot running water and a clean bathroom.

Let's go to the word and see what we can learn about God's plan for our lives.

Turn to Jeremiah 1:5.

How long did God know Jeremiah?

___

___

Now read Jeremiah 29:11-13.

What kind of plans does God have for you?

___

___

He has known you since before you were born. He knows your gifts, talents, and the desires of your heart. He is the One who put them there. If his plans are good and full of hope, then we can trust that his plans for each individual are based on how he designed us. He will place us where we feel energized by his will, not drained or depressed by it.

We've read **Ephesians 2:10** many times during our study.

Why were we created? When did God prepare the works we will walk into?

___

___

The word for workmanship is "poiema." It means a "handiwork or masterpiece." This word is the derivative for our word "poem." Girls, plainly put, we are God's poem! We are his masterpiece!

How does this make you feel?

___

___

Where do we keep the masterpieces in our homes? Where do we hang our most interesting family picture or place our most treasured sculptures? In the basement? No! We put them in a prominent place for all to see and admire. This is what God does with us. He puts us on display. He proclaims to all in the universe that he made us, that he adores us and that we give him great pleasure.

Who or what is a masterpiece in your life?

___

___

Our children, our husbands, our friends are masterpieces made by God and given to us. He puts them on display in our lives to prove his love. If each and every one of us is a masterpiece designed by God for good works since before he created the world, then can we trust him to work everything out in our lives, even in the daily grind?

What if we lose our jobs? What if we lose our spouses through death or divorce? What if a child breaks our hearts?

Write a few "what if"s of your own:

___

___

As we walk through uncertain seasons of life, his promises never will change. His love never leaves us. He hears our cries and his faithfulness is ever-present. Our pain is never wasted in God's economy. He is passionate about his family portrait. God knows who is missing from the picture. He knows each member of his masterpiece and uses us to bring it to completion.

Mary was called to give birth to God's Son. She accepted the unknown and believed his promises would stand. She could only see the "now." Do you think Mary wondered why God allowed such difficult surroundings for his Son's birth?

___

___

One of the treasures of Mary's heart was the Word of God. She sang of God's faithfulness and her gratitude at being chosen for carrying and birthing his Son. As the birth pangs became real, perhaps she silently recalled parts of the Psalms between contractions.

Read Psalm 118:14-17.

How would these verses coach Mary through her pain?

___

___

On this night, she is her own OB/GYN. There are moments during childbirth when a woman feels like she may die in the process. In Mary's day it would have been common for a mother to die giving birth. Here she finds herself utterly dependent on God for her life and that of his child.

Obviously God's favor was with his lovely masterpiece named Mary. He knit her together with strength and a faith-filled heart. Even if Mary never dreamed her baby would be born into the world this way, we still think she trusted Yahweh to keep his promise to her. She would give birth to this child in a field, a cave, or on a street corner. With her very last push, she birthed the living promise of God.

Read Luke 2:7 and describe what Mary does with her newborn:

_____

_____

She swaddled Jesus in strips of cloth and laid him in a feeding trough, possibly made of stone. Ironically, the same type of cloth was used to wrap the dead for burial. Mary then may have fallen back into her makeshift bed of straw and drifted into an exhausted sleep.

What prophecy did she fulfill in **Luke 2:12**? How would the shepherds recognize the newborn Messiah?

_____

_____

Even in the smallest details, God is working out his plan.

By wrapping her newborn securely and putting him in the "crib," Mary was fulfilling the plans of God.

Have you ever felt this way while diapering a baby? Has it felt like holy work?

Not likely. If this one moment in Scripture teaches us anything, it is that we must never disdain the small things of each day. Changing diapers and finding pacifiers, washing "blankies," cleaning toilets, and wiping dirty noses can be sanctified work: holy, full of purpose and used by God to do the impossible. Mothers of young children, don't ever let our culture tell you that what you're doing is insignificant. The next time someone asks "What do you do?" tell them you're in a full-time business position with eternal benefits. You are accomplishing the purposes of God.

MORE FROM THE TIP OF THE ICEBERG

What about the shepherds who received a special visit on the night of Jesus' birth? Shepherds were low on the totem pole of society. They were usually the youngest men in a family, sent out to tend the sheep in the fields, doing the dirty work. Some were known for being liars, thieves, and pickpockets. They were not allowed to give testimony in a court of law. They were perpetually unclean and required to go through a weeklong ceremonial cleansing process before they could enter the temple courts. Israel had waited for 400 years to hear more from God about the promised Messiah, their king and ruler from the line of David. At last the skies broke apart with the news that the Child had been born. The news didn't come to the rabbis or leaders of the Sanhedrin. God chose a group of unclean, lowly shepherds to be his audience that night.

Read Luke 2:8-17.

Where were the shepherds?

_____

Who appeared to them in **verse 9**?

_____

How did they respond?

_____

What news did they receive and what did they see?

_____

How would they recognize baby Jesus?

_____

_____

This unlikely group was visited by angels who told them to look for their Savior in the ordinary. Nothing glamorous here. Nothing of notoriety or fame. Nothing the world would esteem. The kind of things that a simple group of shepherds would understand: Go to a tiny town. Go to a place where animals are kept. Look for a baby wrapped in swaddling clothes lying in a feed trough. The shepherds could have ignored the proclamation, deciding it didn't fit their idea of how the Messiah would enter the world. Instead, they embraced it and hurried to be a part of the adventure.

As for Joseph and Mary, would they have chosen the lowest members of the society to be their first visitors?

LUKE'S INTERVIEW WITH MARY: DAY TWO

Luke: Mary, when you and Joseph saw shepherds approaching, were you afraid? There was the possibility you could have been mugged.

Mary: Honestly I'd been through so much I didn't know what to expect next. A visit from the archangel Gabriel, then being the focus of ridicule and town gossip about being pregnant out of wedlock. Traveling so far, giving birth in a dirty cave to God's Son… then a visit from a group of shepherds. It was quite a lot for a young teen-age girl to absorb!

Luke: What was your first thought when shepherds were the first to visit?

Mary: King David was once a young shepherd boy, the least-likely person to become the most famous king of Israel. So who was I to judge? Jesus often doesn't fit into our preconceived plans of how we think things should be. He didn't arrive in a way any of us imagined. He didn't then and he doesn't now. If we cling to our own agenda, we could miss him.

Luke: Please go on.

Mary: Nothing was predictable. I know it sounds simplistic, but I chose to believe that no matter what happened, God would be with us.

Luke: How would you characterize your conversation with the shepherds?

Mary: In a word, delightful! It was very comforting to talk to someone else who had seen angels. Joseph and I were thrilled by their excitement. Of course, all the talk and noise woke the baby.

Read Luke 2:17-20.

The shepherds lost no time in telling everyone who was born! By appearing to the lowliest of men with the loftiest news, God continued a pattern that marked the life of his Son. Jesus was born to a young girl from nowhere. He would choose nobody fishermen to be his disciples. He would touch the unclean and talk to the ungodly. A Samaritan woman becomes an enthusiastic missionary. Mary Magdalene takes the news of his resurrection to his followers. The last become first, the slave walks free, the poor receives riches, and sinners are given a clean slate in his kingdom.

Mary and Joseph receive other visitors early in the life of Christ. Wise men spend years tracking the new star they've seen in the heavens. They would bring lavish gifts and warnings of political unrest. All of these experiences would be quietly, carefully stored up in the heart of Mary.

Eventually Joseph took Mary and baby Jesus back to their home town in Nazareth. Jesus would have been raised in the traditions of Jewish law. The anonymous years of Christ were spent in this small town in Galilee where everybody knew each other's business.

Read Matthew 13:55-56.

How did the hometown Nazarenes categorize Jesus?

_____

_____

How many other children were in his family?

_____

_____

Mary was one busy mother and wife. She had five sons and at least two daughters (Matt. 13:55-56). She and Joseph stayed in Nazareth, despite the gossip about the mysterious birth of her firstborn. Joseph was a carpenter, working hard for the money while Mary kept the home fires burning. Jesus may have been God's only Son, but he was not Mary's only child. He grew up in a large family and exhibited no signs of being spoiled or doted upon. His "homies" knew him as a carpenter's son.

Joseph would have taken a large role in the religious upbringing of Jesus. It would be the father's responsibility to teach Jesus to read Scripture by the age of five. When Jesus was six, his culture's version of kindergarten would be a local school taught by a rabbi. Young men were trained to memorize passages from the Torah as they grew into manhood. During these formative years, Jesus immersed himself in the study of God's laws, and by the age of twelve we see evidence of his maturity.

Read Luke 2:40.

How does this verse describe him?

_____

_____

What conclusions can we draw about his early years of life?

_____

_____

As the years passed, Mary watched her eldest son grow into a compelling, passionate, brilliant young man. Still, the Word tells us that she did not fully understand his destiny.

Read Luke 2:41-52.

Where did the family travel and why?

_____

How old was Jesus?

_____

What happened?

_____

_____

When my (Bonnie's) son Graham was about six years old, one day he decided to play hide-and-seek while we were in a large department store at a local mall. He managed to get away from me and crawled into a circular clothes rack, sitting in the middle of it where no one could see him. I quickly noticed Graham was missing and my heart fell into my stomach. I began calling his name over and over again and the clerk alerted security. They shut the store doors and everyone began searching for Graham, who sat silently hidden by the long dresses around him. Finally he came out from under the clothes rack and looked up with a "Gotcha!" smile. Immediately I burst into tears of relief and elation. Part of me wanted to pop his behind but gratitude won the moment. I grabbed his sweet body and held him close, crying and thanking God he was safe.

Have you had a similar experience? How did you physically feel when you couldn't find your child?

_____

_____

While traveling home, at some point, the head count revealed a missing Jesus. After three long days of searching for him, all the way back to Jerusalem, where was Jesus found?

_____

What was he doing?

What did Mary say to him?

The Amplified Bible describes Mary's emotional outburst. "Your father and I have been anxiously looking for you (distressed and tormented)" (Luke 2:48).

How did Jesus answer his mother?

LUKE'S INTERVIEW WITH MARY: DAY THREE

Luke: Mary, talk to us about the childhood of Jesus. For example, tell us about his Bar Mitzvah. Describe the time you and Joseph could not find Jesus after the Passover Feast in Jerusalem.

Mary: Losing Jesus.... Oh, I'll need a minute to talk about that.

Luke: Then let's back up a few years. Was Jesus a good student?

Mary: Of course he was! Smartest boy in his class. He began studying the law at our local synagogue when he was just five like every good Jewish boy. He was a very quick study and couldn't get enough of the psalms and the prophets. He particularly liked reading the passages that spoke directly about him.

Luke: Was he an easy child to raise?

Mary: Easy? That's not the word I would choose. Challenging? Yes. Interesting? Daily. He was continually surprising me, saying something that was funny or clever. And he loved to tell parables. Started working on those early! Would you like to see his baby book? I wrote down every sweet thing he ever said.

Luke: And his Bar Mitzvah?

Mary: Oh yes. I remember Jesus' twelfth birthday in particular. I wove him his first prayer shawl and gave it to him that day. We celebrated his entrance into manhood. He wore it to Passover that year.... Oh, my.

Luke: Talk about the trip when Jesus stayed behind at the temple. I don't mean to be rude, but how could you not know where he was when you started home?

Mary: Joseph and I were proud to show off our firstborn that year. As usual, nothing happened as we expected. We traveled in a caravan with friends and relatives from Nazareth. The women and children walked in the front to set the pace. The men and young boys followed behind. Jesus always liked to go back and forth between the groups. He was very social that way. I assumed he was with Joseph and Joseph thought he was with me. Easy mistake to make, don't you think?

Luke: What happened when you realized he was missing?

Mary: Do you see this gray hair? That experience took ten years off my life! Sometimes I still have nightmares of pushing my way through crowds and calling his name. It was three days of sheer panic and sleepless nights before we found him. Three days of feeling utterly helpless. Three days later, there sits my Jesus calmly talking with the older rabbis in the temple, as if he were at home!

Luke: I've recorded your response as being "amazed." Would you mind if I elaborated on this a bit?

Mary: Be my guest.

Luke: I'll probably use the Greek word "ekpletto." This means "to strike out, force out by a blow, but found only in the sense of knocking one out of his senses or self-possession, to strike with astonishment, terror, admiration." Would this accurately describe your amazement?

Mary: You took the words right out of my mouth! You could have knocked me over with a feather. I was breathless with relief, angry… and, yes… proud to see my twelve-year-old Jesus engaged in a lively discussion with a group of teachers.

Luke: He was not arguing with them.

Mary: No, no. The arguments would come later. From their side. He was listening to them talk and asking questions. They were drawn in by how much he knew about the law and of the wisdom of his inquiries. Jesus was brilliant with the way he asked questions.

Luke: Did his answer to your question seem strange?

Mary: Looking back now, I realize that of course this was exactly where he was supposed to be. But at the time it felt so disrespectful for him to scare his father and me so thoughtlessly. It wasn't like him. It was a hellish experience searching three days for my child. Added to this was the terrible guilt we felt.

Luke: What do you mean?

Mary: Joseph and I kept saying, "Oh no! What are we going to do? We've lost the Son of God!"

Luke: As if such a thing was possible!

Mary: Exactly. But I'm a momma. He is my son. We had our moments of just being a normal family, you know. I expected Jesus to rush into my arms with tears of gratitude and relief. Instead he asked, "Why were you looking for me?" I was hurt… and confused. As he grew up, being hurt by his answers became a part of my life. Are you going to put that part in?

Luke: Not without your permission.

Mary: I don't want it to sound like I was a bad mother for losing him for three days, or misrepresented in how I felt. I honestly didn't understand some of his responses until later.

Luke: Did you reprimand him?

Mary: Of course I did! But I could never be too hard on him. He was such a good boy. I was astonished at his wisdom. One might say Jesus was the only teen-ager in the world who really did know more than his parents! I wasn't ready for him to not need me anymore.

Luke: He did return home with you.

Mary: Yes, he was very obedient. I've thought about this moment quite a lot. It was hard at the time. But in looking back, I see what Jesus did that day was one step toward preparing me for another Passover that would come twenty-one years later.

It's going to be sheer delight to interview Mary in heaven! This moment of parenting for Mary was very strange indeed. Jesus expresses surprise that his parents hadn't anticipated he would be busy with the affairs of his heavenly Father. Talk about a precocious child! There was much to ponder and mull over through the years. Did time begin to muddy the clarity of her calling and dim the memory of Gabriel's visit? Or did the words of Simeon haunt her?

Read Luke 2:25-35.

In **verses 34-35**, what did Simeon say would happen in the future?

_____

_____

In **verse 33**, how did Mary and Joseph react to Simeon's response to their infant son?

_____

_____

Up until this day there had been visitors with gifts, messages from angels, and prophesies that focused mainly on the power and glory of Jesus. Simeon's words must have sent chills up and down Mary's spine.

The prophesy of **verse 34** is spoken directly to Mary. It's almost as if Simeon looked directly into her eyes. His other prophecies over Jesus were directed to God. Then Simeon turns to Mary and speaks of the future enemies of her Son. He says, "A sword will pierce even your own soul." *Nelson's New Illustrated Bible* Commentary says, "This image is of a broad sword striking Mary."[62]

Unknowingly, Mary signed up to share the agony and the ecstasy of Jesus' suffering when she accepted God's call to be his mother. She would endure tormenting days and nights, and carry a cross no other mother has carried before or since. The word tells us she struggled with understanding the path Jesus would take. His disciples didn't understand either. There was no way for them to see the complete picture of the joy Jesus saw before him. Mary was a woman who chose to believe God would be faithful. But her soul was pierced through in the process.

What can we surmise about the love Jesus showed to Mary from **Luke 2:51-52**?

_____

_____

A heart only can break if it has first loved deeply. Jesus loved his parents and honored them with obedience. Mary loved her firstborn son as deeply as any mother can love a child. Their hearts were bonded by the Holy Spirit in her womb and this bond was unbreakable as he grew into manhood.

If we truly love our children, what are parents called to do as they reach adulthood?

_____

_____

We must love our adult children enough to let them go. If they fall down, we let them fall. We always are close by to comfort them. The umbilical cord is never completely severed. But as our children grow up, they have to make their own choices. When they are bruised and battered in the process, we trust God's grace to meet them where they are. The only way any of us mature is by walking out our lives humbly before him. Easier said than done!

Mary was a human momma. Letting go of this firstborn special child from heaven must have been extremely difficult. She struggled with the independence of her adult son.

Take a look at another delicious moment in Mary's career as the mother of Jesus. In this snapshot we smile at mother Mary who still wants to be in charge.

Read John 2:1-11.

What is the occasion?

_____

_____

Who was invited?

_____

_____

What was the problem?

_____

_____

What was **Mary's** solution to the problem?

_____

_____

What did Mary tell the servants?

_____

_____

According to **verse 11**, what was the significance of this miracle?

_____

_____

Here we see Jesus doing what so many of us have done: attending a wedding! This puts flesh and bone on the Son of God. He wasn't too busy to attend the wedding of his friends. He was not a recluse but chose to take part in social situations. This should comfort us and cause us to love Jesus more than ever. In our most common experiences, Emmanuel, God himself, is with us.

We don't know who this couple was, but they must have been fairly close to Jesus and his family because Jesus was invited along with six disciples who were following him at the time. Some scholars say the bride was probably related to Mary.

What was a wedding in Cana of Galilee like at this point in history? A closer look reveals how different their customs were from ours and just how high the stakes were when the bride and groom ran out of wine.

Weddings for a virgin began on a Wednesday and lasted seven days. Widows were married on a Thursday. (If you were not a virgin or a widow, you received no celebration.)

Stop here and imagine how Mary felt about weddings. After her betrothal she became pregnant. She had no way of proving she was still a virgin. As rumors spread, her wedding plans would drastically change. There would be little or no public celebration.

Did Mary ever attend a wedding without wanting it be everything hers was not? Does this help us understand her insistence that Jesus act to make things right? Your thoughts:

_____

_____

Mary never had the following experience. During a wedding week, the bride and groom wore crowns and were treated like a king and queen. The family opened their house to friends and relatives.

A SUGGESTED WEDDING MENU FROM THE GOOD BOOK COOKBOOK

Wedding challah
Endive salad with olives and clementines
Dolmas (stuffed grapevine leaves)
Baked sardines in tahini sauce
Roast duck with mulberries and horseradish
Rack of lamb with spicy mint sauce
Sweet millet fruit balls
Almond cookies
Platter of melon balls, raisins, dates, and candied Jordan almonds
Wine, wine, and more wine!

We think a Western wedding is expensive! Jesus came from a poor family. Since the wedding party was likely friends of his family, their wedding budget may have been stretched to the max. There would have been two beverages of choice: water and wine. It was typical to dilute the wine, seven parts water to one part wine to ensure the supply would last.

During a weeklong celebration, the obligation to "wine and dine" was a priority. There would have been relatives from both sides to entertain. It may have been a few days into the celebration when Jesus and his disciples arrived because the host had run out of wine. Female relatives were expected to help in the kitchen (some things never change) so Mary was right in the middle of things when the wine shortage was discovered.

Did she suggest they call the local liquor store and buy some more cases of wine? No. She goes to her son and tells him what has happened. She has not yet seen him work a miracle, but chooses this moment to expect one.

Why do you think Mary felt Jesus could remedy the situation?

_____

_____

In the East, good hospitality was important, especially at a wedding. It would be highly embarrassing if you fell short of your duties as a host. You might run low on finger foods, but never wine. Did Mary tap Jesus on the shoulder while he was dancing and pull him off to the side? "Son, we've got a problem in the kitchen!"

Her faith in him is absolute, even at this early stage in his public ministry. She is content to simply tell him about the problem and wait for his solution.

What does Jesus call Mary when he answers her request?

"Woman." To our modern way of thinking this may sound harsh, but in his day it was a term of endearment, more like saying, "Dear woman" or "Dear Ma'am." He says, "Dear woman, what is that to you and me? My hour to act is not come yet."

Jesus responded to his mother as the Messiah, not a son. He was now working on his heavenly Father's timetable when it came to the revelation of his power. Yet something in the tone of his voice and the expression in his eyes must have reassured Mary. Jesus would not let this young couple be publicly humiliated on their wedding day. Mary's wedding day was riddled with humiliation and questions. Perhaps Jesus had heard Mary speak of this day with Joseph from time to time. Did her eyes move his heart to compassion? "Son, do something, anything to make this wedding celebration a sweet one."

Mary goes back into the kitchen, confident that God was moving in her son. She tells the servants to do whatever Jesus asks.

LUKE'S INTERVIEW WITH MARY: DAY FOUR

Luke: Mary, walk us through what happened when Jesus saved the day at the wedding celebration in Cana.

Mary: Oh, the servants were baffled by what Jesus asked them to do. Six stone jars had to be filled with water. Each jar held ten to twenty gallons. Normally they were used for ceremonial cleansing. You should have seen the frowns on their faces when they were told to fill them. One man muttered, "What's this? We don't need water, we need wine!"

Luke: What convinced them to obey Jesus?

Mary: Jesus had such a commanding yet gentle way with everyone. They did what he asked. What did they have to lose? The head waiter nearly jumped for joy when he saw the water had turned to the finest wine!

Luke: What treasure could our readers store up after reading about this miracle?

Mary: There are many situations in life that cause us to think our world is falling apart. Like the host of this wedding, we have a fear of being humiliated. It's comforting to know that even if your needs might seem unimportant on a grand scale, they are very important to Jesus. Bring anything and everything to him. In his own way and time, he always will answer your prayers.

This miraculous provision took place because of obedience. The servants obeyed Jesus even though they didn't know why, or how filling the jars with water would help the situation. A case could be made that Mary's faith in Jesus prompted him to act even before his hour of public declaration. Her faith activated something in the heavenly realms that caused the Son of God to answer her request. It's also a show of the tremendous respect and love of Jesus for his mother.

Not long after this, what does Jesus tell his disciples in **Mark 9:23**?

_____

_____

All things are possible with God. Do you and I have the courage of Mary to ask and believe even in the oddest situations?

The miracle at Cana flew under the radar of public knowledge. Only Mary, the wedding servants, and Jesus' disciples knew what had happened. Yet this first miracle from the Son of God represented the purpose of his life.

"Jesus' miracle of turning water into wine was loaded with implications. For Jews, wine represented life and abundance. No proper wedding would be without it. Wine symbolized the life of the party and the expectation of a good life to come for the newlyweds.... Just as the young couple prepared to launch a new life, the unthinkable happened: They ran out of wine. The party immediately began to wind down.

But Jesus used the moment to reveal to his followers something of who he was. By producing wine from water, he astounded his disciples and encouraged their faith. ... The product was not merely wine, but the best wine. In the same way Jesus was the new wine bringing abundant life to Judaism, which, like the wedding, had run out of life and become spiritually empty."[63]

We would add that Jesus is the life of the party! It is significant that his first miracle took place at a wedding, an occasion for joy. He came to earth and betrothed unto himself a virgin bride: you and me!

Over the next months and years, his public ministry unfolded. There would be times when his responses to Mary and his family were more complicated. Mary's heart would be pricked here and there as she watched the mission of Jesus lead him farther away from home and into the depths of his calling. How do we feel when our children don't need us in the ways they used to and begin to launch out and away from us? It's what we want for them, but it doesn't happen without a little pain.

There would be many other priceless memories of joy to balance out the times she could not understand.

Early in his ministry, Jesus was baptized by his cousin John in the river Jordan. He was tempted by Satan in the wilderness. He came out of this critical forty days filled with the Holy Spirit. During this time, he was embraced by many. For Mary this would have been a thrilling time to be his mother. His fame spread throughout Galilee and surrounding regions.

Read Luke 4:14-30.

Where is Jesus teaching?

___

Who is his audience?

___

By citing Isaiah 61, Jesus is claiming to be a royal figure and to have a prophetic mission. Mary watched her son's public ministry grow by leaps and bounds. He was the talk of Judea. He was the man of the hour.

LUKE'S INTERVIEW WITH MARY, DAY FIVE

Luke: Mary, describe one of the most pivotal days in your son's ministry.

Mary: The Sabbath when Jesus opened the Scriptures to read in our local synagogue was quite an unforgettable day! I could hardly breathe as Jesus read the words of Isaiah 61.

Luke: To remind our readers, you were sitting in the women's section of the synagogue along the outside walls of the room.

Mary: Yes, I was sitting with the other women. But I could see my son take the scroll and open it. His eyes were filled with so much emotion. They were riveting eyes, the eyes of my Jesus. There's no way to describe their color and the power they contained. When he looked straight into your eyes, the most liberating, beautiful feeling washed over you and I just....

Luke: Mary, excuse me for interrupting, but I'd love to hear the rest of what happened that day in the synagogue.

Mary: Oh, yes. Forgive me. There are so many things about my son that no one but me will ever know. Of course those who believe in him know. Anyway, on that morning the people in the synagogue were astonished at his reading. He read the very passage in Isaiah that described the coming of God's Son. After reading, he closed the scroll, sat down, and looked out at the people who had seen him grow up, the ones that had known him all his life. He said, "Today this Scripture is being fulfilled while you are present and hearing." The reaction to him at that moment was....well...

Luke: Mary, what are you remembering?

Mary: Don't you see? Jesus told our hometown synogogue that he was the one they had waited for! He wanted to heal the broken-hearted, to save the lost, to gather them under his wing as a mother holds her own... as I held him as a baby.... He sometimes wept because this calling of love consumed him.

Luke: And?

Mary: That day marked the beginning of watching people turn on my son. It was the first of many times I heard him mocked, disgraced, accused of being an illegitimate child, lied about, rejected....And at the last... the arguments turned to bitter rage.

Now read Luke 8:19-21.

What does Mary want?

___

___

How does Jesus answer?

___

___

Luke: Mary, describe for our readers how you felt when Jesus left home and began his public ministry.

Mary: Looking back now, I realize our family didn't understand much of what he was doing at the time. There was a lot of friction at home when Jesus left us and it broke my heart to see our family separated by his ministry.

Luke: Please go on.

Mary: As you know, in our culture, the eldest son is the one expected to become the head of the house when the father has died. Joseph was such a great husband and it was extremely hard to lose him. I became a widow and there were so many responsibilities.

Luke: Feel free to be specific.

Mary: We had a family business to look after. There were my daughters' dowries to be negotiated. It was strange to have Jesus leave us when he did. And the men he chose for his inner circle... they were... fishermen.... Quite a rowdy bunch.

Luke: Yes, Jesus had a salty group of disciples!

Mary: I had hoped one of his brothers would be included in his work. And the biggest shock was that John the Baptist, who had prepared Israel for his coming, was beheaded in a prison. It was so baffling.... Life and death all spiraling together at once.

Luke: You always were there for Jesus. What kept you going through the difficult days when you heard the religious leaders insulting your son?

Mary: I knew who he was. I knew he was part of something much bigger than Joseph or I, or his brothers and sisters could comprehend. There were priceless moments of utter joy, like hearing my son teach! Parables, stories that turned lives upside-down and right side up! He set people free from the bondage of the law. He spoke words of life into the souls of thousands of our people.

Luke: Jesus was so popular with the crowds. How did you manage to have time with your son privately?

Mary: I did what I could. But his ministry wasn't about me. It was about his work. I tried to make my peace with what I saw happening. His love for me was never a question. I missed him terribly, but he knew I was close by.

Luke: Did you keep a record of his miracles?

Mary: There were too many to write down. But there's nothing like watching your son touch a blind man's eyes and have him see, or heal the lame, the lepers, the unclean. And oh, how he healed women! Jesus forever changed the lives of women, you know.

Luke: Anything more you would like to share?

Mary: Dr. Luke, when your book is published, make sure people know it's not enough just to know stories about Jesus. They need to know Him.

Luke: I promise I will do what you ask.

Mary: Please use my memories to guide them to Him. Once they know Him, they will begin to store up priceless memories of their own.

Mary saw her son grow from being a powerful teacher to a man who claimed to be the Son of God. More than anyone alive, she knew this to be true. Mary received the first eyewitness newsflash from heaven at his conception. Now she watched the impact of this revelation. The secret was out: Her son boldly taught that he was the way, truth and life. When one saw him, one saw his Father: God. Jesus held back nothing and offered everything. The baby Mary carried, the child she raised, the son she watched sleep at night, the man who grew into favor and fame, was at last stepping into the full calling for which he was born.

As his mother, Mary would have the primal, maternal instinct of protection. What happened next would be out of her control.

"We are not necessarily doubting that God will do the best for us; we are wondering how painful the best will turn out to be."[64]

TODAY'S DATE: _____

YOUR HEADLINE:
_____
_____

Week Eight
BREAKING NEWS

Calgary Chronicles

PILATE ORDERS EXECUTION OF NAZARENE TEACHER
Shocking Release of Barabbas

Calgary Chronicles is the first to report that Jesus of Nazareth is scheduled to be executed this morning outside the city of Jerusalem.

Early in the morning hours, the beloved teacher was arrested and tried for high treason. Pilate, caught in the political crosshairs of the Sanhedrin's demands for his death, has yielded a sentence of death by crucifixion.

In one last effort to spare Jesus' life, Pilate offered a prisoner swap. This is Rome's customary olive branch of peace offered during the Jewish Passover celebration.

Barabbas, a known murderer, was brought with Jesus before the crowd outside Pilate's court sometime after sunrise. Pilate's face went pale when the crowd unexpectedly demanded the release of Barabbas and shouted for the crucifixion of Jesus.

"I wash my hands of this man's blood!" Pilate announced. "I can find no wrong in him!" He washed his hands before the crowd and retreated into his offices.

Jesus is presently being flogged by Roman guards. His followers have scattered in the chaos surrounding his arrest. Two unnamed thieves are to be crucified with Jesus this morning.

With confusion and controversy swirling around his execution, it's sure to be one for the history books.

TODAY'S HEROINE:
Mary, part three

"To say that God is a mystery is to say that you can never nail him down. Even on Christ the nails proved ultimately ineffective." Frederick Buechner [65]

No mother wants to outlive her child. In this chapter our heroine has the full thrust of the sword pierce her heart. Mary now endures the torturous, public murder of her son.

The young teen-age mother whose spirit rejoiced with elation at the birth of Jesus now faces the brutal agony of watching him die. Could she possibly have known her son's calling would one day lead to death by crucifixion?

Could God himself have known the price of watching his heart nailed to a cross?

Ponder Revelation 13:8.

Before the foundations of the world God knew exactly when and where Jesus would be crucified. God knew the price. Jesus embraced the call. The Holy Spirit ensured the strength.

"Emmanuel would stand at the crossroads of life and death, and make a choice. The author knows well the weight of that decision. He pauses as he writes the page of his own pain. He could stop. Even the author has a choice. But how can love not love? And so the author completes the story. He drives the spike in the flesh and rolls the stone over the grave." [66]

Mary had no advantage of hindsight. She was simply a mother watching every dream she had for God's Son nailed to a cross.

What were Mary's dreams for Jesus?

Ponder the list below.

Dreams for his life to be long, God-centered, and full of glory.

Dreams of his marriage, for a godly daughter-in-law, and grandchildren. Would Gabriel appear again to describe the birth of the seed of God's Son? How would his children further the work of his kingdom? What joy would Mary feel holding the children of the Son of God in her arms as a grandmother?

Dreams of his glorious calling. The Messiah would restore Israel's hope. Jesus would usher in a new season.

Dreams that his kingdom would be strong and received with gratitude and celebration.

What are some of the dreams you have for your family, children or grandchildren?

_____

_____

Mary knew that Jesus was the Promised Child from heaven. She knew God had a mighty mission in bringing his Son to earth. She dreamed big dreams for her miraculous son. Never in her worst nightmare would she have pictured a torturous murder.

Only a week earlier, Jesus had ridden into Jerusalem for the Passover celebration to the cheers of his people: "Jesus, son of David! Hosanna to the king of the Jews!" Crowds came to touch his robe, to hear him teach, to hang on his every word. Now he hangs naked. God nailed down.

As she stands at the foot of his cross, Mary represents every woman who has experienced loss. Losing something or someone we love is our greatest heartache on earth. We often are surprised by loss and can react with shock, guilt, and anger.

The flesh wars with the spirit. We were not made for a world in which the innocent suffer and die. Often we wonder why God allows the levels of pain we see around us. Will the sadness ever go away? Will fear overwhelm our hearts? Will our faith survive?

Do you see any of your losses in the list below?

A relationship breakup
Loss of health
Loss of a job
Loss of financial stability
A miscarriage
Divorce
Death of a pet
Loss of a cherished dream
A loved one's serious illness
Loss of safety after a trauma

What has been the deepest loss in your life?

_____

_____

All losses are valid, and pain is pain. Yet Mary's heart suffered a loss like no mother before or since.

THE TRIAL AND SENTENCING OF JESUS

In **John 18:1-4**, where is Jesus?

_____

How did Judas know where to find him?

_____

_____

Who was with Judas?

_____

How did Jesus react in **verse 4**?

_____

_____

Jesus left the Passover dinner with his best friends and walked through the Kidron Valley to one of his favorite places, the Garden of Gethsemane. Knowing full well "all that was about to befall him" (Amplified Bible), **Jesus walked out to engage** Judas and the men who would put him on trial. Mary raised a son who was fearless, strong, and confident.

In **John 18:4-8**, Jesus replies three times with what three words?

_____   _____   _____

Fully human and full of God's spirit, Jesus repeats the words, "I am he." God spoke these words first to Moses in **Exodus 3:14.**

The power of this proclamation knocks the guards to the ground.

Does Jesus try to escape? Does he use his power to stop his arrest? He knows who he is and that his hour has come. He never loses sight of his purpose. Jesus **allows** the men to bind and arrest him. Thus begins the mockery of a trial and sentencing of Jesus to death by crucifixion.

In **Mark 14:56**, how is the trial of Jesus described?

_____

Jesus was taken from one ruler to the other, from Herod to Pilate to the leaders of the Sanhedrin, raked over the coals during the process of six different trials. All of this happened during the early hours of Friday morning, where at some point Mary would have been alerted about the fate of her son.

Mary knew the history of Jewish law. Her son had memorized the book of Deuteronomy and knew the procedure for a fair and godly trial.

According to **Deuteronomy 19:15**, no one could be put to death unless what conditions were met?

_____

_____

Over the months leading up to this Passover, Mary would be aware of the rising hatred for Jesus among certain powerful men in Jewish leadership. Her son's teachings and public healings convinced many of what she had always known. Jesus was not only her son, but also the Son of God. Yet why did his great love incite such bitter hatred?

Read John 11:43-46.

What miracle happened here?
_____
_____

Verse 45 records what response from many?
_____
_____

Read John 11:47-48.

Who met and what did they decide?
_____
_____

Finish reading John 11:53-57.

From this day on, what was the focus?
_____
_____

What did Jesus do differently?
_____
_____

What order was given in **verse 57**?
_____

Did Mary wonder: *Son, could you not have remained quiet during the Passover? You knew the leaders were plotting to kill you. Why didn't you put up a fight? You were raised in a carpenter's shop. You are strong and fit. Why did you go out to meet these men? Why did you allow Judas to stay in your inner circle? How could this happen?*

Consider the following laws that were broken in order to arrest, try, and nail Jesus to a cross:

An arrest could not be made at night.

The time and date of trial could not legally take place on the eve of the Sabbath.

The Sanhedrin was without authority to instigate charges. Its only purpose was to investigate, never formulate charges.

The court did not meet in a regular meeting place (during daylight hours) which was required by Jewish law.

Jesus was permitted no legal defense.

The Jews could not impose a death sentence without Rome's permission.

"The Jewish method of execution was stoning. However, Jesus had already indicated that he would be crucified....The Jewish leaders' inability to impose capital punishment themselves fulfilled Jesus' prediction describing his death." [67]

Read John 12:32, 33

Jesus had a respectful, loving connection with his mother. He honored her and grew up as one who gained favor with God and man. At one point during his ministry, Mary traveled with him and remained close to his followers. Jesus explained to his disciples exactly how he would die. Point by point, he spelled out the horror of what would happen.

Knowing this, do you think perhaps Jesus had a private conversation with Mary about what was coming?

_____

_____

How would Mary have felt when she realized Jesus had been brought before Pilate for sentencing?

_____

_____

Carol Kent writes about the suffering of her heart during the trial of her only son, Jason.

"There are moments in our lives when we can't think. We simply feel the pain, the heartache, the brokenness, and the sorrow. Everything felt like it was whirling in slow motion. I looked at the judge and wondered if he believed the verdict was fair and appropriate. My eyes swept over the faces of the members of the jury. I looked at my son, child of my womb, and wondered if he would be tormented....What would happen to my boy?" [68]

Mary had no control over how her son would be treated. However, Jesus maintained perfect control throughout each interrogation. Before Herod, he chose silence; refusing to dignify any of his questions with a response. Before Pilate, he spoke with bold, searing clarity.

What does Jesus say about his kingdom in **John 18:36**?

_____

_____

Jesus points out that though he is a king, he poses no threat to Rome. His kingdom would not come by any type of worldly revolution.

What does Jesus say about his kingship in **verse 37**?

_____

_____

His arrest was made in the dark of night. Charges against Jesus mounted as he was dragged from makeshift courtrooms to private interrogations. Not one of the players in this sham of a trial could find a leg to stand on. The Roman authorities threw Jesus back to the Jewish authorities and then back and forth again. Day began to dawn and the madness intensified. At last Pilate washed his hands of the entire ordeal and settled on old Jewish custom to bring down the gavel.

Read Luke 23:13-17.

What does Pilate say to the chief priests?

_____

_____

In honor of the Jewish Passover, Pilate will release a prisoner.

How is the crowd described in **Luke 23:18-23**?

_____

_____

Imagine Mary in the crowd of people who held the fate of Jesus in their hands. The Amplified Bible reads "but they all together raised a deep cry (from the depths of their throats)." Mary's voice would shout out, "Give us Jesus! Give me my son! You don't know who He is! Jesus! Jesus! Jesus!" until she had no voice left. With her body shaking, exhausted with fear, she would hear the insistent, loud cries drown out everything but one name and one decision.

LUKE'S INTERVIEW WITH MARY: DAY SIX

Luke: Mary, when Pilate offered to release a prisoner that morning did you have a glimmer of hope that Jesus would be set free?

Mary: For a few seconds I believed God was using Pilate to save my son's life. Then the crowd began to shout: "Away with this Man! Release to us Barabbas!"

Luke: Barabbas was …?

Mary: A prisoner who incited riots and committed murder. He was guilty and deserved to be in prison. He was exactly the kind of man my son died to save. One could say all of us were like Barabbas… until that day.

Luke: Please go on.

Mary: Every human heart is sinful and trapped in a prison of one kind or another. On that day, on that cross, Jesus took those sins and died in our place. He threw open the prison doors for all who will believe.

Luke: This sounds so simple.

Mary: It is. It's the simple, holy miracle of having faith. Jesus came to give the greatest sacrifice of his life that day. Many cannot accept the simplicity of a God who would love and forgive so completely.

THE MOST PUBLIC DAY OF HIS LIFE

Crucifixion: Excruciate, to cause great agony, torment. Latin: ex: out of, from cruciate (cross) "from the cross."

This day would be the greatest public appearance of Jesus' life. He had performed miracles and taught before thousands. But the most noted event of his life would be the day he was crucified on a hill outside Jerusalem.

Let's try to get inside Mary's skin for a moment as she stood with the unforgiving noonday heat beating down on the battered body of her firstborn child. She would have been around forty-eight years old. She was a widow and financially insecure. Her other children did not believe Jesus was the Messiah. Except for a few of his followers, Mary would have been utterly alone.

SO THIS IS PLAN A?

The words of Mary's Magnificat would have been impossible to speak on this dark Friday. Did she think instead: *God, is this is what you asked of me when Gabriel brought me the news that I was to bear Your Son? Lord, was this the plan from the beginning, the kingdom plan assigned to Jesus from before the foundations of the world?*

What did Pilate order in **Luke 23:16**?

_____

_____

Pilate hoped that a public scourging of Jesus would satisfy the crowd and tame the self-proclaimed king of the Jews. To tame the Lion of Judah, the King of Kings, is a laughable quest. Satan and his minions certainly were cheering as Jesus was beaten to a bloody pulp.

Many victims died from the brutality of a flogging alone. The victim was tied to a post, with his back entirely exposed. The Romans used what was called a "flagrum." It consisted of small pieces of bone and metal attached to a varying number of leather straps. The beating would shred the back and sometimes tear internal organs. Roman law had no limits as to how many times the criminal could be beaten. Thirty-nine strikes of the whip were believed to be one short of death.

After being flogged, Jesus was humiliated further. Mocking, spitting, sneering, and laughing guards threw a scarlet robe over the bleeding wounds of his back and placed a stick in his hand as a scepter. Only one more thing was needed for this "king of the Jews." They twisted together a thorny crown and fastened it onto his bleeding head. The crown of thorns is thought to have potentially covered his entire scalp. The scourging would have caused severe bleeding to this most vascular part of the body.

Mary's son was not the thin, fair-skinned, waif of a man portrayed in far too many paintings and films. Jesus would have been a healthy, strong Jewish man in his early thirties. He grew up working with wood in a carpenter's shop and was accustomed to extensive travel on foot.

After a sleepless night where he prayed with such intensity that great drops of blood and sweat fell from his forehead, he was tied up, dragged from one location to another, and given a beating to the brink of death. Before making the two-and-a-half-mile walk up the hill of Golgotha, he lost even more blood from the thorns stabbing into his skull. Many scholars believe his good health explains why he was still alive at the time of the crucifixion.

Turn to Luke 23:27-28.

Who accompanied Jesus as he took each painful step to Golgotha?

___

What did he say to them?

___

This was the final lament from the lips of Jesus to the people of Israel. Every warning, every entreaty, every parable and prayer, had been spoken. Decisions to accept his offer for eternal life and forgiveness would be received or rejected. He tells the daughters of Jerusalem to save their tears for the future children of Israel.

Did Mary remember the prophecy of Isaiah as she gazed with shock and grief at the unrecognizable face of her son?

"He was despised and rejected and forsaken by men, a man of sorrows and pains, and acquainted with grief and sickness; and like one from whom men hide their faces.... Surely he has borne our grief (sickness, weakness, and distress) and carried our sorrow and pains of punishment" (Isa. 53:3-4 Amplified Bible).

The promises of Gabriel would ring cruelly in Mary's memory as she watched the crucifixion of her son. What good could come from such a torturous death? Where was God when Jesus needed him most? If Jesus must die at this young age, why would God allow Him to be crucified?

Read Deuteronomy 21:23.

How was crucifixion viewed by the Jewish people?

___

The Romans perfected crucifixion to make it a method of execution which would cause the maximum amount of pain and suffering over the longest period of time. Most men condemned to this death were slaves, provincials, and the worst criminals. Roman citizens, except for a soldier turned traitor, were exempt from crucifixion.

The crucifixion site was set apart from the city for sanitary purposes. Many times the body was left to rot on the cross as a disgrace and warning for passersby.

The path to the hill of Golgotha is called the Via Dolorosa (the "way of suffering"). The distance is estimated at about 650 yards, down a narrow street of stone, most likely surrounded by markets. Crucifixion involved carrying a cross bar through the Via Dolorosa, up Golgotha to Calvary, the highest point of Jerusalem; 777 meters above sea level. The cross bar weighed from eighty to 110 pounds. At some point Jesus fell under its weight. Matthew's gospel describes how Simon the Cyrene was chosen from the crowd to carry this heavy crossbeam in his place.

Did the words of **Psalm 22:16-17** rush through Mary's mind?

"Dogs have surrounded me; a band of evil men has encircled me, they have pierced my hands and feet. I can count all my bones; people stare and gloat over me" (NIV).

The cross bar would be laid on the ground. Jesus was placed on his back with his arms outstretched. Nails, about seven inches long and roughly three-eighths of an inch in diameter, were driven into the median nerve of his wrists, causing shocks of pain to radiate through the arms. (The wrist was considered part of the hand at this time.)

In the center of the upright posts (about seven feet high) was a crude seat that served to support the victim. The cross bar would then be lifted onto the post and the feet nailed to them. To allow this, the knees had to be bent and rotated laterally in a tremendously uncomfortable angle.

The cross being erected upright brought an arduous strain on the wrists, arms and shoulders. Dislocation of the shoulder and the elbow joints followed, while the arms, forced up and outward, pushed the rib cage into a tight position. This made breathing, especially exhalation, nearly impossible. One could only take short, shallow breaths, which may explain why Jesus made his profound last statements in short phrases.

How could Mary bear the pain of watching? Why didn't she leave?

Read John 19:25-26.

Who stood with Mary at the cross of Jesus?

_____

Now read Luke 23:35-37.

Who else is standing by?

_____

What do they say?

_____

_____

What is written in three languages and placed above his head?

_____

Luke's description in **verse 35** is one of the most unsettling verses in Scripture. Like people out for a day in the big city, a certain group watched his death with apathy as though it was commonplace or entertainment and nothing new.

"Now the people stood by (calmly and leisurely) watching…" (Amplified Bible).

Mary sees the naked body of her son writhe in agony on a cross. All around are the mocking shouts from Roman guards. And worst still, were the calm, casual eyes of others who mocked him with apathy.

Take a moment to ponder: Are there times when we are calmly removed from Jesus? Do we find ourselves taking a step back from the fullness of Jesus when he's too painful to follow?

_____

_____

Did **Psalm 56:8** come to her mind?

How would this verse give her strength?

_____

_____

Mothers have a visceral response to seeing their children hurt. When our children break a bone, or bleed, we feel pain in our bodies. Can you comprehend for a moment Mary's torment as she watched the body of Jesus nailed to a cross?

Did she recall the words of **Isaiah 50:6**?

"I gave my back to those who strike me, and my cheeks to those who pluck out the beard" (NASB).

Describe the prophecy of **Isaiah 52:14** and how it related to the day Jesus was crucified:

_____

_____

One cannot over-emphasize that the most public act of Jesus' life is found here on the cross. He was led like a lamb to be slaughtered. Mary's son was humiliated and tortured for all to see.

The custom of the time was to crucify criminals two to three feet from the ground. Did Mary touch his bleeding feet and weep, unable to stop his pain? Often, wolves and jackals would begin eating the feet and legs of the criminal long before they were dead. The longest crucifixion on record took thirteen days; the shortest lasted thirty-two hours. Mary had no idea how long Jesus would suffer. Maybe she stayed to make sure the wolves wouldn't get near him. Maybe his feet were the only place she could protect.

When Jesus said, "Father, forgive them for they know not what they do," how did Mary respond?

Forgive them? My Son! Forgive this? How? When? By what power?

"Father, Father, why have you forsaken me?"

Yes! God! Where are you? Why will you not help him? Why have you turned your face away from us?

Read John 19:26-27.

Looking down at the crowd, he saw the tormented face of his mother and his beloved disciple, John.

What did Jesus manage to say to them?

_____

_____

Most biblical scholars believe John was about fifteen or sixteen years old when he began to follow Jesus. When he stood beside Mary at the foot of the cross, he was probably no more than nineteen years old. Yet Jesus chose him, not one of his siblings, to care for Mary. John must have been honored by this request. The word tells us that from that moment on, John took Mary into his home.

Even in his physical anguish, Jesus sees Mary's needs. He calls her "woman" again. It is the same term of endearment he used when she came to him at the wedding in Cana.

How Mary's heart must have ached hearing these words of affection from her son as he hung dying on a cross. It was as if Jesus said, "Most precious mother, from now you will be taken care of by one of my best men, John. John, watch over my mother and love her as your very own."

Time would drag on as the sun rose into the sky.

At some point during his excruciating hours on the cross, Jesus would have gone into an acute state of dehydration.

What did Jesus say in **John 19:28**?

_____

_____

Mary had fed and bathed her son. She had brought him drinks of water and seen him turn water to wine! Now she is helpless to offer him the simplest drink of water. The first wine offered to Jesus was a mixture used by Jewish women as an act of mercy for the suffering victim. It was laced with myrrh to help deaden the pain. Jesus refused this wine. He would meet death in its fullest dread and defeat it without medication.

The second drink offered to Jesus was a form of wine vinegar, soaked on a sponge. The sponge was then put on a stalk of the hyssop plant and lifted to his lips. It was a poor man's wine; Christ received this drink.

Why take this second drink? Jesus came to fulfill every part of God's promise, even while dying on a cross. The hyssop plant was used every year during the Feast of the Passover.

Read Exodus 12:22.

How was the hyssop plant used?

_____

_____

Hyssop literally means, "that which is soured," and is related to the Hebrew term, "that which is leavened." In the terminology of Christ's culture, both yeast and leaven were symbolic of sin. With his act of taking this drink, it's as if Jesus puts an exclamation point on his death.

After drinking from the hyssop plant, he cried out loudly to his Father and to all humanity:

"Father, into your hands, I commit my spirit!"

Creation responded with Mary's heart at his death. The one who held creation together had died. The Son of God was dead. One part of the holy Trinity breathed his last breath. It was as if the entire universe shook with spiritual implications.

What is described in **Luke 23:44-45**?

_____

_____

What else happened according to **Matthew 27: 51-53**?

_____

_____

For three hours in midday, from noon to three o'clock in the afternoon, there was darkness across the entire world! We have Luke to thank for this detail. The ground split apart; dead people rose from their graves and made a few house calls to family members. The veil in the temple that had separated man from God was torn in two from top to bottom.

LUKE'S INTERVIEW WITH MARY: DAY SEVEN

Luke: After Jesus was put into the tomb provided by Joseph of Arimathea, what did you do?

Mary: With all due respect, I'd like those two days to remain private.

Luke: Certainly.

Mary: I will say that grieving for me was a roller coaster of extremes. Watching his crucifixion…there are no words to describe it. Then three days later, he has risen from the tomb! Then before I knew it, he was gone again! Thankfully the Holy Spirit was poured out on all of us who believed in him. His sweet spirit sustained and comforted me.

Luke: What was the first thing you did when you saw him alive again?

Mary: I couldn't speak. Honestly, he stood there smiling in the doorway and I tried to speak but nothing would come out. The harder I tried to talk, the more he laughed. Then he picked me up and swung me around! I buried my face in his neck! And I couldn't stop touching his hands and feet.

Luke: Were the nail marks still there?

Mary: Yes, of course they were! Thomas had to go and make a big fuss out of seeing them in person. But Jesus was hungry. Right away he wanted to know what I had to eat.

Luke: Did He ever mention going to the Roman authorities to prove his claims of being the Messiah?

Mary: No. Not once. He made no visits to the Sanhedrin or to Pilate or Herod's palace. Jesus only appeared to those of us who knew him to be Christ. He was full of joy and bold teaching. He kept quoting Isaiah, like he did as a little boy: "Behold, I make all things new!"

Luke: How long was he on earth before he left for heaven?

Mary: Not long enough for his mother!

There is no written record of it, but we are convinced that Jesus would have appeared to Mary after his resurrection. Take a moment and write some words of comfort and encouragement that he might have shared with her during this visit:

_____

_____

Read Acts 1: 1-3.

What did Jesus do during the forty days after he rose from the dead?

_____

_____

Luke: What are your favorite memories about Jesus after his resurrection?

Mary: There are so many it's hard to say. He taught all of us so much about what role we would play after he left for heaven.

Luke: He told you all to wait in Jerusalem for what purpose?

Mary: We were to wait for the gift of the Holy Spirit to fall upon us. Cousin John had baptized with water. Now we were to receive the gift of his Holy Spirit! Then we would take the great news about him to all people of all nations!

Luke: Did some of his followers expect him to stay and restore his kingdom in Israel at last?

Mary: Yes, and you can understand why. He had died and risen from the dead. He had proven he was God's Son. Some of his friends assumed the next logical step would be for him to establish an earthly kingdom.

Luke: How did he reply to this request?

Mary: He was patient and explained that the time for his kingdom and second coming was better left in God's hands. I had learned not to ask too many questions, because God only let me see one piece of the puzzle at a time. I'd like to add one thing.

Luke: Please feel free.

Mary: If you believe in Jesus, then trust him in the process of life. He is into the details. Over time, the picture becomes clear. He will never forsake you. He will never leave you without hope.

Luke: Do you think being his mother was worth all you went through?

Mary: Are you serious? Would I have done it all over again? We'll have to wait until heaven to talk that through. Did I miss Jesus after he ascended? Yes. Did I miss his physical presence and laughter, his brilliant teaching, and his eyes of compassion and love? Yes.

Luke: Were you ever able to erase the memories of his crucifixion from your mind?

Mary: Would any mother ever forget such horror? No, I could never forget that day. But with his death came the gift of eternal life. None of us should ever forget the price of his cross.

Luke: Was it hard to say good-bye… even knowing you would be with Him again?

Mary: Yes, of course. But I like to call it an "interlude." The glorious truth of his resurrection gave me beauty for ashes. My life is filled with the promise of what is coming.

After his resurrection, Mary became part of the faithful new believers worshiping in Jerusalem (Acts 1:14). How respected and honored she must have been among the people of that young church. She was the first to know him, to hold him, and could tell them stories of his childhood and answer questions about his early years on earth.

Luke: In your scrapbook of memories, what did you look at most after Jesus returned to heaven?

Mary: Oh that's easy. Any time I missed him too much or had a disappointing day, I remembered the empty tomb.

Luke: The tomb?

Mary: Oh, yes! The stone was rolled away. The cloths placed on his body were neatly folded. Mary Magdalene and I often spoke about the two angels who sat on either side where his body laid…. Just like in the Ark of the Covenant.

Luke: This is your favorite memory?

Mary: Isn't it yours?

Luke: Yes, I believe it is.

Mary: The night before he was crucified, he said something no one understood at the time. He said it was better for him to go away. Of course being his mother I thought, *What could be better than seeing your sweet face each day?*

Read John 16:6, 17.

Luke: How did he explain his departure?

Mary: Later we came to see that he wanted each of us to have a gift only he could give. Jesus was filled with the presence of God's Holy Spirit. It strengthened him, gave him insight and the ability to see beyond earth and into heaven. When he left this gift would be shared with all who believed in him!

Luke: This gift of the Holy Spirit comforted you in the days after his ascension?

Mary: I still had to grieve my loss and walk through some painful days of missing my son. Just like you and everyone else who suffers loss; we must give ourselves time. Gradually the Holy Spirit will lift us out of our heartache.

Luke: So the empty tomb represents the gift of the Holy Spirit and eternal life?

Mary: Yes, among a thousand other blessings. My son said not to worry about the little things. He left us with his peace. He said there are many rooms in his father's house and he has gone to prepare a place for all who believe. When I was a young girl, I carried Jesus in my body. I felt him kick and tumble in my womb. Little did I know he would be born in me again! This time it's not for nine months. Because of that empty tomb, I have him with me forever.

The empty tomb changes everything for you and me as well.

What would Jesus say to you in your greatest moment of sorrow? When you are in a dark season, a place of confusion and pain or battle, feeling that God is deaf to your cries, remember the empty tomb. Jesus lived through every loss we ever will suffer. He lived a human life and died a human death. He understands. He's been there.

He walked out of that tomb to defeat every enemy—even death.

We met Mary when she learned of the news of Jesus' birth. As we leave her, she has made the journey through birth to death and back to life again.

Turn to John 16: 21-22.

Jesus continues to reassure us by talking about childbirth! He talks about the travail and sorrow and anguish of labor. He says when a woman is in labor, "her hour has come." That is where we are now: we are in labor. Our hour has come! We are in travail on this sinful planet in our weak and very human bodies until he returns.

In the middle of it all, he is with us. While we walk out one difficult day at a time, he lives inside us, guiding us and comforting our beating hearts.

Mary lived to see some of the fulfillment of the prophecies concerning her son, but not all of them. She died knowing there was more to come. She is one of the women in the Hebrews Hall of Faith who "from weakness was made strong" and "received back their dead by resurrection." She gained approval through her faith, but she did not receive all that is to come. Mary is part of the cloud of witnesses cheering us on. She waits for us to join her at the consummation of the ages.

Gabriel's promises will come true, one by one.

Jesus will reign forever on the throne of David.

In the final chapters of his earthly life, Mary went through the fires of personal hell. The mother of our Lord was not spared grief, and neither are we. It's part of what it means to be human.

When Jesus became sin on the cross it forever marked the pages of history. From that pivotal day forward, the cross of Jesus will require a response. His cross defines the story of every man who dares to look upon it and believe.

"You wonder how long my love will last? Find your answer on a cross, on a craggy hill. That's me you see up there, your maker, your God, nail-stabbed and bleeding. Covered in spit and sin-soaked.

That's your sin I'm feeling.

That's your death I'm dying.

That's your resurrection I'm living.

That's how much I love you!" [69]

Imagine how he looked from the cross into the face of Mary and John to give them hope. Imagine him looking from the cross into your eyes to reassure your heart.

"I took sin to the cross. It's here with me.

It's nailed to my body and not yours.

I've walked through life and have seen what you face.

I hate injustice as much as you.

My love overrides hate.

You will be with me in heaven.

Dare to look this way. If you look long enough and listen closely you will hear angels singing above the noise of the mockers.

Dare to live without the burden of a cross.

Dare, my beloved, to believe!"

Never again will you or I be separated from God. Jesus sits at the right hand of God and speaks your name and mine. He is coming back for us again.

When the time comes, we'll share in Mary's wedding feast.

He will come for his bride, for Mary, his disciples, for you and me.

The privilege of studying the Scriptures about Mary means that when we meet her in heaven, we won't need to be introduced. We'll already recognize her and it will be more like a high-five than a handshake. She won't want us to glorify her and put her on a pedestal. Instead, she'll probably say, "Let me tell you something about my son! I have a few pictures. Where would you like to start?"

TODAY'S DATE: _____

YOUR HEADLINE:
_____
_____

WEEK NINE

EVICTION NOTICE

Served: Adam and Eve

Removed: From Garden of Eden

When: Genesis 3:23-24

With a heavy heart, the Lord God has posted the following notice of eviction: Adam and Eve are hereby given notice that Elohim is terminating their day to day tenancy of the premises of the garden of Eden located at the headwaters of the Tigris-Euphrates River, to be effective immediately. Adam and Eve must leave their residence and travel east of the Garden and never return. Holy angels have been dispatched to stand with flaming swords at the Garden's gates, to protect and guard the way to the tree of life.

There is no re-entry available at this time.

Adam and Eve should seek marriage counseling as soon as possible. They also will benefit from the practice of a trustworthy OB/GYN. Their days of walking freely with God in the Garden are presently over.

Elohim has promised not to leave or forsake them. Plans for restoring the Garden and its inhabitants are in place and moving ahead on schedule. All should prepare for eternal life in a new garden, per his invitation only.

Details of a new housing contract have been negotiated.

TODAY'S HEROINE:
Eve

Now the Lord God said, "It is not good (sufficient, satisfactory) that the man should be alone; I will make him a helper meet (suitable, adapted, complementary) for him" (Gen. 2:18 Amplified Bible).

She is the crowning and final work of his creation: Eve. The first woman. Eve, the mother of all the living, the first beloved daughter of God, the first mother and wife on earth.

How and why did Eve come to be?

Eve's story has everything to do with relationship. God always has been and always will be about relationship.

Before the words "in the beginning" were written, God was. And he was not alone. John 1:1 tells us that before all time, before Genesis 1:1, God existed in harmony with Christ and the Holy Spirit. From this perfect union of God the Father, Son, and Spirit, the world was created.

"The author opens the large book. It has no words. It has no words because no words exist. No words exist yet because no words are needed. There are no ears to hear them, no eyes to read them. The author is alone…. So he takes his quill and spells the first. T—i—m—e. Time did not exist until he wrote it. He, himself, is timeless, but his story would be encased in time. The story would have a first rising of the sun, a first shifting of the sand. A beginning… and an end. A final chapter. He knows it before he writes it.

Slowly, tenderly, the author writes the second word. A name. A—d—a—m. In my image, I will make you. You will be like me. You will laugh. You will create. You will never die. And you will write.

For each life is a book, not to be read, but rather a story to be written. The author starts each life story, but each life will write his or her own ending. What a dangerous liberty. How much safer it would have been to finish the story for each Adam. To script every option. It would have been simpler. It would have been safer.

But it would not have been love. Love is only love if chosen." [70]

Elohim creator God spoke the heavens and the earth into being.

All it took was one word from his mouth and the process of life began.

The earth was without form and void. It would now burst to life at the sound of his voice.

Let's blow our minds a bit here. **Read Hebrews 1:3.**

Who is the sole expression of the glory of God?

Who is the perfect imprint and image of God?

___

Who propelled the universe by his mighty word of power?

___

Over the brooding empty waste of darkness, the Holy Spirit of God hovered to birth order, to change chaos to cosmos. This same Holy Spirit hovered to birth Jesus into the womb of Mary. God's Spirit was given as a gift to all who believe. He longs to hover and continually birth truth into the inmost places of our hearts. Chaos to cosmos to completion.

In the first five days of creation, the Creator speaks light into existence, the seas and sky, and land and tress and all plants in the earth. He calls forth the birds into the air and the fish teeming in the waters.

> Light, come forth out of darkness.
> Day, separate yourself from night.
> Waters and sky find order and be named universe.
> Earth and heavens be defined.
> Vegetables, fruit and seed bearing plants be abundant.
> Season, days and years be set in motion.
> Sun, moon and stars blaze in perfect union.
> Birds and fish, leviathan and every living creature breathe, run free, play and abound.
> Livestock and beasts enjoy the lush magnificence of earth.
> Oceans be filled with a sea of colors and life all your own.
> Yes, it is good! All is good!

He calls it good and speaks a blessing, telling his creatures to be fruitful and multiply and fill the earth.

Read Genesis 1:26-27.

Who did God make on day six?

___

In whose image?

___

Man was made in the image of God the Father, God the Son and God the Holy Spirit. God's love was too great to stay silent. The glory of the Son, too radiant not to be seen by millions. The creativity of the Holy Spirit, too incomprehensible to be tamed.

What existed before man and woman? Fellowship. God with the Son and the Son with the Spirit, fellowship reigned.

"Freedom ran free. Freedom was nothing less than Christ himself. Nothing existed except the Godhead. All was reality. The only reality that ever existed, existed there.

The Trinity moved in a realm of absolute freedom, which is a natural, innate part of God.

The God head was having a wonderful time!

….a corporate fellowshipping of the Trinity just may be the key to everything." [71]

All of life was created by God's Word. The Word made flesh. In Christ and through Christ, the universe was made and held together by his being.

On day six, God stoops down and puts his hands into the dust. Again he creates, only this time, like a sculptor on the beach, he molds the dirt of his earth into the shape of a man.

Then I AM bent down to breathe life into the nostrils of man. Adam's eyes opened first to see the face of his God. They gaze at one another. When Adam looked at God, he could see a resemblance. He knows he is made in the image of his Creator.

"This breath may be the narrator's way of describing the infusion of the human spirit, with its moral, intellectual, relational, and spiritual capacities. God showed tender care and intimate concern in the way he shaped man…. the breath of life makes humans distinct from all other creatures." [72]

The name "Adam" is translated as "Ish," or earthly. Earthly had much to take in and a great assignment after seeing his Maker.

Read Genesis 2:8.

What did God plant?

___

Where was it located?

___

Who did he place there?

___

God created man in the wild of nature and the animals. After he made Adam, he created a garden in Eden called "Delight." Adam was not created in the garden, but in the marvelous adventurous world of God's glorious creation. Thus the spirit of man has always been thrilled by the sacred call of the untamed. Woman would be created in the garden, in the environment of flowing rivers and beautiful flowers, a place of order and lush protection. Thus the spirit of Eve would always be drawn to places of safety and loveliness.

Read Genesis 2:15-25.

Why did God put Adam in the garden?

___

Please don't miss this point. Eden was perfection. In this perfect place God's pleasure was to allow Adam the pleasure of dominion over the earth. Work would not be drudgery, but an honorable, fulfilling part of life. Tending the garden would be rewarding to man. Taming and protecting creation would be a source of endless enjoyment.

Read Genesis 1:26-31.

Describe the privileges God gave to Adam and Eve:

_____

_____

"And God saw everything that he had made… and he approved it completely" (Amplified Bible).

WHERE'S MY GIRL?

Read Genesis 2:18.

What statement did God make about Adam's solitude?

_____

_____

The only questionable review of creation came from God's own lips. He always had been and would be in fellowship with the Son and Spirit. Every aspect of creation was pronounced "good." But on day six of creation, something was missing: Man was lonely. The author of relationship knew Adam needed a mate to complete the picture of human fellowship.

Then God does something interesting. He parades the animals before Adam and asks him to name them. Adam was able to sit beside God and enjoy the brilliance of his creativity as he observed the unique and fascinating nature of all God's creatures.

Adam not only sat by God, but may he also have run with God from one habitat to another, viewing the natural surroundings made for each of God's vast members of creation? Imagine God taking Adam from sea to mountainside, from riding the backs of dolphins to racing bareback across meadows on a stallion.

Gene Edwards writes in his book *Wild Goose Chase:*

"I don't think God paraded the animals past Adam in a single-file line; I'm guessing God let Adam discover them in their natural habitats. Imagine how thrilling it must have been for Adam to catch his first glimpse of wildebeests stampeding, mountain goats climbing, or rhinos charging. Few things compare to the thrill of seeing a wild animal in its natural habitat. There is something so inspiring about a wild animal doing what is was created to do. Uncivilized. Untamed. Uncaged." [73]

We can imagine Adam marveling at the regal beauty of a lion, or picture him laughing with God at the antics of the monkey and applauding the colorful feathers of a peacock. God enlists Adam's participation in the naming of all his creatures. It is part of Adam's role and privilege as ruler over all God has made. Adam learns to govern and have dominion over the earth. Like his Father who rules with love over all, man joins the invitation to imitate his Maker.

It seems that the animal naming process had a two-fold purpose. God wanted Adam to name the creatures, and he also wanted Adam to look carefully at each pair that passed by—each pair. The animals were in relationship with each other and able to multiply as God had commanded.

In **Genesis 2:20** what does Adam realize?

_____

There seems to have been a subtle psychology to what God had in mind for Adam in this naming exercise. Adam saw there was no one like him. The literal translation of "suitable" is "corresponding to."

As the animals passed before God and Adam in pairs, did Adam look at God and say, "Each creature has a mate; why don't I?" Put into modern terms, there was not one animal in the bunch who could possibly be his "soul mate."

It has been said God's great love necessitated the creation of woman. It was not just enough for God to be with man. Man was made in the image of God. God creates. He ordained the animals to create. So also man must create. To create, he would need a partner on his journey. Creation required relationship. Relationship was completed in the creation of Eve.

God made man and woman in his image. Adam carried many of God's attributes. Woman would complete the creation of God's nature. What existed before Genesis 1:1 would be fulfilled in one last miraculous act.

God caused Adam to take a nap. He fell into a deep sleep.

Let's read the account of this first surgery.

Read Genesis 2:21-23.

What body part from Adam did God use to form Eve?

_____

What did Adam say when he saw her?

_____

When Adam woke, he would decide on the most important name yet; he would name his mate. "Woman," he declared. In the Hebrew, her name is "Ishsah." William Young notes Adam might have exhaled the 'ahhhhhh' to show how the sight of Eve thrilled his heart. The Hebrew word for man is "Ish." The literal translation is "this one shall be called Ishshah because she was taken out of Ish." In any language, there is no doubt that Adam declared Eve was indeed very good.

When God brings Eve to Adam we find the first recorded words from man. Perhaps the sight of his bride inspired man's first poem!

"This is now bone of my bones
And flesh of my flesh;
She shall be called 'woman,'
For she was taken out of man" (NIV).

Adam knew Eve was made from part of his own flesh. He needed a companion. He needed another like him with a high intelligence, a sense of humor, someone to share the love of God's good earth, someone who spoke his language. Someone who could ensure that man would begat mankind.

It's interesting that God didn't use the dust of the earth to create Eve. He used part of Adam's body and Adam knew it. In the future, no matter how much his wife might confuse, frustrate, or baffle him, Adam could never doubt where she was "coming from." Eve came from him!

In their relationship we see the first marriage. What was it like in the beginning for man and woman to live in a sinless world, in harmony with each other and their God?

Read Genesis 2:23-25, the description of earth's first marriage.

How would you paraphrase their vows?

_____

_____

Naked, unashamed, cleaving in joy to each other, united in purity and celebration, Adam and Eve begin their journey together in the innocence of childlike abandon. Perhaps God chose the rib to form Eve because he wanted to make sure Adam knew she was to be treated as his equal. Bible commentator Matthew Henry made the beautiful statement so often used today, inspired by the end of Genesis 2.

"Woman was created from the rib of man.
She was not made from his head to top him,
nor from his feet to be trampled on.
She was made from his side to be equal to him;
from under his arm to be protected by him;
from near his heart to be loved by him.[74]

Let's stop for a minute and imagine what Eve might have looked like. This has been a delightful source of fascination for many of us. Before there were wrinkles or age spots, hair sprouting in unwanted places, or PMS, what was Eve like?

How do you think she looked?

_____

How do you think her voice sounded?

_____

What was her temperament?

_____

How was her intimacy with Adam?

_____

How would she have related to God?

___

How would Eve have enjoyed the garden? Think specifics!

___

___

Who knows? Maybe Eve was a full figured Rubenesque lady. But it's a stretch to believe she had stretch marks. Eve was gorgeous. She had no dysfunctional family in her background. No cellulite. No memories of geeky junior high school years or acne. No baggage of failed romance or need for counseling. Eve was loved at first sight by her man. She was the innocent, ultimate woman married to the innocent, ultimate man.

When Adam said, "This is now," he was literally saying, "At last!" Finally he was looking at someone who was just like him and yet different in all the right ways.

Marriage began in the garden as a representation of God's great love for humanity. Jesus holding creation together was slain before the foundations of the world to show his undying commitment to his Bride, the Church. Therefore Adam would be asked to love Eve in such a manner: as if she was worth dying for. This is the greatest relationship apart from God in a man's life.

The apostle Paul often is accused in modern circles of being a chauvinist. Let's look at what he said about women.

Read 1 Corinthians 11:7.

"Woman is the _____ of man" (NIV).

He calls us the "glory" of man.

What does Paul call man in Ephesians **5:22-23**?

___

If man is the "head" of the woman, then woman is the crown that honors the head.[73] This doesn't sound like women are the lesser creature. It sounds more to us, as the French would say, that she is "the piece de resistance!"

When the Scriptures say God made the first woman, the verb "made" means "to build." *Nelson's New Illustrated Bible* Commentary makes the point that with today's understanding of molecular structure and DNA, the expansion of one small part into a complete body makes perfect sense. God took one rib from Adam and made an entire woman, from her beautiful head to her cute little toes.

They were unashamed and openly enjoyed sexual intimacy, created by God for their pleasure. They were fully known by God and each other, finding in this unbroken sharing a completeness of their souls. For a short while, Adam and Eve experienced the perfect marriage.

In Mike Mason's book, *The Mystery of Marriage,* he writes:

"Secretly we long to perpetuate that one astounding moment in the Garden of Eden. We long to stand in awe of one another, just as Adam and Eve must have done when they first locked gazes. We long for our whole body to tingle with the thrill of knowing that this one fascinating being, this being of a different gender, has been created specifically for us and given to us unreservedly for our help, comfort and joy." [75]

WHAT GOD HAD IN MIND WHEN HE SAID, "LET THERE BE….."

The first two humans on earth knew what all followers of Christ know. The answers to the two most fundamental questions of life are found in **Genesis 1 and 2**:

Who am I?

Why am I here?

Adam and Eve were marked for life by the hand of God. They were image bearers given permission to reign as his representatives on earth. His most-prized possessions, given free will and access to all the glories of creation. Filled with the creative spirit of God, man and woman were given intimacy, the freedom to walk openly with their Maker and to rejoice in being alive.

This first marriage is the blueprint God had in mind for his people. In the two opening chapters of Genesis we have guidelines for a healthy marriage relationship. Man is to leave his parents and cling to his wife.

The two become one flesh.

In the Ephesians 5 passage, Paul calls us to be subject to one another based on a reverent fear of Christ.

What is the marriage between a man and woman a spiritual picture of?

_____

How are husbands to love their wives?

_____

How are wives to love their husbands?

_____

This is a beautiful picture of the way Jesus gave his body for us and how he nourishes and cherishes the Church, his Bride. It's also the correct interpretation of a highly abused word, "submission." If a man treats his wife as if she was worth dying for, if he listens to her and lovingly creates a safe environment, then a woman gratefully responds with respect. Any woman treated with God's Plan A will find herself in awe of her man. Aretha got that right. Good marriages are all based on what Christ modeled: "R-E-S-P-E-C-T." Respect requires sacrifice, dying to navel-gazing and demanding rights. Respect for God demands we give ourselves to a higher purpose and cause; to love another as we are loved.

Paul goes on to quote Genesis 2:24: "Therefore a man shall leave his father and his mother and shall become united and cleave to his wife; and they shall become one flesh" (Amplified Bible).

Christ and his Bride will forever be inseparable. Even in the garden, God was painting a picture in human flesh of the coming relationship between Jesus and his Church. To be "one flesh" in marriage is representative of being "in Christ."

Our western culture is all about individual rights and separate lives. Submission to one's husband flies in the face of a liberated woman. To die to oneself and to be "one" with another human smacks of losing one's identity. Yet nothing could be farther from God's plan.

His call to us in marriage and in our relationship with Christ is one of true liberty. He says, in essence, "Lose yourself in Jesus and you'll find me. Lose your life for another and you'll find true fulfillment. Lose your will and let me knock your socks off! Let there be perfect unity, perfect oneness, as the Father, Son and Spirit enjoy."

"For God is not one independent person, but three, a Trinity which co-exists in perfect unity, all the partners being perfect reflections and expressions of one another. Our God, if you like, is a marriage, a family whose members are not the least bit ashamed of being utterly like each other and in total agreement about everything.

If just one of them (let us say Jesus) had ever for a moment sought independence from the others in order to "be his own person," then there would certainly be no such thing as Christianity. In fact, we can presume that the whole universe would have fallen apart."[76]

Adam and Eve experienced this lack of self-protection or a demand for independence. They were rapturously caught up in being one flesh, having a sexual union as well as an emotional and mental one. They were naked and comfortable with their physical bodies—in the light and in the dark—without any self-consciousness or timidity. They were truly children of Eden, innocent and playful. It is an amazing insight into the character of God that he chose to build into their lives the enjoyment of sexual activity.

The enemy of this world has perhaps had the most success with distorting God's good blessing of sexual pleasure. Nothing in God's creation has been so abused, distorted, and trashed as the sexual relationship God intended when he said, "Let there be!" Because of the way the world has perverted sex, because of the painful experiences many have suffered from rape, incest, and abuse, it's difficult to remember that God created sex in a marriage relationship for our comfort and pleasure. Scientific studies show that sex within marriage enhances good health and longevity. Isn't that like our heavenly Father?

He gives us something for our pleasure and then makes it good for us too!

If you're married, stop for a moment and ask God to continue to reveal the joy he has for you in your marriage. It's good to take inventory of how to replicate the playful openness and beautiful freedom Adam and Eve once shared.

BUFF, BRAVE, AND BEAUTIFUL

When we try to picture Adam and Eve as God created them to live, we must picture them in a world uncorrupted by sin. They were created as physically perfect human beings without genetic deterioration in their DNA.

Imagine having a photographic memory. Imagine always using every single brain cell you've been given. Imagine being able to do any complex math problem in your head without the aid of a computer or calculator. Imagine being able to name the animals God made in one day and remember them! Imagine never feeling physically tired or stressed out. Imagine backs that never hurt, necks that are never stiff, and feet that are never tired. Imagine never having hurt feelings, sleepless nights, guilt, shame or regret. Imagine never having a toothache or infection. No cancer, no divorce courts. No freezing rain or scorching sunburns. Perfect intelligence. Perfect talent. Perfect skill. Perfect body.

Not even Jesus, when he walked this earth was immune to the curse of a fallen world. He was perfect in righteousness but experienced all the sorrows and temptations that we do. He knew fatigue, sadness, hunger, thirst, rejection, pain, and death. That is what makes him the perfect Lamb and Intercessor on our behalf (Hebrews 4:15-16).

Adam and Eve are the only two people to walk the earth who knew for a brief time what it was like to experience God's original plan.

Knowing this makes the loss of Eden impossible to imagine.

THE BITE HEARD AROUND THE WORLD

Read Genesis 2:16-17.

What was God's one and only rule in the garden?

_____

Who was not yet created when God gave this rule?

_____

What would happen if they chose not to listen to God's warning?

_____

Eve obviously learned God's rule about this particular tree from Adam. She wasn't created yet when God warned Adam of the consequences of eating from this tree. They could eat from the tree of life, but not from the tree of good and evil.

Let's start first with the tree of life.

Adam and Eve could eat from this tree any time they pleased. One has to pause here to recall how God told his people to choose life and not death. Jesus is the way, the truth, the life. We are offered life on all sides, but human nature pushes the boundaries like a disobedient toddler. The grass deceptively appears greener on the other side. Yet the tree of life is the very tree God guarded after Eve and Adam sinned.

This tree is mentioned in other places in Scripture.

Turn and read Revelation 22:2.

Where is the tree of life?

_____

What is its purpose on the new earth?

_____

When will it yield its fruit?

Time is measured in some way in heaven. Every month the tree of life yields fruit with a fresh crop. New fruit for a new earth.

Read Ezekiel 47:12.

What grows on the trees?

How are their leaves described?

New fruit grows how often?

What does the fruit produce?

"The tree of life in the original creation was in the middle of the Garden of Eden, from which all of humanity was excluded after sin entered the world. Ezekiel's apocalyptic vision included trees bearing fruit every month with medicinal leaves. Since only one tree of life is mentioned here—even though it is on both sides of the river—it is probably meant as a parallel to Genesis 2, implying that a new, better, and everlasting Eden has come."[77]

A new and everlasting Eden will come. It helps to remember this as we ponder Eve's culinary choices. It seems that all believers will one day enjoy what Adam and Eve tasted in Eden. Once attained, it will be accessible, no longer guarded by the cherubim with flaming swords.

INTERESTING SIDEBAR: Where was the Garden of Eden located?

Read Genesis 2:10-14.

No one knows for sure the exact location of the Garden of Eden. The river that flowed out of it and divided into four branches now flows through modern-day Syria, Iraq, and Turkey. Scholars believe the garden was in the eastern part of the Fertile Crescent near the junction of the Tigris and Euphrates rivers. These rivers have changed dramatically since Noah's flood, so all we truly have is an educated guess.

NOT WIRED FOR EVIL

Why do you think death was the result of tasting from the tree of good and evil?

God wanted Adam and Eve to avoid the tree of good and evil because he did not want them to have experiential knowledge of sin.

He wanted his children to grow gradually in wisdom and knowledge through a firsthand relationship with him. By taking fruit from this tree, Adam would be taking a shortcut to knowledge without the guidance and perfect timing of God. He also would have firsthand personal knowledge of evil. The promise that it would lead to death did not mean an instantaneous loss of life, but a gradual slide into decay.

I (Bonnie) have spent a lot of time mulling over this tree thing. God seems to be very invested in trees. They clap their hands in praise of his creation. His Son was nailed to a tree out of love for mankind. And in the beginning and the end of his Word, trees are both dangerous and healing. After my divorce, on the heels of clinical depression I wrote the following:

"There is so much we weren't supposed to know.

We were made after his good. We were not gods ourselves, but we were made after his likeness. With one exception: We were not made to understand evil.

Don't eat of the tree because the tree is full of fruit that only God can handle. God wrestles the devil down and fights battles we cannot understand. Humans fail miserably in this venue, this drama. God has been rescuing us ever since we barreled into scenes never meant for our presence.

We were made to love and laugh and enjoy good things, like children innocent of the potential to destroy those very things made for our pleasure. Things like food, sex, love, nature, intimacy, and possession.

Emotionally, physically, and spiritually, we weren't made for rape, disease, injustice, torment, prejudice, divorce, or single parenting, or depression. Yet God the Father is able to deal with it. He walks beside us, bowing his head in pain with us, wishing that the gift of free will hadn't backfired.... He is unwilling to let what we cannot handle eat us alive." [78]

We weren't wired for sin. God created Adam and Eve to walk with him in the cool breezes of the evening and to enjoy his creation without fear or shame.

Before time began, the enemy of God rebelled in heaven and a third of God's angels followed Lucifer into the darkness of evil. The matter was settled long before Adam or Eve took their first breath. Yet only God can comprehend the loftiness and depth of good and evil. Only Christ could defeat evil with love on a cross. Only the Holy Spirit of God is able to send the devil's minions screaming as they run for cover.

Man and woman....Adam and Eve....They were created only to find joy and pleasure in God's company. Humans never were wired to deal with evil. For the sons and daughters of God, the only antibiotic for sin is the blood of Jesus.

THE EMPTINESS OF EDEN

What happened to the Garden when Adam and Eve left?

Read Genesis 3:22-24.

Who was left to guard the garden?

Why do you think angels were sent to bar anyone from the entrance?

___

Why do you think God would bar the way to the tree of life?

___

The tree of life prevented Adam and Eve from aging. Once they sinned, they could no longer enjoy unbroken fellowship with God. Sin would be at enmity with him. God did not want them to live forever in this condition. Verse 22, in the Amplified Bible, ends with a sentence that is not finished. It reads: "And now, lest he put forth his hand and take also of the tree of life and eat and live forever…." There's a footnote on this verse that says, "This sentence is left unfinished as if to hasten to avert the tragedy suggested of men living on forever in their now fallen state."

This truth is a beautiful picture of God's father heart. The sentiment here is similar to things we would do for our children in order to avert tragedy. "I had better put that baby gate up, lest my child come to the top of the stairs and…." Or, "I had better put the safety lock on the medicine cabinet lest my child get the lid off the aspirin bottle…." Or, "I must teach my daughter the importance of saying 'no' lest she be out on a date and is tempted to…." Or, "I will teach my son how to drive carefully, lest he be out with friends and become distracted and…."

God's is the heart of a parent longing for the best for his children and doing all he can to ensure their safety and well-being. So God takes a gamble on his children in Eden. But before they were created, he put a plan in place to ensure their eternal safety. That's how great his love. That's how great and wide is his mercy. Jesus would be slain before the foundations of the world, a decision that reverberates to this day throughout the unseen places, outweighing every bad choice and evil presence in existence.

"The star maker turns to us one by one, and says, 'You are my child. I love you dearly. I'm aware that someday you'll turn from me and walk away. But I want you to know, I've already provided a way back.'

Emmanuel would stand at the crossroads of life and death and make a choice.

The author knows well the weight of that decision. He pauses as he writes the page of his own pain. He could stop. Even the author has a choice. But how can a creator not create? How can a writer not write? And how can love not love? So he chooses life, though it means death, with hope that his children will do the same.

And so the author of life completes the story. He drives the spike in the flesh and rolls the stone over the grave. Knowing the choice he will make, knowing the choice all Adams will make, he pens, "The End," then closes the book and proclaims the beginning.

Let there be light!" [79]

God is the father who isn't put off by the prodigal's rebellion but looks longingly, achingly at the horizon to see any glimpse of the child's return. Ready for a welcome celebration, he holds the robes of righteousness bought at his price, by his sacrifice, to dress his beloved in the finest garments for the feast prepared. Though Adam and Eve shook their fists in his face and said, "No, thanks, I'll do it my way," God still loved them so much he took eternal steps to ensure their salvation.

When they disobeyed him by eating from the tree, God sent them away from the garden. He did not uproot or kill the tree. He guarded it with cherubim.

Why the cherubim? Why not one angel? The cherubim are the protector of God's majesty in a holy and special way.

Turn to Isaiah 6.

What is Isaiah describing?

_____

Who sits on the throne in the temple?

_____

Who surrounds him in **verse 2**?

_____

What are they saying and doing?

_____

How did Isaiah respond in **verse 5**?

_____

Who touched his mouth and gave him hope?

_____

Angels also are seated on either side of the mercy seat in the Holy of Holies in the tabernacle. This was where God met with man during Israel's Old Testament period. God would dwell between the cherubim.

When Adam and Eve disobeyed the Lord, could it be that God's life-giving, holy presence in Eden was no longer easily accessible once sin entered the world?

Before man and woman ate from the tree of good and evil they were able to talk freely with God, without pre-conditions, without sacrifice. Sin changed everything. The blood of an innocent animal would be required … until the blood of Jesus was shed.

Scripture says that God "drove" Adam and Eve out of the garden. Surely they did not want to go. He had to force them. But with the tree of life still there guarded by the angels, Adam and Eve must have hoped that one day they would have access to it again.

Indeed they will, along with all of us who wait for the appearing of Jesus in the clouds!

What happened to cause such a bad decision? What choices were made that brought about the eviction of God's created ones from his presence? A closer look will be like seeing the face in our mirror.

As daughters of Eve, we are far too familiar with sin.

THE SERPENT DECEIVED ME

Let's look at the very first sin and see how it all came down.

Read Genesis 3:1-6.

Who was in the garden with Eve?

_____

How is he described?

_____

What did he ask Eve?

_____

How did she answer?

_____

Why did Eve eat the fruit?

_____

Why do you think the serpent went after Eve instead of Adam?

_____

Why do you think the serpent tempted her to eat?

_____

If any of you are enthralled with the possibility that you will see your pets in heaven, here's ample proof that you're on the right track. Before the fall in Eden, there was open conversation between Eve and the serpent. Nothing about this seemed out of place in her world. (As with Balaam's ass, God allowed the animal kingdom to converse easily with humans.) It's no stretch of the imagination to believe we will live in a "Narnian" new earth where our cats, dogs, horses, and hamsters will tell us exactly what's on their mind.

Like Dr. Doolittle, Eve could talk to the animals, and in the first four words the serpent utters, we find the root and source of all rebellion against God. Like a badly scratched recording, the enemy of God uses the same lie over and over again, ever the wannabe imitator: slick, quick, but always predictable.

"Indeed, has God said…" (NASB).

"Crafty" is the word used to describe him. Can you say, "understatement?" Satan has made questioning the authority of God his full-time profession. He loves to plant the same seed of doubt in our minds, just as he did with Eve.

Turn to 2 Corinthians 11:2-3.

What does Paul say he's jealous for?

___

What does he pray against?

___

Some things never change. At least until the end of the beginning comes around. The enemy of God appeared to Jesus with nerves of steel. He tempted Christ three times in the wilderness, hoping to throw God's plan off course. Knowing Jesus was God in the flesh, still Satan threw his full weight of deception and lies into the ring. He left a bit discouraged but decided he'd come back to taunt Jesus at a better time!

Take a moment and think through how the enemy came at God's girl.

THE QUESTION/ANSWER GAME THAT CHANGED THE COURSE OF HISTORY

Satan arrived uninvited. Without announcement he appears and strikes up a conversation. He starts by planting doubt in Eve's mind. No "Hello" or "How are you." He begins by asking why God is limiting her access to the good things in life. Right out of the box, he asks: "Can it really be that God has said, 'You shall not eat from every tree of the garden?'" (Amplified Bible)

SIDENOTE: Satan did not use the name "Yahweh." Seems to have stuck in his throat.

His question was a total distortion of the truth. God had not forbidden them to eat from every tree in the garden. There was one tree he warned them to stay away from, for the health of their bodies and souls. The rest of the garden was open for exploration and eating. The very nature of Satan's distortion of the words was an attempt to get Eve to believe God was unkind and withholding.

Doubt: Strike one.

Eve responds by affirming that God has said she and Adam are free as the birds to eat anything they would like. But he had a point. Eve fell for it. She responds with adding her own distortion to God's command. "We may eat fruit from the trees in the garden, but God did say, 'You must not eat fruit from the tree that is in the middle of the garden, and you must not touch it, or you will die'" (Gen. 3:2-3 NIV). Eve falls into legalism by adding to God's word, and Satan's got his foot in the door now.

In **verse 4**, Satan tells his first (recorded) lie. He is the Father of Lies. Lying is his specialty (John 8:44).

"You will not surely die."

Doubt doubled: Strike two.

Eve is silent as he continues. She's in way over her head now. Satan is leading her toward thinking about what she doesn't have, and about her physical death. He knows her sin would include not only physical but also spiritual death. Most importantly, he knows if he can pull this off, Eve will be caught in an immediate spiritual tailspin. Still she doesn't get it. She doesn't leave or back away.

He sees the interest in her eyes and moves in for the kill. He leads her down the path of doubting God's character. He wants her to know God has an ego problem.

"For God knows that in the day you eat of it your eyes will be opened, and you will be like God, knowing the difference between good and evil and blessing and calamity" (Amplified Bible).

Doubt topped with accusation against God: Strike three.

Eve begins to feel left out of the loop. She's a little insulted by the insinuation that God wants to know more than she does. At this point we want to push pause and say, "Please Eve, wait a minute! You know God. You walk with God. He's not like that. And besides, if he knows something you don't, that's fine! He's God. You're not!"

In reality, Satan was inviting Eve to join him in his arrogant hatred of God. He's the one who left God's glory because of jealousy and pride. He is furious that God is more powerful and that love triumphs over evil. He is livid that God has created mankind and given them a desire for intimate fellowship. He cannot bear the thought that here is a God more powerful than him. So he invites Eve and all of us to follow him. He can't do anything to God but he can certainly try to take down as many of God's beloved as possible.

He longs to be God but is a miserable, washed-out wannabe.

So he roams the earth and tempts all of us to hate God just as much as he does. "If I can't be like God, then neither will you!" he cries like a spoiled brat. Satan's only delight is to hurt God by trying to destroy the ones God gave his Son to save. And it all started with Eve in the garden.

Eve looks at the lovely fruit. She looks back at the lovely serpent. What an insightful creature he is! How good of him to share secrets of the garden she had yet to discover. Well then, why not?

For us, the question "did God really say that?" undermines everything we believe. For someone who places faith in Jesus and believes the Bible is the word of God, questioning his authority and faithfulness is not an option. We say we believe him, and we try to live out this faith. Satan delights in bringing up an issue of doubt especially when we say it's a done deal and a settled matter.

Can you name a recent time when you've had a "crisis of doubt?"

_____

_____

Then you can relate to Eve. Satan loves a good debate. He loves to argue, to startle, to rattle the cage. He whispers and winks and distracts.

His oldest trick is to make us think that God is holding out on us. He loves to plant the seed of doubt saying, "If God really loved you, he wouldn't let this happen. If he was really good, he would give you what you ask for. If he was God, life wouldn't be hard. He doesn't have your best interest at heart, so you'd better take care of things yourself. You'll be sorry if you don't and the parade will surely pass you by."

In essence, what Satan did was call God a liar.

He once was the most beautiful angel in heaven. Yet he chose to leave heaven, and a third of the angels followed him. It's impossible to understand why any being would leave the presence of God, and why a third of heaven's angelic force would make the same stupid decision. But this should give us a clear picture of how far the enemy of God will go to run from truth. He knows he is defeated. He knows his days are numbered. He knows he will spend eternity in the abyss of fire. Still he prowls the earth like a lion trying in his last desperate attempts to destroy God's beloved.

It's a comment on human nature that Eve, who had everything she could ever want or need, even the physical ongoing presence of God in her life, was able to be tempted to want more. How often do we see the same invitation in the media and advertising?

You deserve this.
You need that.
You will be happy if you choose…

What's the most obnoxious current commercial you've seen promising heaven on earth?

_____

We don't live in Eden, but through Christ's blood and the Holy Spirit, we have access to unbroken fellowship with God. He has promised to give us everything pertaining to life and godliness (2 Peter 1:3). Yet still we are tempted to look elsewhere for satisfaction and wonder if God is holding out on us.

Would you make the case that Eve was naïve?

_____

_____

She had never been around evil. She only had been in the companionship of God and of Adam, another sinless human. Is it accurate to conclude that the subtle craftiness of Satan was something she had never before encountered?

"Some theologians have claimed that the serpent approached the woman because her weaker mental and spiritual powers made her more susceptible to temptation. Others maintain that, on the contrary, her more active intelligence led her to experiment with the tree of knowledge. Everything we know as human civilization… came from her experiment. From wisdom to war, it's all there, wrapped up in that one inquisitive mouthful." [80]

"Did God say that?"

Let's stop for a moment and park on a big truth. Skilled liars always mix a little deception in with a little truth. Sweet sisters, it's high time we became skilled at spotting the lies. Do you know how FBI agents train themselves to handle counterfeit money? They begin by handling only the real thing. They spend hours touching and examining real money. Then when they touch the counterfeit, they recognize it immediately.

The same is true for us. We need to immerse ourselves in the real thing. We need the word of God every day. Then when Satan comes with his half-baked truths we'll spot them a mile away. The days are evil and the times we live in are desperate. They call for women of wisdom who refuse to give Satan one moment of conversation or even the hint of an opportunity to get his foot in the door.

The Trinity took a great gamble when they allowed free will into creation. God knew that his people would face evil… and he knew who would have their back. Still, the blame game began with Eve's choice to bite into the forbidden fruit and share it with her husband.

Eve was the first to believe a lie. Her name has been linked for centuries with causing the destruction and painful fall of man. But it takes two to tango. By the way, where was Adam when Eve and the serpent spoke?

As far as Scripture tells us, Adam wasn't off playing golf or taking notes during quiet time. He was an arm's length away from Eve and put up no resistance to the fruit she offered to share. He was the one who first received God's direct command to steer clear of the tree. He was the first to take Eve up on her offer to disobey God's caution.

Eve saw. She took. She offered.

"Adam sinned with his eyes wide open. He did not even ask a question. He knew as well as she that the fruit was forbidden. Adam and Even had broken faith with the Lord, and the world was forever changed."[81]

LEAVING HER GARDEN

Turn to 1 John 2:16.

According to this verse, what does the world have to offer?

The beloved disciple John tells us to watch out for the three things that caused Eve to fall into sin:

The lust of the flesh. (That fruit smells good and I'm hungry.)
The lust of the eyes. (It's so pretty.)
The boastful pride of life. (Why can't I be like God?)

The tasty fruit seduced her body. The beauty of it seduced her soul. The idea that it would make her wise seduced her spirit. These three temptations face us around the clock. Satan cannot create; he only can repeat and imitate. Remember he mouthed off with Scripture when he attempted to trip up Jesus. We will have more victory in these areas if we can see his lies for what they are and shoot him down with the word of God.

By the time Eve discovered that Satan was lying to her, it was too late. She rationalized her choices and had her husband join in. Their decision immediately bore fruit of another kind. The result of their sin was the loss of innocence. Instantly they were ashamed of their nakedness.

Read Genesis 3:7-8.

What did they make?

When they heard God walking toward them, what did they do?

No one was in the garden but the two of them and the Lord. Yet they hid for the very first time, covering themselves from each other and from God's presence. For a few brief moments in Eden after they ate the fruit, perhaps they felt smart, cool, and bit worldly wise. But these feelings were quickly replaced with a flood of stress, shame, fear, and regret.

Making "coverings" for themselves was the beginning of religion. It was futile for them to try to take care of themselves. The fig leaves would not work. Neither does religion. Religion continues to be man's attempt to "cover himself" with works, when all God has ever desired is relationship.

Do you understand the difference between religion and relationship?

God created mankind for relationship, for intimate interaction between himself and his people. His great love motivated the act of creation, and all he has ever wanted from you or me is to be in us, to live through us and to give us life. Religion separates us from the love of God. Jesus committed himself to us before time began to make sure that nothing would keep us from eternal relationship with our Maker. If you're caught up in the trappings of religion, you will miss the beautiful possibilities of relationship. The mystery of the gospel is so simple that it staggers our minds. Believe in Christ and be his woman. Believe in God's love and receive his covering. Believe in the work of the Holy Spirit and join his adventure. Believe, beloved. Dare to believe.

Now read Genesis 3:9-24.

Who did God speak to first?

How did he reply?

What did God say about this condition?

Who brought the truth into the light?

Describe the blame game:

_____

_____

It's heartbreaking to imagine God approaching his children as he watched them attempt to hide themselves among the trees, hiding from his eyes.

"Every mother of a teen-ager knows what it feels like suddenly, overnight, to be perceived as 'the enemy' by these darlings on which we have lavished such care. It is then that we learn how much of a catastrophe the fall was, not just for the human race, but for God; how he must have suffered when he sent those original children forth to make their own way in the world." [82]

If we're honest, we admit to identifying with Adam and Eve. When we sin, our first response is not to run to God for help. Most of the time we try to hide, deny, rationalize, or make "coverings" for our sin. We hide behind what we think are good works, or an excuse for how what we've done wasn't really harmful. We feel uneasy when we think about him and fantasize that he's angry with us. Before long, we're hiding like the first couple, avoiding our relationship with God all together.

God is the same today, yesterday, and forever. It still breaks his heart if we run in the opposite direction when we are hurting or have fallen into a messy, dark place. He's aware of every millisecond of our lives. He knew us before we were conceived. Playing hide and seek with God will result in only one outcome: being found. And nothing could be better than being found by your Maker, the one who loves you more than height or depth or breadth can measure.

When God asked "Adam, where are you?" He wasn't asking for help. He was asking, "Adam, will you please talk with me? Will you walk with me again? I'm still here, and we need to work this out." It was a spiritual GPS, the cry of a broken-hearted Father longing for close intimacy he had enjoyed with his children. "For the Son of Man came to seek and save that which was lost," Jesus said in Luke 19:10. Here it begins in the garden. The Father seeks the lost. His Son completed the task. The Spirit awakens the dead heart. And so it continues until every one of his children is home again.

Where did Adam and Eve hide? (See **verse 8**.)

_____

What was Eve's response to God's question?

_____

How long did they think they could hide from God Almighty? They were only humans. He made every square inch of the garden and every tree they tried to use for covering. Did they think God wouldn't miss them? Did they hope God would soon lose interest in their lives and put his focus elsewhere? Did their hearts break at this point, too, or later?

When God confronted Adam, he blamed God and Eve. He said, in essence, "You gave me this woman and she gave me the fruit and I ate it." At last Eve responded. "The serpent tricked me and I ate." The Amplified Bible substitutes the word "tricked" with "beguiled" and adds the words "cheated, outwitted, and deceived." There it is. Eve told it like it was. When God confronted her, she told him the truth: "I was lied to. I did what you told me not to do."

How does her response strike you?

Eve made the wise choice to come clean without excuses. We would do well to learn from her example. When we've messed up, it's best not to try to hide the obvious. God knows where we are, and what we're about. He says he will be faithful to forgive when we come to him as little children with honest, open hearts.

Eve did her best to represent the truth. At this point, God turns his full attention toward the enemy he knows so well. He doesn't waste precious breath asking about what the great deceiver has done. He simply tells Satan about the nail in his coffin, the eternal punishment that has been put in place for enticing Adam and Eve into sin.

Read Genesis 3:14-19.

What kind of judgment did God bring upon Satan?

What did God tell Eve?

How would Adam's future change?

God promptly declares open war on the enemy of our souls. He curses the serpent. He condemns him to crawl on his belly and to eat dust. Ashes to ashes, dust to dust. Satan hoped that mankind would be cursed by sin and lose all hope of eternal life. But God's great love always outweighs pain. Satan hadn't factored in love. Love isn't in his vocabulary. Adam and Eve will leave Eden. Death will come to the garden. But that's not where God's story ends.

What does God say to Satan in **verse 15**?

"I will put enmity
Between you and the woman
And between your seed and her seed;
He shall bruise your head,
And you will bruise his heel" (NKJV).

What does this riddle mean? God announces a perpetual hostility between the children Eve will bear and the Serpent. Even as God judges sin, he gives the promise of a coming victory as the seed of Satan battles the seed of Eve. God must bring judgment on the sin of Adam and Eve. But he also brings mercy. War is declared on Satan and God proclaims that his redemption will come through the child of a woman.

Who is the seed?

_____

How will Satan bruise his heel?

_____

"The seed of the woman is the Promised One, the coming Messiah of Israel. Seed continues to be used throughout the Bible as a messianic term (Gal. 3:16). This is sometimes called the 'first gospel' because these words, as direct as they are, promise the coming One whom we know to be the Lord Jesus, the Messiah."[83]

The bruising of the heel refers to the crucifixion of Jesus. Christ would suffer by becoming sin on the cross and dying as God's perfect sacrifice. But the crushing of the head refers to complete destruction. When Jesus rose from the grave, the last great enemy of man was defeated. With his resurrection, death was destroyed and relationship with God and man came to new life. Eternal life would be the destiny of God's chosen beloved. A new heaven and earth would come again, and the Enemy of God would be chained in the pits of hell forever.

For Adam and Eve, it was time to leave their garden in Eden. Adam would have to work hard to keep his head above water and his family fed. He would one day die and return to the dust from which he was made. But God would never forget his people.

Eve would leave the glory of the only home she'd ever known. In pain she would bear children, and for a long while, the sting of being known as the woman who ushered sin into the world.

How did Eve feel as she left the presence of God? What did she feel as the flowers and flora and leafy trees, the orchids and roses and calla lilies faded to black? How shocking was the first tear that fell from her beautiful eyes? What were the racking sobs of regret? How did she handle anger and frustrating emotions? Did she know where to put hurt when Adam shot her the first glance of disapproval? Did she cry out with fear and agony during the birth of Cain, Abel, and Seth?

Everything changed for her as she followed Adam farther and farther away from the gates of her beautiful paradise. Fear of the unknown must have been one of the first emotions she battled. This would be followed by waves of guilt, regret, and loss.

We wonder if Eve ever felt the consequences of her sin were too much to bear. Did she despair to the point of wishing she could die?

In the coming years she would lose two sons. Abel would be killed. Cain would be banished from her sight.

Are you living with consequences that feel overwhelming?

_____

Are you living with consequences of someone else's sin?

_____

Some consequences are short-term. Others last a lifetime. Certainly Eve's suffering removes her from being a symbol of the fall of man and makes her more real to us. We see her pain as she comes sharply into focus.

Of course the memories of paradise, of knowing she was still loved by God, would bring her courage. There would be moments of joy, holding her first child to her breast and watching Adam take pride in making them a new home. Traces of Eden would stay in their hearts, for God had not forsaken them.

Nothing is wasted with God. And so with Adam and Eve, he did not leave his children without hope.

Eve could take comfort in knowing that through her a seed would be born. Christ would redeem the cycle of sin she had set in motion. With the punishment for sin came the hope of redemption. God's great love for man always outweighs pain. Because he is merciful, he is willing to forgive.

God is the eternal optimist, forever wooing the broken, calling the hopeless and making a way to bring his children back home. A new Eden has been prepared. A new heaven and earth were in his plans before he spoke, "Let there be!"

> **Star:** What is that, which is dark where it should be light?
> **Wind:** It is a hill.
> **Star:** What is that upon the hill?
> **Wind:** It is a tree
> **Star:** What is that upon the tree?
> **Wind:** It is a man.
> **Star:** But I do not understand.
> **Wind:** You need not.
> **Star:** But I am because he spoke, because he is spoken.
> **Wind:** Yes.
> **Star:** I thought that it was dark upon that hill, and now it is so bright that my light is nothing. O Wind, why do I feel pain?
> **Wind:** From the nails.
> **Star:** It is not my pain.
> **Wind:** Yes, it is yours, because it is his.
> **Star:** For you too?
> **Wind:** Creation groans.
> **Star:** Wind?
> **Wind:** Yes.
> **Star:** It is over.
> **Wind:** It has begun. [84]

Read Revelation 13:8.

Who was slain?

___

When did this take place?

___

In the beginning, in the Garden of Eden, God had the last word. Regardless of man's sin, God would not be satisfied until his children were restored. He would deliver the children of Eve through his Seed and once again restore the earth and make all things new. It would cost him everything. It cost him his heart. It would be worth every drop of red.

We'd like to think Eve held on tightly to the loving God who delighted with her during their innocent romps through Eden. She would not hear him walking in the cool of the day near her new home. But in the dark of night, as she lay down to rest, when her eyes closed, there were moments when she felt him watching over her. And perhaps an ancient version of Isaiah 58:11 lulled her to sleep.

> "And the Lord will continually guide you,
> and satisfy your desire in scorched places,
> and give strength to your bones;
> and you will be like a watered garden
> and like a spring of water whose waters do not fail" (NASB).

TODAY'S DATE: _____

YOUR HEADLINE:

_____

_____

WEEK TEN

New Earth Garden Party

Where: The Estate of Eve
Speaker: Eve
Lecture: "Beyond the End"
Reference: Colossians 1:15-17
Gathering Time: Eternity

Menu

(subject to heavenly additions)

hot apple spiced cider

apples with assorted cheeses

apple butter served on apple-cinnamon rolls

hot apple pie served with honey ice cream

apple fritters and cobbler

caramel apples for the children

apple crisp a la mode

Eve is delighted to be giving a short lecture on her early adventures in Eden. You will hear the rest of the story about her encounter with the Enemy and eating of the tree of good and evil. She is thrilled to explain the bigger picture and reveal the mysteries of Christ hidden in her before time and beyond the end.

A guided tour of her garden in the new heaven is open to all inhabitants of God's kingdom. Come and walk with Eve and Jesus as they describe the endless heavenly variety of flowers, trees and flora, and colors blooming on the grounds of her estate.

At the conclusion of the tour Eve will take questions from the audience. (Women in particular are encouraged to ask about "the curse").

She feels you will be especially interested to hear about the day Christ strode into hell after his crucifixion, crushing the gates of death to reclaim and redeem those who waited his coming.

No RSVP required.

You're home now.

Come as you are and rejoice!

TODAY'S HEROINE:
Eve, part two

Now he is the exact likeness of the unseen God (the visible representation of the invisible): He is the firstborn of all creation. For it was in him that all things were created in heaven and on earth, things seen and things unseen, whether thrones, dominions, rulers or authorities; all things were created and exist through him (by his service, intervention) and in and for him. And he himself existed before all things, and in him all things consist (cohere, are held together) (Col. 1:15-17 Amplified Bible).

Before creation, Christ was. And in him were each of the ones who would be created. He is called the firstborn of creation, the last Adam. All who belong to the Father were in Christ before they breathed their first breath on earth.

"Firstborn in Greek, prototokos, can indicate 'first in time' or 'first in place.' The Son of Man is the 'chiefbearer' of all God's creatures. This designation in no way indicates that Christ himself was created by God; the verse moreover asserts that all things were created in, through, and for Christ. As a participant in the creation of all things, Christ cannot be a created being. Instead, he is the Son of God, the second person of the Head, who has existed from eternity."[85]

This is the mystery of the ages.

The mystery described in **Colossians 1:22 and 26**.

What did Jesus accomplish in verse 22?

_____

Sweet reconciliation of man, the circle completed. From the fallen Garden of Eden in Genesis to hope of the new earth in Revelation 22.

How are those in Christ presented before God?

_____

Per **verse 26**, what had been hidden for ages and generations?

_____

The mystery kept even from angels is now revealed. Christ, the eternal Son of God, lives now in the ones predestined to be his from before time.

Using your well-tuned sanctified imagination, how would the unfolding of this mystery have been especially sweet to Eve?

_____

_____

What does it mean to your heart today to know that you are in Christ, in him from before the foundations of the earth and in him forever?

_____

_____

It's nearly impossible to fill in that blank. It's a mystery that leaves us breathless with anticipation and astonished by such love. It's the love Adam and Eve experienced in person in a perfect garden with God.

Adam and Eve were given the horrible, precious gift of free will. They failed the test. Eve's name carried with it the blame of every fallen aspect of earth. Her first bite into the forbidden fruit began a ripple effect of death unleashed. Walls of innocence cracked, sewers of injustice spilled into the earth's virgin soil. Pandora's box flew open wide and every pain-drenched experience of man and woman was laid at Eve's feet.

But God so loved his world.

He knit Eve together as intimately and lovingly as every one of his beloved daughters. She was the first woman, his first baby girl, his first daughter and mother on earth. How his heart must have broken when she chose disobedience. Yet he knew before time began what the gamble of free will would cost.

Adam and Eve experienced in their earthly bodies what we will experience in the new earth where righteousness dwells. Hallelujah!

(One of our favorite books in the world is *Heaven* by Randy Alcorn. If you want to get excited about what you have to look forward to when you leave this world, then we highly recommend this book.)

The life Eve enjoyed in the garden with God before the first sin is a glimpse of what we have waiting for us when eternity begins. The three of them enjoyed unbroken fellowship in a world totally free of corruption. Adam and Eve had the work of caring for a perfect garden, made especially for them and were given dominion over all the works of God's hands. They walked with him in the cool of the day and had face-to-face access to the Creator of the universe.

All Eve knew was good health, beauty, strength, and peace. All she knew in those days before the fall was that she was completely cherished by God and her man. She knew nothing but acceptance… and infinitely more. Eve understood the smile of God. She heard him laugh and knew his voice and her heart skipped a beat with delightful anticipation when she heard his footsteps approaching.

Yet one conversation later, one lie believed, one act of disobedience shared with her man, and her life in the garden was over.

For Eve, the reversal of the curse on earth must have been especially profound. To understand all she lost, let's look at the ways her life with Adam changed when sin entered the world.

LIFE UNDER THE CURSE

One day the first Adam would be redeemed by the last Adam. Jesus would come to conquer death and sin and his blood would run from the cross in both directions. In the meantime, the first father and mother of the human race would leave Eden. They entered a groaning creation. They would find out what it meant to age. The ground would be twisted with weeds, thorns, and thistles.

Read Genesis 3:20.

What does Adam call his wife for the first time?

_____

In our last lesson we learned of Eve's original name. Do you remember it?

_____

"Ishshah" was her name, the feminine form of Adam's name, "Ish."

Adam uses his former skill of naming creation to give his wife a new name. In doing so, he bestows honor on Eve. He proclaims that she is the first of many. Adam looks at her as they prepare to leave their garden paradise and knows she will be the mother of all the living. God has promised to bring his seed through her to crush the serpent's head. Eve now has a name that means "life spring" or "living" as she faces the world outside of Eden.

Now read Genesis 3:21.

What tender act does God perform for his children?

_____

Knowing they would face weather changes and all manner of physical challenges, God clothes them with the skins of animals. He knows so much still that they have no way of comprehending. Eating the fruit made them more foolish, not wise. God wants them to survive. He makes garments to protect their bodies as well as to cover their shame. Until this time, there is no record of an animal being killed for any reason. The act of slaying an animal is a picture of the coming animal sacrifices required by God to atone for sin. This also points to the Perfect Lamb who has already committed his life to die for the children of Eve when his time arrives.

Our heavenly Father doesn't give up on us even when we disappoint ourselves. He knows everything we need even before we ask. This picture of his loving hands crafting their clothes reminds us of the intimate provision God always has shown to his people. He knows our spiritual needs as well. Have you ever bundled up a child before they went out into the cold? Have you prepared countless meals for your children and said, "Eat this. It's so good for you?" Have you spent sleepless nights praying for a child who was struggling? Have you sent a teenager out into the world to make it on their own, and turned to grieve your empty nest? When you do all you can for someone you love, you have much in common with your heavenly Father.

"… how brave he was to let them go. In motherhood, we come as close as any human can to both the joy and agony of God Himself." [86]

Though hard and excruciating for everyone involved, his goals for his children would not be compromised. Nothing, no one, no sin, no fallen state, would keep him from carrying out his Plan A of salvation. When the time came, his covenant would be made. But for now, it was time to send Adam and Eve into the rest of their story. They had chosen sin, and with it came consequences.

How did God describe childbirth as a consequence of Eve's sin?

_____

What otherwise would have been nothing but joy will now be a mixture of sorrow and pleasure. Can the mothers among us say a hearty "amen?" Had God only been speaking of labor pains, the curse might not really be so bad. But the bittersweet experience of motherhood goes on from the delivery room to kindergarten, from college graduation and beyond. Thanks to our fallen condition, children are capable of bringing us the sweetest joys in life as well as the greatest heartbreak and anguish.

How does the relationship between man and woman change?

The battle of the sexes now began. "Your desire will be for your husband and he will rule over you." The Hebrew word for desire is "teshuga" and it also can be interpreted as "an attempt to usurp or control." Ultimately what God is saying is that Eve would have a desire to dominate Adam but Adam would be inclined not to appreciate that very much, thank you, and would respond by ruling over her.

Eve's mind would have been reeling with unanswered questions: *What was I thinking when I ate from that tree? Where did these funny lines on my face come from? Why is the sun so hot today? Cain and Abel are always fighting, fighting, fighting. How I wish Adam would look at me just once the way he used to in the garden.* Perhaps the most painful thought for both she and Adam would have been, *We miss our God.*

For Adam, the ground outside of Eden would be unforgiving. With sweat he would now work hard day and night to grow food to feed his growing family. The land that once so easily yielded its fruit would now resist him. His wife's perfect body was changing before his eyes, as was his own once chiseled physique.

Regret would now fight hard against the hope of God's coming seed. We only can imagine the deep regret Eve felt when reality set in.

Have you ever had a moment in your life when the cold reality of your sin hit you square in the face? Ever wished, like Superman, you could spin the planet backwards, turn tack time and have a 'do-over?'

_____

Deep sorrow over sin in our lives is a hard truth for all of us. No need to point the finger at Eve.

Turn to 2 Corinthians 11:14-15.

How does Satan disguise himself?

_____

How low will he go? As low as it takes. In Eve's eyes, Satan appeared to be an angel of light. He presented himself as someone who had her best interest at heart. We are surrounded today by a culture full of deception masquerading as angelic light. We must have eyes to see behind the masks.

Eve's breaking point came when the Enemy promised she could "be like God." She wanted to know the difference between good and evil when she'd had no experience whatsoever with evil. It's important to note that Eve wasn't starving. She could eat anything, anytime she wanted. But the one thing God withheld from her had a powerful allure.

We must learn from Eve's mistake. If God says stay away from something, then he has a good reason. By reaching for wisdom apart from God, we could say Eve was "dabbling in the occult." God is emphatic in Scripture about staying away from the occult. Why? Because there are spiritual powers in the world that are bent on destruction. He wants us to stay protected by coming to him alone as the source of all knowledge.

Read Leviticus 19:31 and 20:6.

Who did God tell the Israelites to avoid?

_____

In **verse 6**, how did God describe the behavior of someone who turned to a medium for guidance?

_____

Going to a medium or spiritist was "playing the harlot." In other words, we are being unfaithful to our first love when we go elsewhere for input. God feels betrayed when we turn from him and trust someone else for what he alone can give us. It's also because there are dark powers and danger involved with consulting a medium.

When I (Nan) was a young teen, I had a friend several years older who had a fascination with the occult. This young lady grew up in a godly home and went to church three times a week. She was young and immature in her faith and was into consulting Ouija boards. When I would come to her house to hang out, she would get out the Ouija board and we'd place our hands on the heart-shaped piece of plastic with the clear circle in the middle and start asking questions about the future. "Who am I going to marry?" "Will I marry soon?" And on and on.

One day she told me she'd started going to a fortune teller. She went regularly for a while and even said she'd like to take me with her. Thank God she never did. Eventually she quit going. I guess it got too expensive after a while.

I loved this friend. She had been my babysitter. She was tall and beautiful and smart. She had everything going for her. For some reason, all the good things she had were not enough. She was finding it difficult to walk by faith and not by sight. She was desperate for knowledge of things God was not ready to give her yet. So she went elsewhere to find it. The Ouija board and the fortune teller are tools of Satan. Certainly the fortune teller was robbing my friend of her money and masquerading as an angel of light.

Years later, she apologized for having been a negative influence on me in this way. She had repented of dabbling in the occult and was sorry she ever did it, and hoped I hadn't been harmed by it. She grew into a godly and mature woman of God. In his mercy, he delivered her. Thankfully, the occult things she introduced to me were not something that held my interest.

In a very real way, Eve was also playing with the occult. She didn't know it, but she was listening to Satan. He convinced her to reach for knowledge outside the will of God for her life. With the Internet at our fingertips, we don't have to reach for a Ouija board to play with the darkness. We can virtually tap into countless sources of so-called knowledge that draws us away from intimacy with God. We need to find peace with the "No" of God and realize his concern is always for our best. The sooner we stop doubting his goodness, the sooner we can fully trust him with everything in our lives.

Trusting God is our great gift to him. Faith delights his heart. Eve had to learn to trust God in the light of the garden and the darkness of earth. She learned the brutal lesson that pride always goes before a fall. But we know God was with her through the years of adjusting to "real life" and the agony of having Cain murder Abel. The final son she birthed was named Seth.

"Adam and Eve had no son to carry on their line for good and the promise of the Messiah. Hence the importance of the birth of Seth. His name is related to a Hebrew verb meaning 'to place' or 'to set,' for he was appointed to take the place of the murdered son in the plan of God."[87]

God doesn't abandon Adam and Eve and he doesn't abandon us in the middle of our consequences. We are assured that nothing can separate us from his love, not even our own poor choices (Romans 8:38-39). He sent his Holy Spirit to live inside us to make sure that we would never be apart from his presence. He also is in the business of restoring what we have lost.

Adam and Eve's third son, Seth, had a son named Enosh. Enosh was a godly man whose life ensured the promise of God would continue. Enosh lived in a new era, a new day when the Bible records that "at this time men began to call (upon God) by the name of the Lord." This was the first worship of God in 1,000 years. Perhaps Enosh grew up hearing about the faith of their grandmother Eve and grandpa Adam. Perhaps Grandma Eve rocked Enosh in her lap and sang songs over him describing the mighty God she had seen face to face.

What had life taught her? To trust God. One can imagine she found a way to sing a hymn of trust over her grandson as he slept.

> "Blessed is the man who trusts in the Lord
> and whose trust is the Lord.
> For he will be like a tree planted by the water,
> that extends its roots by a stream
> and will not fear when the heat comes;
> but its leaves will be green,
> and it will be not anxious in a year of drought
> nor cease to yield fruit" (Jer. 17:7-8 NASB).

At last Adam and Eve died and returned to the dust of the ground. But God was alive and well. His covenant was made clear with Abraham, Isaac, Jacob, and Joseph. Down through the ages the prophets continued to tell of the coming Messiah first mentioned in the opening chapters of Genesis. Finally the time came and Jesus was born just as God had promised, through the line of Eve. His life was given and in his resurrection, all hell literally broke loose.

THE CURSE REVERSED!

Madeleine L'Engle, the celebrated author of *A Wrinkle In Time* and great lady of faith in Christ, writes about the spectacular redemption of Adam and Eve. In the following piece she takes us to the Saturday after the crucifixion of Jesus, to the day between his death and resurrection. The Scriptures tell us in 1 Peter 3:18-20 that Christ was put to death in body but he was "made alive in the spirit, through whom also he went and preached to the spirits in prison who disobeyed long ago when God waited patiently in the days of Noah while the ark was being built" (Amplified Bible).

We know that the cross of Christ has a shadow falling across every direction of history, bringing to salvation all who have believed in God's covenantal promise and Son.

The following piece from Ms. L'Engle thrills us as we imagine the spirit-filled perSon of God in Christ striding through the darkness of hell. On every side he reaches out to take the saints of God held for centuries as prisoners to sin and death. At last Jesus reached Adam and Eve. The following words are Ms. L'Engle's imagination of how Adam felt as Christ approached and took him from death to eternal life.

> "The light was brutal against my shaded eyes,
> blinding me with brilliance.
> I was thousands of years unaccustomed to the glory.
> Then came the wrench of bone where the bone had been dust.
> The shocking rise of dry bones, the burning fleshing,
> the surge of blood through artery and vein
> was pain as I had never known that pain could be.
> My anguished scream was silenced as my hand was held
> in the grip of such authority I could not even try to pull away.
> The crossed gates were trampled by his powerful feet
> and I was wrenched through the chasm
> as through the eye of a hurricane.
> And then—O God—he crushed me
> in his fierce embrace. Flesh entered flesh;
> bone, bone. Thus did I die, at last.
> Thus was I born.
> Two Adams became one.
> And in the glory Adam was.
> Nay, Adam is." [88]

The cycle of sin that started with Eve had been broken. The empty tomb dealt the death blow to Satan's plan to forever ruin Eden. The sin nature that we inherited from Eve was paid for on the cross. Thanks to Jesus, we are assured of a home in Eden restored when God makes all things new and gives us back what we lost through sin. Oh, let's shout hallelujah!

"Then I saw a new heaven and a new earth… and I heard a loud voice from the throne saying, 'Now the dwelling of God is with men, and he will live with them. They will be his people, and God himself will be with them and be their God. He will wipe every tear from their eyes. There will be no more death or mourning or crying or pain, for the old order of things has passed away.' He who was seated on the throne said, 'I am making everything new.' Then he added, 'Write this down, for these words are trustworthy and true'" (Rev. 21:1, 3-5 NIV).

Eve had seen the world when everything was new. But then came the deception and everything changed. Now we have the promise that once again God will make a new earth and new heaven. There will be no enemy of his to fight against, no temptation to reach for phantom dreams. He will be the light of the city and we will walk again with our Maker. Perhaps no one will be more grateful for this eternal freedom than the mother of all living.

Turn to Revelation 22 and read as much as your heart desires.

When the Garden of Eden disappeared, where was the tree of life transplanted?

_____

How is the city described?

_____

The Garden of Eden contained only a few precious stones. Now count the numerous jewels and ways they are used in the new garden:

_____

Will we eat in heaven? How about the celebration feast of the Lamb!

Will we have bodies? Jesus said we would have bodies like his own resurrected body.

Something is coming, girlfriends, that is better than our eyes have seen or ears have heard or minds have imagined! Earth is but a shadow. Heaven is the source. Those who put their faith and hope in Christ will live in the new earth, where nothing but righteousness will dwell. We will walk along a crystal clear river and eat from a tree that will keep us from aging! Imagine that! No wrinkles. No sagging. No age spots. No flabby muscles. No cancer. No disease. No sorrow. No pain.

NO SIN!

Eve, our sister-friend will be there. We'll assure her there are no hard feelings. We'll be able to hear from her lips what it meant when Jesus rose from the dead. Of all women, she waited for that moment the longest.

Our minds cannot completely wrap around the wonders of heaven, but we can glimpse it by reflecting on our sweetest moments here on earth. Take those memories and place them in a context completely void of sin.

"The most ordinary moment on the new earth will be greater than the most perfect moments in this life—those experiences you wanted to bottle or hang on to but couldn't. It can get better, far better, than this—and it will. Life on the new earth will be like sitting in front of the fire with family and friends, basking in the warmth, laughing uproariously, dreaming of the adventures to come—and then going out and living those adventures together. With no fear that life will ever end or that tragedy will descend like a dark cloud. With no fear that dreams will be shattered or relationships broken."[89]

Eve and all our "fore-sisters" we've studied from Scripture are waiting for this moment to come. Together we will spend eternity having girl gatherings, sharing our stories, enjoying what our Savior has prepared for us from the foundations of the world.

Will you see loved ones there? Children who left too soon? Parents or friends and relatives? John recorded in his vision of heaven the astonishing view of a great gathering of people from every nation, tongue, tribe and people. This implies that personal identities remain intact in our new bodies.

There is so much about heaven yet to explore. We encourage you to read and study and ask God to reveal to your heart the glories that await you. Most importantly, we must dare to believe God's promises are unshakable. If he says it will come to pass, then it will. And this world is just a foretaste of what lies ahead. Resist the call of our culture to try to find heaven this side of paradise. It's not going to happen. Eve would testify a "yes and amen" on that subject. We live in a fallen garden and see through a glass dimly. But God has set eternity into our hearts. In the oldest book of the Bible, with no mention of Israel or the history of God's people, Job declared, "I know that my Redeemer lives. And I shall see God!" (Job 19:25)

Our mother of all living was not a faceless symbol of the fall of man. Eve was flesh-and-blood real. She experienced the greatest joy and the greatest loss. Of all the women who have ever lived, perhaps Eve suffered the most because she tasted heaven and then had to leave it.

What did the crown of thorns Jesus wore mean to Eve? Thorns entered the world with her sin of disobedience. Roses that were easy to hold and gather in her arms would now be riddled with thorns that would tear the flesh. Thorns symbolize death and decay for all of creation.

When the crown of thorns was placed on the head of Jesus, he bore the penalty of Eve's sin. He bore the penalty of all our sins, and one day every thorn and thistle will be banished from this earth.

What does the empty tomb mean to Eve? The curse has been reversed! Our lives have been redeemed, and she carries the blame no more. The groans of creation will turn to shouts of praise as the trees clap their hands again and the lion lies down with the lamb.

What do his crown of thorns, his death, his empty tomb mean to you today?

_____

Is there someone or something you would lift up to God for redemption and restoration?

_____

_____

Now write a prayer of faith and thanksgiving for what God did in Christ before time began. Thank God for the gift of believing! He gives us the gift of faith. Are you grateful for a heart that believes he **IS** and you are now **IN HIM** forever and ever?

_____

Turn and read Leviticus 26:12.

What does God long to do with his people?

_____

"I will walk among you and be your God" (NIV)

God longs to take those walks with us. He is preparing a place for us, better than Eden, where we will live in unbroken fellowship with him in a world in which righteousness reigns.

Eve will walk in that garden again with God. So will we. There will be no cherubim with flaming swords guarding the way to the tree of life. Like a heavenly tour guide, Eve can show us around, pointing out her favorite fruit! She might even be quick to laugh and say, "Don't be afraid; take a bite out of this one. Believe me, none of it is forbidden!"

Then the King will say to those on his right, "Come, you who are blessed by my Father; take your inheritance, the kingdom prepared for you since the creation of the world" (Matt. 35:34 NIV).

TODAY'S DATE: _____

YOUR HEADLINE:

_____

_____

"Marked for life in the womb of Eden

Marked for life by God's own hand

The spirit of creation breathed into the soul of man

You are the pure intention of heaven's heart

You can hear the angels sigh

Walk on my children,

You are marked for life."[90]

Leader's Guide and Study Questions

We all know it's one thing to read the Bible or do a study on your own, but quite another to share it with your best girlfriends. Because we've learned so much about God, ourselves, and each other through our three-decade, hand-in-hand walk, we wanted to give you the same opportunity. After you complete each week's session, be sure to gather with other women who dare to believe. We promise it will be worth your while.

These gatherings can be informal, but it might help to designate a facilitator, just to make sure the conversation keeps on track. It's also OK to switch up the facilitator each week. Regardless, a few things to keep in mind:

- Start each meeting in prayer, fully expecting God to move. Follow with a brief recap of the previous week's lesson in case someone was unable to keep up or attend.

- Allow the Spirit to lead. Realize that some of these lessons may necessitate times of personal confession, ministry, or prayer. Find a balance between staying on track and taking care of business!

- Consider setting an ending time for your gatherings. Formally dismiss at that time, but note that people can still stay around and chat further (as long as it's OK with the hostess).

- Encourage some sort of communication during the week. It doesn't have to be official prayer partners, but do find a way to touch base.

- Draw out those who aren't participating by creating a safe, respectful atmosphere. Be sure, though, that nobody feels put on the spot.

- Don't feel like you have to get through all of the questions during a meeting. We've included a lot here, knowing that some will work better for your group than others. These are just jumping off points. Sometimes a discussion will lead to unexpected revelation. Go with it.

- Remember to have fun!

    Most humbly in Him,
    Nan and Bonnie

WEEK ONE DISCUSSION QUESTIONS: Naomi

- Read Genesis 19:30-38 and discuss the origin of Moab. Why did God want his people to stay clear of the Moabites?

- In the beginning of their relationship, Naomi taught Ruth about Yahweh and showed her a better way than idol worship. Then, when Naomi was bitter and hopeless, Ruth was there for her, helping her in her darkest moments. Discuss the give-and-take of friendship and how we can best help one another during our good and bad seasons of life.

- We all make the choice to cling to something. Ruth clung to Naomi and held on for dear life to everything Naomi stood for. What are you clinging to? Is it worthy of your devotion?

- Read Judges 2:10. What stories must be passed down in our families for faith to keep growing in the next generation?

- Why do you think God chose to include a story in Scripture about a woman who was deeply depressed? God is not put off by your emotional darkness. He doesn't want you to stay there, and he is not angry at you for being there. Just as he brought Naomi into a glorious Chapter Four, so he also wants to do the same for each of us.

- The Israelites tried to worship Baal, Ishtar, Chemosh, and Asherah along with Jehovah. It didn't work. Are we tempted to do the same? What are our false gods? What, plus God, do we tend to worship?

- What do you think of Naomi's choice to move her family to Moab? Was it wise? What do you think of her choice to allow her sons to marry Moabite women?

- Has God ever allowed a "famine" in your life? Share the experience with a trusted friend.

- Read Psalm 38:15. How do we hope in God?

- Read 1 Peter 5:9-10. Discuss the fruit of our suffering. Would you say it was worth it?

- Read Psalm 56:8. What do you think God will eventually do with your bottled tears?

- What do you think Ruth saw in Naomi that made her want to stay with her?

- Read Ruth 1:13, 20-21. How does Naomi see God's hand in her suffering? Do you think she was accurate in her conclusions? Why or why not? How do you see the hand of God in your life today?

- The word "return" is used nine times in Ruth 1. Do you see any significance in this?

- Ruth represents the Gentile bride of Christ. Naomi represents the nation of Israel. What is the church doing for Israel today? How can we extend hope to Israel?

WEEK TWO DISCUSSION QUESTIONS: Ruth

- Ruth had much to be depressed about. How did she finally end up responding to her personal tragedies?

- Why do you think Ruth chose Naomi over her own biological mother? What did staying loyal to Naomi cost Ruth?

- How do you think Ruth learned of Yahweh?

- Read Proverbs 20:24. What examples of the sovereignty of God do we see in this story?

- How does this truth encourage you?

- Read Ruth 2:12. What does it mean to take refuge under his wings?

- The story of Ruth and Naomi shows us once again that while people are in the middle of the most desperate situations, God is still at work fulfilling his purposes. Ruth had no idea she was part of fulfilling God's promise to Abraham to bring the Messiah to earth. She simply was faithful. How does this encourage you today in your times of struggle?

- By partaking in flesh and blood, Jesus became our Kinsman-Redeemer. How is Boaz like Jesus in his relationship with his Bride?

- The words "redeem" or "redeemer" are used fourteen times in the book of Ruth. To us, our redemption is free. From God's point of view, how costly was it?

- Naomi's closest relative was afraid of "jeopardizing his inheritance" if he married Ruth. Boaz was not afraid of this, but took Ruth into his household and willingly married her. What does Ephesians 1:11, 18 say about Jesus and his inheritance?

- Discuss some of the women in Boaz's genealogy and why this may have made him willing to marry Ruth.

- How did the names of Boaz and Ruth become famous?

- How is Ruth a picture of every Gentile who comes to faith in Jesus?

- The nature of our current culture is similar to the times of the Judges. Discuss the different "fields" in which God has sent you to glean. What is our calling and responsibility to our culture?

- The book of Judges ends with these words: "There was no king in Israel, and everyone did what was right in his own eyes." How is the story of Ruth a shining example of righteous living in the midst of a pagan culture? How does it apply to us today?

- How do we see the attribute of God as a rewarder in the book of Ruth?

- God's law was very specific about how he wanted his people to treat the widow, orphan, and the alien. Why do you think God wrote this into his laws?

- The fields where Ruth gleaned also were the fields where David cared for his father's sheep and where the angels announced the birth of Jesus. The places where you are faithful will be places of blessing for coming generations. Where are you gleaning today?

What does it take to believe God has a harvest and a new season ahead?

- Ruth had to go behind everyone in the field and pick up the leftovers. Her job was menial and humiliating, seemingly insignificant. What "insignificant" tasks are you responsible for and how can Ruth's story encourage you to continue in faithful obedience?

- The first person Jesus declared to be full of faith was the woman who was willing to receive even the crumbs that fell from the master's table. Ruth was willing to glean in the fields and pick up what was left for the poor. On a spiritual level, what do Ruth and this unnamed woman in the New Testament have in common?

- Ruth gleaned barley in the fields of Boaz. We also glean from the harvest of God's work in our lives. How do we glean wisdom and knowledge from the past and from our present circumstances?

- After her ten years of heartache in a foreign land, discuss what it would have been like for Naomi to have been surrounded by her old friends in Bethlehem as they met to name Obed.

- Ruth started out a childless widow. She ended her life as an ancestor of Jesus Christ. Discuss the saying, "God is never finished."

- Every Naomi should have a Ruth in her life. Be sure you have one. If you don't, pray for one.

WEEK THREE DISCUSSION QUESTIONS: Anna

- God used a very senior citizen to break his 400-year silence. What inspires you most about Anna? Do you know anyone like her? How do you feel when you're with her?

- There are forty-three references to women in Luke's gospel. What does that reveal about Luke's character and personality? What does it reveal about the priority God gives to women?

- What do you think the people who knew Anna said about her? Is it possible some thought she lived a wasted life? Was she considered a fanatic? A crazy old lady? Discuss the ways we label or marginalize people today.

- When Anna was serving in the temple courts, God had been silent for 400 years. She waited most of her lifetime to receive answers to some of her prayers. What does Anna tell us about persevering when you feel God is silent in your life?

- How could Anna have responded to being widowed after seven years of marriage? We wonder how many relatives and friends she outlived. What did it cost her to keep believing? What do you think she would say about the timing of God?

- What do you think Anna would have to say about the focus of our culture on the pursuit of youth? On entertainment? On our many diversions?

- What was Anna's platform or sphere of influence? What is yours? How should we view the people who come in and out of the place where we serve him?

- It's interesting to note that God had given Simeon a special revelation. Simeon knew God was going to allow him to see Jesus before he died. Did Anna have such a promise? Discuss the role of faith in Anna's life.

- Ask the women in your group who are sixty-five or older to share some of their wisdom on the process of growing older in Christ Jesus. Ask how our culture makes them feel.

- F.B. Meyer once confided to his friend F.A. Robinson of Toronto, "I do hope my Father will let the river of my life go flowing fully until the finish. I don't want it to end in a swamp." What do we fear most about growing old?

- Read Titus 2:3-5 and discuss creative ways mature women can encourage the younger generation.

- Anna spent her life pursuing one thing. Discuss the process of making priorities when it comes to the use of our time and talents. What are the time-stealers in our lives and how do we rid ourselves of them?

- Discuss the struggle to believe what God says about old age with what our culture says about it.

- What is the secret to living positively and productively in an aging body?

- What do you think it would have been like to be a "Messiah Watcher?" How are we Messiah watchers today?

- Read Proverbs 16:31 and Isaiah 46:4. How does God view our aging in Jesus? What does God promise his senior citizens?

- Anna took no spiritual retirement. How do we stay spiritually energetic? How do we train our senses to see the extraordinary around us? Anna "pressed forward with great eagerness to see him." Do we?

WEEK FOUR DISCUSSION QUESTIONS: An adulteress

- Why do you think that it was God's timing to have this event take place when thousands of people were in the temple courts and could witness it?

- Why do you think the Pharisees considered Jesus a threat?

- How was Jesus different from many people's preconceived notions of who the Messiah would be?

- The Pharisees used the law as a point of argument to trap Jesus. Four hundred years of silence had brought hundreds of laws into their religion that God never gave them. In the absence of the Spirit, there is only law and the law brings death. Are you relying on adherence to the law to justify you before God?

- Why do you think Jesus stooped and wrote in the dirt when the adulterous woman was thrown at his feet?

- The Pharisees cared nothing for the woman or the real truth of the situation. They only wanted to trap Jesus and discredit him. What does it mean to be a spiritual bully? Are we ever guilty of this? How? Do you have any stones to throw?

- Jesus was not put off by the mess the adulterous woman had made of her life. He was put off by the self-righteousness of the Pharisees. What lesson is in this for us?

- Why do you think the adulterous woman stayed behind to be with Jesus after all the other people left? What do you think was going through her mind?

- We have all been "caught in the very act" of sinning, whether our sin was made public or not. For Jesus to heal us, our sins must be exposed to his merciful gaze. What would Jesus have you bring under his gaze today?

- How do you see yourself in this story? Do you identify with the Pharisees? With the woman?

- All of us need what Jesus offered in John 7:37-38. Read these verses and spend time in prayer, asking Jesus to apply his living water to your life.

- Do you think the adulterous woman would have said that being caught was a good thing for her? Why or why not?

- Jesus' discernment in this situation allowed him to see below the surface and address the real problem. When we find ourselves in a difficult dilemma that requires wisdom and discernment, we can rely on the Holy Spirit to help us see below the surface and get to the heart of the matter. What are you facing that requires Holy Spirit eyes to see? Is there an issue in your life that needs to be brought to the feet of Jesus?

- Before the moment when the adulterous woman was brought before Jesus, he had spent the night in prayer on the Mount of Olives. He was spiritually ready to face the Pharisees. What can we learn from Jesus' example in this?

- Jesus was the only one who could have condemned her that day, but He didn't. Why is it a good idea to always stay in full view of our Good Shepherd?

WEEK FIVE DISCUSSION QUESTIONS:
A woman with the issue of blood

- Describe the life of a person who was "unclean." What does it mean to be an "untouchable" in today's culture?

- What do you think of the "cures" offered for women with an issue of blood? What false hopes or "cures" can we run to for the deep need in our lives?

- Do you have a feeling of hopelessness about any type of ongoing issue in your life? Do you feel you are letting God down because you still struggle?

- Read 2 Corinthians 1:19-20. When our prayers do not seem to be answered, how do we stand in the "yes" of Jesus Christ?

- What did it cost the woman with the issue of blood to leave her house that day to pursue an encounter with Jesus? What did she need even more than physical healing? Where is true peace found?

- When she was healed, what effect do you think this had on Jairus?

- What did Jesus call her? What is the significance of this name?

- Why do you think Jesus made her tell her story in front of the crowd?

- When she touched him, he could have gotten angry at her for making him unclean. Instead, he welcomed her and healed her. What does Jesus want us to do with our unclean condition?

- What is the difference between just brushing up against Jesus and touching him in faith? How are we guilty of being near Jesus instead of encountering him deeply?

- What did the woman with the alabaster box, the woman with the issue of blood, and Mary Magdalene all have in common? How did Jesus respond to each of them? Do you identify with any of them? How do their testimonies comfort you or give you hope?

- Jesus often broke from the religious traditions of his day. Rabbis were not even supposed to speak to women or have eye contact with them. A woman's testimony had no legal value in ancient Israel. How do you feel about the fact that when Jesus rose, instead of holding a press conference or arranging a meeting with the Sanhedrin, he appeared first to a woman? What message does this send to all women?

- Read Psalm 107:2, 20-22. Spend some time together sharing some of the wonders of God in your lives. Practice letting the redeemed of the Lord "say so!"

WEEK SIX DISCUSSION QUESTIONS:
Mary, the mother of Jesus

- Discuss what it means for the Author of time to enter his own story.

- Why do you think God chose an unknown virgin from a town with a bad reputation to be the mother of Jesus?

- Discuss what Mary had to give up in order to be the mother of the Messiah. What price did she pay?

- Why did Jesus have to be born of a virgin?

- What information did Gabriel give Mary? What information about the future of her child did he not tell her? Why do you think he made this choice?

- Do you sense God's presence hovering over you, birthing within you the hopes and dreams he has for your life? How do we cooperate with God in fulfilling his purposes for our lives?

- Mary knew Elizabeth would understand the miracle that was happening within her. Take a moment to reflect on the friendships in your life. Do you have a friend who encourages you in Jesus? Are you that friend to someone?

- How do you think Elizabeth's words to Mary made her feel?

- From the words of the Magnificat, what truths about the character of God did Mary know? What aspects of the character of God sustain you?

- Discuss what it means to be "the handmaid of the Lord."

WEEK SEVEN DISCUSSION QUESTIONS: Mary, part two

- Mary learned to ponder life's rich moments and treasure them in her heart. What moments in your walk with God have you treasured in your heart? Share one with a friend.

- How do you think Mary felt about the conditions surrounding Jesus' birth? Do you think she felt the mother of the Son of God deserved better accommodations?

- Does it ever frustrate you that God does not ask your opinion on how to accomplish his purposes? How willing are you for God to do things his way in your life? How do we become a "handmaid of the Lord?"

- Read Jeremiah 1:5, 29:11-13 and Ephesians 2:10. God's plans for you are based on how he designed you. Discuss how these verses can help you in a walk of submission to God's purposes for your life.

- If you or your friend is in the middle of a difficult situation, read Psalm 118:14-17 over each other and pray for one another.

- Why do you think the angels appeared to lowly shepherds to announce the birth of the Messiah?

- The angels told the shepherds to look for Jesus in ordinary circumstances. How can we find Jesus in the ordinary? How can clinging to our own agenda cause us to miss Jesus?

- Read Luke 2:49. If you had been Jesus' mother, how would you have reacted to his response?

- Read Luke 2:51-52. From these verses, what can we surmise about the love Jesus showed to Mary and Joseph?

- Mary's wedding plans had to change when she became pregnant during her betrothal year. How do you think this affected her desire to help make things right when the wedding couple at Cana ran out of wine?

- For Jews in the Middle East, wine represented life and abundance. By producing wine from water, what did Jesus reveal to his disciples about his character?

- Jesus spent much of his life in anonymous obscurity. Then his public ministry began only in the last three years of his life. Do you ever feel anonymous? Overlooked? How does the iceberg equation apply to our lives?

- Discuss with a friend what you would like to know about the unrecorded years of Jesus' life.

- What fruit results from putting God's agenda ahead of our own?

WEEK EIGHT DISCUSSION QUESTIONS: Mary, part three

- Mary had Jesus within her for only nine months. Because of the empty tomb and through the power of the Holy Spirit, we can have Jesus dwelling within us forever. How does it change your day to have Jesus within you?

- When in Mary's life do you think she fully understood Jesus' purpose and calling?

- Have you had to give up any of your personal dreams for a higher calling of God in your life? Share these with a trusted friend. Speak words of encouragement over one another.

- Read Luke 23:35-37. Some people watched passively as Jesus was crucified. Are there times when we are calmly removed from Jesus? Do we find ourselves taking a step back from the fullness of Jesus when he's too painful to follow? What does it mean to press in to Jesus when life is hard?

- What do you imagine Jesus would have said to Mary after he rose from the dead?

- Read John 16:21-22. Are you in an hour of travail? Are you laboring in your spirit over circumstances that are difficult? What is promised you in these verses that no one can take away from you?

- The grave clothes in the empty tomb were not randomly tossed aside. The linen face cloth was neatly folded. Ever wonder why Jesus did this? Some scholars believe Jesus did this to send a message. It was the tradition for the head of the house to toss his napkin onto the table if he was finished and not returning to eat any more. If he intended to come back, he would neatly fold it. What message could Jesus have been sending?

- What would Jesus say to you in your greatest moment of suffering? How has God redeemed your circumstances or turned your mourning into dancing?

- How did the empty tomb change everything for Mary? How does it change everything for us?

- What questions about life as the mother of Jesus would you like to ask Mary one day?

WEEK NINE DISCUSSION QUESTIONS: Eve, Part One

- Adam and Eve had all they needed, but Satan tempted them to want more. Can you relate? How? What can this lead to in our lives?

- What does it mean to be deceived by Satan?

- How are we tempted to "make coverings" for ourselves when we sin?

- What is the difference between religion and relationship with God?

- How is the Trinity a picture of relationship?

- How important do you think relationship is to God? Why?

- How is relationship with God begun? How is it cultivated?

- How does being made in the image of God make us different from the animals?

- As Christians, how do we exercise dominion over the earth? What has God given you to rule?

- What privileges has God given you?

- Apart from childbearing, what does it mean to "be fruitful and multiply?"

WEEK TEN DISCUSSION QUESTIONS: Eve, Part Two

- How does Genesis 1 and 2 answer the fundamental questions of: Who am I? Why am I here?

- Discuss Satan's choice of words when he tempted Eve.

- How does Jesus' temptation in the wilderness in Matthew 4 compare with Eve's temptation in the garden?

- Discuss how we learn to spot the lies of Satan.

- Discuss the losses Eve experienced when she and Adam left the garden. What hope and promise for the future did God give her before she left the garden?

- If you could ask Eve one question, what would it be?

- What does it mean to come to God alone as your source of knowledge and wisdom?

- Why would it have been important to Eve to know that nothing can separate us from the love of God in Christ Jesus? Why is it important to you?

- As Eve raised her sons, what do you think she would have taught them about the character of God?

- How are we tempted to find paradise this side of heaven?

- How is God expanding your view of our future life on the new earth?

- What in your life would you like to see God redeem and restore?

Epilogue

Thank you for taking this amazing journey with us through the hall of faithful heroines in Scripture. Our hearts are forever knit to yours. We thought about you each moment of the writing process for the studies and the related musical. Our greatest hope and prayer is that you have met God on every page and will be encouraged to live your lives bravely in him during these last days.

Our study of women in the Bible has made each one leap off the page to us and come to life in living color. We now see them as flesh-and-blood sisters, not much different from us, separated only by time but united with us in our womanhood. When we meet them in heaven, we won't need to be introduced. Each one will immediately be familiar to us, like being reunited with an old friend. We'll look into each other's eyes with joy, and if grateful tears are allowed in heaven, they surely will flow.

Instead of a handshake, it will be a high-five. And then the laughter will begin and dancing and the sharing of stories. We can hear it now. One of us will say, "Oh, I loved it when you stood before the king and pointed to Haman and said, 'He is the man!' That was awesome!" And Esther will say, "Oh, I loved it when you stood before your television and turned it off and told your children, 'No I won't let you watch that tonight! It's ungodly.' That was awesome!"

You'll meet us there and we'll have the ultimate girl party. We'll be amazed at all the times we thought no one was watching as our faith played out before the cloud of witnesses. Their voices cheered us on just as we cheer back our gratitude for the trails of faith they blazed before. We can be trailblazers now for those who come after us. Don't doubt it, sweet sister. Your faith matters. Your courageous obedience is seen in the heavens. You have a heavenly fan club of women praying for you and singing your praises.

Writing, recording, researching, producing, and birthing this project has been our act of daring to believe God.

If there is one thing we could wish for you in the days to come, it is that you will dare to believe him with us. We pray you are enabled to stand strong against the tide of our culture that seeks to undermine your faith. We pray that you will shine like the stars in the sky, undimmed by the ups and downs of the unknown, holding fast to the unchanging hand of God.

Like us, are you yearning to walk down this path of courage?

Good for you! Let's walk it together.

Let's be women who dare to risk,
to love
to hurt for the things of his heart
to push through
to enjoy life
to believe he is the I AM
to know we are loved
to believe our lives have a specific plan and purpose
to know we will not miss him
to believe he hears our prayers and answers them
to believe God cares about the little things
to believe Christ lives in us
to believe the Spirit dwells in us
to be mothers, sisters, and daughters of God!

In our Jesus we do wildly and continually hope,

        Nan and Bonnie

ENDNOTES

Week one

1 Joseph Parker, (British Congregationalist minister and commentator, circa 1830-1902), Amplified Bibliography, page 1949, Bible Commentary, by James C. Gray and George M. Adams, 5 Volumes, Zondervan Publishing, Grand Rapids, MI, Amplified Bible footnote on Judges 21:25, page 406.

2 Earl D. Radmacher, Ronald B. Allen, and H.W. House, *Nelson's New Illustrated Bible Commentary: Spreading the Light of God's Word into Your Life*, Thomas Nelson, Nashville, TN,, 1999, page 335.

3 See 2 Kings 3:26-27.

4 Bonnie Keen, *A Ladder Out of Depression,* Harvest House Publishers, Eugene, OR, 2005, page 30.

5 Ibid, pg 37

6 Bonnie Keen, *A Ladder Out of Depression,* Harvest House Publisher, Eugene, OR, 2005.

7 *Amplified Bible,* Zondervan Publishing, Grand Rapids, MI, 1987, footnote page 408, Ruth 1:14, William Gurnall, cited by James C. Gray and George M. Adams, Bible Commentary.

8 Earl D. Radmacher, Ronald B. Allen, and H.W. House, Nelson's New Illustrated Bible Commentary: Spreading the Light of God's Word into Your Life, Thomas Nelson, Nashville, TN, 1999, page 339.

9 Bonnie Keen, Mirandi Herrenbruck and James Hollihan, "Behind the Seen," *Evidence of Love,* Julie Rose Music, Inc., 2007, ASCAP

Week Two

10 Linda Dillow, *Calm My Anxious Heart,* NavPress, Colorado Springs CO, 1998, page 26.

11 Earl D. Radmacher, Ronald B. Allen, and H.W. House, *Nelson's New Illustrated Bible Commentary: Spreading the Light of God's Word into Your Life,* Thomas Nelson, Nashville, TN, 1999, page 336.

12 *Nelson's New Illustrated Bible Commentary,* page 339.

13 Virginia Stem Owens, *Daughters of Eve,* NavPress, Colorado Springs, CO, 1995, pages 84-85.

14 *Daughters of Eve*, page 86.

15 Andrew E. Hill and John H. Walton, *A Survey of the Old Testament,* Zondervan Press, Grand Rapids, MI, 1995, pages 184-185.

16 *Nelson's New Illustrated Bible Commentary,* page 340.

17 Ibid, page 340, chapter 3:4

18 *Nelson's New Illustrated Bible Commentary,* page 342, chapter 4:16-17

Week three

19 Richard Bauckham, "Anna of the Tribe of Asher," (Luke 2:36-38), *Revue Biblique* Volume 104, 1997, pages 161-191; www.godward.org/archives.

20 "The Book of Tobit," Jared L. Olar, *An Introduction to the Apocrypha – Part Six,* Editors, Doug and Sherry Ward, Oxford, Ohio, July 24, 2002, pages 2:6, 13:1-17, 14: 5-7.

21 Doug Ward, "Anna the Prophetess, And the Hope of All Israel," http://www.godward.org/archives,

22 Martin Luther, *The Sermons of Martin Luther,* Baker Book House, Grand Rapids MI, 1905, pages 284-289.

23 Ibid.

24 "Prophet," *Unger's Bible Dictionary,* Moody Press, Chicago, IL, 1966, page 890.

25 *US News & World Report,* 29 July 1996. Baby Boomers

26 Earl D. Radmacher, Ronald B. Allen, and H.W. House, *Nelson's New Illustrated Bible Commentary: Spreading the Light of God's Word into Your Life,* Thomas Nelson, Nashville, TN, 1999, page 1132.

27 Ibid, page 1253.

28 *Our Daily Bread,* Discovery House Publishers, Grand Rapids MI

29 Kristi Overton Johnson, *Running the Course: Becoming a Champion in God's Eyes,* Broadman & Holman Publishers, Nashville, TN, 2003, pages 141-143.

Week four

30 Beth Moore, "Living Beyond Yourself" Bible study, page 123, Lifeway Press, Nashville, TN, 1998

31 Earl D. Radmacher, Ronald B. Allen, and H.W. House, *Nelson's New Illustrated Bible Commentary: Spreading the Light of God's Word into Your Life,* Thomas Nelson, Nashville, TN, 1999, page 1217-1218.

32 *Nelson's New Illustrated Bible Commentary,* page 1217.

33 *Nelson's New Illustrated Bible Commentary,* page 1332.

34 Elizabeth Fletcher, *Women in the Bible:Stories from the Old and New Testament,* "The Adultress"The Scene is Set, www.womeninthebible.net , November 2009

35 Virginia Stem Owens, *Daughters of Eve,* NavPress, Colorado Springs, CO,1995, page 122.

36 Anne Lamott, *Traveling Mercies,* Random House Inc, NY, NY, 1999, page 128

37 Warren Wiersbe, *Wiersbe Bible Commentary New Testament,* David C. Cook, Colorado

Springs, CO, 2007, page 256.

38 Earl D. Radmacher, Ronald B. Allen, and H.W. House, Nelson's *New Illustrated Bible Commentary: Spreading the Light of God's Word into Your Life,* Thomas Nelson, Nashville, TN, 1999, page 1325.

Week five

39 Earl D. Radmacher, Ronald B. Allen, and H.W. House, *Nelson's New Illustrated Bible Commentary: Spreading the Light of God's Word into Your Life,* Thomas Nelson, Nashville, TN, 1999, page 1264.

40 Joyce Anderson-Reed, *Break the Chains Bible Study,* Year 2, Session 1, 2008 American Baptist Women's Ministries, posted November 11, 2008.

41 Ibid.

42 Crosswalk.com, lessons on Luke 8:43-48

43 Joe Focht, "Talmud Cures for Flow of Blood" sermon "Touching the Master", Luke 8:43-48, http://www.blueletterbible.com,

44 Crosswalk.com, lessons on Luke 8:43-48

45 Philip Yancey, *The Bible Jesus Read,* Zondervan Publishing, Grand Rapids MI, 1999, page 205-206.

46 Virginia Stem Owens, *Daughters of Eve,* NavPress, Colorado Springs, CO 1995, pages 230-231.

47 Victor Journey Through the Bible, Cook Communications Ministries, Colorado Springs, CO, 1996, page 256.

48 "The Tallit: Hem of His Garment," http://www.The RefinersFire.org.

Week six

49 Max Lucado, *A Gentle Thunder,* Thomas Nelson, Nashville, TN, 2006, pages 50-51.

50 Earl D. Radmacher, Ronald B. Allen, and H.W. House, *Nelson's New Illustrated Bible Commentary: Spreading the Light of God's Word into Your Life,* Thomas Nelson, Nashville, TN, 1999, page 1143.

51 *Unger's Bible Dictionary,* Moody Press, Chicago, IL, 1966, Page 779

52 Nelson's Commentary, page 1250.

53 Max Lucado, *A Gentle Thunder,* Thomas Nelson, Nashville, TN, 2006pages 59-60.

54 Virginia Stem Owens, *Daughters of Eve,* NavPress, Colorado Springs, CO, 1995, page 29.

55 Max Lucado, *A Gentle Thunder,* Thomas Nelson, Nashville, TN, 2006, pages 25, 60.

56 Bonnie Keen, "Born a Sacrifice," First Call's *Beyond December* (Warner-Alliance), ASCAP,

Julie Rose Music 1996.

Week seven

57 Alicia Britt Chole, *Anonoymous,* Integrity Publishers, Nashville, TN, 2006, pages 6-7.

58 Virginia Stem Owens, *Daughters of Eve,* NavPress, Colorado Springs, CO, 1995, page 30.

59 Madeleine L'Engle, *The Irrational Season,* Harper San Francisco, 1977, page 120.

60 Victor Journey Through The Bible, Cook Communications Ministries, Colorado Springs, CO, page 200.

61 Earl D. Radmacher, Ronald B. Allen, and H.W. House, *Nelson's New Illustrated Bible Commentary: Spreading the Light of God's Word into Your Life,* Thomas Nelson, Nashville, TN, 1999, page 1252.

62 Ibid. page 1254.

63 Ibid, Page 1317.

64 C.S. Lewis, *The Quotable Lewis,* Letters from C.S. Lewis, 29 April 1959, para 1. pg 285. "Pain", pg 469 Tyndale House Publishers.

Week eight

65 Frederick Buechner, *Wishful Thinking: A Theological ABC,* Harper San Francisco, A Division of Harper Collins Publishers, NY, NY, 1973, page

66 Max Lucado, *One Incredible Moment,* quote from "In the Grip of Grace", Word Publishing, Nashville, TN, 1996, pages 49-59.

67 Earl D. Radmacher, Ronald B. Allen, and H.W. House, *Nelson's New Illustrated Bible Commentary: Spreading the Light of God's Word into Your Life,* Thomas Nelson, Nashville, TN, 1999, page 1354.

68 Carol Kent, *When I Lay My Isaac Down,* Carol Kent, NavPress, 2004, page 143.

69 Max Lucado, *One Incredible Moment,* quote from "In the Grip of Grace", Word Publishing, Nashville, TN, 1996, pages 60-61.

Week nine

70 Max Lucado, *One Incredible Moment,* Thomas Nelson Publishers, Nashville, TN, 1996, page 49-50.

71 Gene Edwards, *Christ Before Creation,* Seedsowers Publishing, Jacksonville FL, 2003, page 9.

72 Earl D. Radmacher, Ronald B. Allen, and H.W. House, *Nelson's New Illustrated Bible Commentary: Spreading the Light of God's Word into Your Life,* Thomas Nelson, Nashville, TN, 1999, pages 8-9.

73 Gene Edwards, *Wild Goose Chase*, Multnomah Books, Colorado Springs, CO, 2008, page 5.

74 Warren Wiersbe, *Wiersbe Bible Commentary Old Testament*, David C. Cook, Colorado Springs, CO, 2003, page 21

75 Mike Mason, *The Mystery of Marriage*, Multnomah Books, Colorado Sprigs, CO, 1985, page 27.

76 Ibid. *The Mystery of Marriage*, page 161.

77 Earl D. Radmacher, Ronald B. Allen, and H.W. House, *Nelson's New Illustrated Bible Commentary: Spreading the Light of God's Word into Your Life*, Thomas Nelson, Nashville, TN, 1999, page 1767.

78 Bonnie Keen, *Blessed Are the Desperate*, Harvest House/Julie Rose Music, Inc., Eugene, OR, 2000, page 113-114.

79 Max Lucado, *One Incredible Moment*, Thomas Nelson Publishers, Nashville, TN, 1996, combination of quotes from pages 53 and 59.

80 Ibid, pages 49-50.

81 Virginia Stem Owens, *Daughters of Eve*, NavPress, Colorado Springs, CO 1995, page 15.

82 Earl D. Radmacher, Ronald B. Allen, and H.W. House, *Nelson's New Illustrated Bible Commentary: Spreading the Light of God's Word into Your Life*, Thomas Nelson, Nashville, TN, 1999, page 11.

83 Virginia Stem Owens, *Daughters of Eve*, NavPress, Colorado Springs, CO 1995, page 17

84 Nelson's Commentary, page 12.

85 Madeleine L'Engle, *The Irrational Season*, Harper San Francisco, 1977, page 166.

86 Ibid.

Week ten

87 Earl D. Radmacher, Ronald B. Allen, and H.W. House, *Nelson's New Illustrated Bible Commentary: Spreading the Light of God's Word into Your Life*, Thomas Nelson, Nashville, TN, 1999, page 1562.

88 Virginia Stem Owens, *Daughters of Eve*, NavPress, Colorado Springs, CO, 1995, page 15.

89 Earl D. Radmacher, Ronald B. Allen, and H.W. House, *Nelson's New Illustrated Bible Commentary: Spreading the Light of God's Word into Your Life*, Thomas Nelson, Nashville, TN, 1999, page 16

90 Madeleine L'Engle, *The Irrational Season*, Harper San Francisco, 1977, page 96.

91 Randy Alcorn, *Heaven*, Tyndale House, Carol Stream, Ill., 2004, page 472.

92 *Marked for Life*, Bonnie Keen, Spring Hill CD release, Marked For Life, Nashville, TN, 2000, Julie Rose music, Inc. ASCAP